Classroom Assessment and Learning

Classroom Assessment and Learning

Margaret E. Gredler
University of South Carolina

An imprint of Addison Wesley Longman, Inc.

New York • Reading, Massachusetts • Menlo Park, California • Harlow, England
Don Mills, Ontario • Sydney • Mexico City • Madrid • Amsterdam

Vice President/Editorial Director: Rich Wohl
Acquisitions Editor: Art Pomponio
Marketing Manager: Renée Ortbals
Project Coordination, Text Design, Art Studio, Photo Research,
and Electronic Page Makeup: Thompson Steele Production Services, Inc.
Cover Designer/Manager: Nancy Danahy
Full Service Production Manager: Eric Jorgensen
Print Buyer: Denise Sandler
Printer and Binder: The Maple-Vail Book Manufacturing Group
Cover Printer: Coral Graphic Services, Inc.

For permission to use copyrighted material, grateful acknowledgment is made to the copyright holders on page 269, which are hereby made part of this copyright page.

Library of Congress Cataloging-in-Publication Data

Gredler, Margaret E.
Classroom assessment and learning / Margaret E. Gredler. — 1st ed.
p. cm.
Includes bibliographical references and index.
ISBN 0-321-01335-2
1. Educational tests and measurements—United States.
2. Examinations—United States. 3. Examinations—United States—Interpretation. 4. Examinations—United States—Design and construction. I. Title.
LB3051.G66698 1999
371.26—dc21 98-9248
CIP

Please visit our website at http://longman.awl.com

ISBN 0-321-01335-2

12345678910—MA—009998

To my husband, Gilbert

Preface

The purpose of *Classroom Assessment and Learning* is threefold: (1) to present the full array of assessment methods available to the classroom teacher in an interesting, engaging format; (2) to broaden the preservice and inservice teacher's understanding of related assessment issues, from Individual Educational Plans (IEPs) for special needs students to ethical and legal issues in testing; and (3) to place assessment in a meaningful context. An example is Chapter 1, which conveys a sense of the public political nature of assessment, from Dr. Rice's first informal (and poorly constructed) spelling test to the current "Dow Jones" indicator role of test scores.

As described in the overview at the end of Chapter 1, the text consists of three major parts: Overview of Assessment, Classroom Assessment Tools, and Related Assessment Issues. However, the text chapters are designed to be used in flexible ways. For example, some instructors may prefer to address "Interpreting Norm-Referenced Tests" (Chapter 13) after "Validity and Reliability" (Chapter 3). Others may wish to address "Ethical and Legal Issues in Assessment" (Chapter 14) after an introduction to the trends in assessment in this country (Chapter 1).

The text is designed to facilitate learning in several ways. First, consistent with current views of learning, the material is structured to assist the learner in making connections among important concepts. For example, validity and reliability are introduced in Chapter 3. Then validity and reliability are discussed in relation to the different types of assessments discussed in later chapters. In this way, the concepts acquire practical meaning. Further, Chapter 2 presents an overview of assessment methods and this information is then expanded in later chapters. Also, later chapters refer to examples in earlier chapters, where relevant. To the expert, the instructor, this approach may seem to be redundant. To the learner, however, this approach helps to counter the problem of inert knowledge—information learned in a course to pass a test, but that does not become part of the learner's knowledge base.

Other learning aids include the list of key topics preceding each chapter and the opening excerpt related to the issues in that chapter. Some are real-world incidents and others are insightful observations of assessment issues. Also, each major chapter section concludes with a summary and each chapter includes thought-provoking questions. Finally, the instructor's manual includes exercises and tasks for additional exploration and practice.

This text developed for the introductory course in classroom assessment for the classroom teacher, at either the undergraduate or graduate level. The approach is to address important topics accurately and in a meaningful way, but free of technical terminology. Basic statistical calculations are in the Appendix for those who want this information.

I would like to thank the reviewers for their feedback on the early drafts of the text:

Elizabeth L. Bringsjord, SUNY Albany

J. Linward Doak, Eastern Kentucky University

Betty E. Gridley, Ball State University

Steve Hoover, St. Cloud State University

Carl Huberty, University of Georgia

Richard G. Lomax, Northern Illinois University

Rosalyn Malcom–Payne, University of Alabama-Birmingham

Sherry Markel, Northern Arizona University

Craig A. Mertler, Bowling Green State University

Peggy Perkins, University of Nevada–Las Vegas

Cynthia Peterson, Southwest Texas State University

David E. Tanner, California State University–Fresno

Lesley Welsh, West Chester University

Elizabeth Witt, University of Kansas.

In particular, I want to thank my husband, Gilbert Gredler, Professor of Psychology, for his invaluable assistance with the chapter on special needs students and Mrs. Janet Hawkins for her patience and hard work in typing this manuscript.

Margaret E. Gredler

Part One

Overview of Assessment

Chapter 1

Introduction

Chapter 2

Assessment Methods

Chapter 3

Validity and Reliability

Chapter 4

Teaching and Assessment

Chapter 1

Introduction

As the twenty-first century approaches, the coming years will likely witness an explosion of the forms of assessment in schools

–Cizek, 1993, p. 14.

Nevertheless, "news of the death of the multiple-choice test is somewhat premature"

–Armstrong, 1993, p. 17.

Major Topics

In the past, the term "assessment" was likely to conjure up an image of a six-weeks test in English or the Scholastic Aptitude Test for college admission. Assessment, however, includes a wide range of methods and activities that are used to obtain information about behavior. For example, the forms of classroom assessment include student demonstrations in hands-on situations, teacher observations, and others.

Moreover, assessment is an important component of instruction. In the public school classroom, teachers use preassessments to determine students' knowledge about a unit, informal assessments during instruction to monitor and guide student progress, and formal assessments to obtain systematic information about student learning (Taylor & Nolen, 1996).

Becoming knowledgeable about assessment is important for several reasons. First, as already stated, assessments assist teachers and administrators in making decisions about students. Assessments should reflect curriculum and classroom priorities, fit the decision that is being made, and also be fair.

Second, assessments inform students about what is important in a discipline. For example, if a history student knows that the requirement is to know dates, names or places, he or she will memorize that information and not spend time on conceptual understanding (Taylor & Nolen, 1996).

Third, assessments inform students about themselves. They provide feedback to students about how well they are progressing in a subject area. Therefore, selecting or developing assessments that are fair and that address the central learnings in the discipline is important. Inadequate assessments can impact students in negative ways. In the early and middle grades, inadequate assessment robs students of an accurate estimate of their capabilities. More importantly, students are deprived of feeling in control of their academic lives (Wiggins, 1988, p. 366).

Fourth, the focus of curriculum development and, therefore, the nature of available assessments have evolved over the years. The early focus of schooling was on the memorization and recall of information. Then, beginning in the 1970s, the focus gradually began to change. In science, for example, teaching progressed toward an activity-based, process-oriented curriculum. In addition, mathematics and writing have evolved to a current focus on cognitive processes and developing growth in thinking. However, developing assessments that tap the student's growth in thinking is a different task from that of measuring the recall of facts, rules, or procedures.

Fifth, assessment impacts both teachers and administrators as well as students. An example is Public Law 94-142, which guarantees the right to students with disabilities to a free and appropriate public education. This legislation led to the practice of incorporating exceptional children into the classroom. Essential to this practice is the development of an Individual Educational Plan (IEP) for each special student with goals and accompanying assessments tailored for him or her.

In addition, standardized testing has been assigned a major role in reporting to the public about education. At least 14.5 million students were tested in 1992–1993 in statewide testing programs. This number represents at least 36% of all students. [Almost half of the students were tested in grades 4 and 8 (Barton & Coley, 1994).] Results of these tests are often reported in the form of school and district rankings, with varying effects on the curriculum and the classroom.

Assessment, in other words, influences the lives of students, teachers, and administrators. Therefore, a major purpose of this text is to provide individuals with (1) an understanding of the richness and diversity of assessment practices, and (2) the knowledge and skills to use and interpret assessments for different purposes. Another purpose, and the major focus of this chapter, is to develop an understanding of the events that have led to changing assessment practices and an increasingly major role for large-scale testing in school life.

✦ Trends in Achievement Testing

The routine use of large-scale assessment is light-years away from the priorities in the early days of American education. At that time, reporting to the public was not a focus of educational assessment. The country was largely rural, and social and political life, including education, was local. Universal secondary education had not yet been mandated by law. Most students completed only a few years of elementary school, and then left education for the world of work.

The major form of assessment was recitation. Pupils were called on in turn by the teacher to respond to different questions or to demonstrate their reading skills by reading sentences aloud. The focus of the content-related questions was on the memorization of information. The student's grade, of course, was influenced by whether or not he or she received a difficult or an easy question. The concept of standardizing tasks so that all students respond to the same items was not thought of as essential at that time.

Written examinations were not widely used until paper, pens, and pencils became readily available in classrooms (the nineteenth century). These examinations, however, consisted of simple spelling and arithmetic tests and essay questions that tested factual knowledge. These simple tests, although imperfect and limited to facts, were sufficient for the purposes of public education at the time. Schools were expected to teach basic reading, writing, and ciphering (computational skills).

Measurement Enters Education

> *Children who are taught spelling for 30 minutes in a day for 8 years spell no better than children in other schools who are taught only 15 minutes a day (Rice, 1897).*

These conclusions were the result of an informal study conducted by Dr. Joseph M. Rice, a physician who hoped to reform education. After making up a spelling test of 50 words, he spent 5 months going from town to town administering the test (1200 classrooms in 36 cities) (Skates, 1947). Many educators denounced Dr. Rice's report ["The Futility of the Spelling Grind" (1897)] as "foolish and reprehensible" (Ayres, 1918, p. 11). The value of spelling, they contended, was not in spelling accuracy, but that it disciplined children's minds!

Of course, simply selecting a group of 50 words at random is not an appropriate way to construct a test. Nevertheless, Dr. Rice's study was a landmark event because it challenged the time-honored methods of deciding curricular emphasis through discussion and argument (Skates, 1947). Instead, he used actual data on student performance as the basis for recommending that less time be spent on spelling drills. Unfortunately, one immediate effect of his findings was an *increase* in the amount of time spent on spelling drills (Linn, 1992). In other words, his findings initially had the impact of focusing instruction on a trivial outcome.

Gradually, the negative attitudes of educators toward measurement in education changed, largely as the result of two unrelated movements. One, the efficiency movement in education, is discussed in the following section. The other, referred to as the scientific movement in education, involved the development of systematic and verifiable methods for measuring achievement. Initiated by E. L. Thorndike, the first examples were his arithmetic test and his scale to measure the quality of handwriting.

The measurement of student characteristics gained further credibility through the standardization of the Binet-Simon intelligence scales by Lewis Terman. Known as the Stanford-Binet, this test reflected the model developed by Sir Francis Galton in his measurement of physical characteristics such as height. Galton found that, in a large adult population, (1) individual heights were spread across a broad continuum, and (2) few individuals were found at the tallest and shortest heights while a large number clustered around the mid-point or average of the population height.

The Stanford-Binet, and the broad achievement tests modeled after it, consist of a range of tasks designed to spread students along a continuum of performance. The tests, referred to as norm-referenced, assess a broad domain of knowledge and report individual student performance in relation to average performance in the population on whom the test was standardized. The rationale for the use of these tests was the selection role of education in the early twentieth century. That is, of the students entering the educational system, approximately 5 percent were considered to benefit from higher education (Bloom, Hastings, & Madaus, 1971, p. 21). Education formed a pyramid, with many at the bottom and few at the top. Those who scored well above average in comparison to their peers were identified as well suited for further schooling. Until the 1960s, these tests were used for the placement of students and the selection of students who were to go on to higher education.

Efficiency: The New Priority

Even the church is having its methods subject to rigorous criticism from the standpoint of efficiency. Should education, the most important of human industries, be any different? (Melcher, 1918).

The decade in which Joseph Rice conducted his spelling study was also the beginning of broad economic and social change. Rapid industrialization was replacing the family as the center of economic life. Home-based industries, such as textile weaving, disappeared. Production methods were mechanized and housed in large mills. Farmworkers migrating to the cities in search of jobs and a large influx of European immigrants swelled the populations of the country's major cities.

The apprenticeship model, in which new workers learn from skilled craftsmen, was obsolete in an industrial setting. Also, early production methods were clumsy, inefficient, and costly. Into this void stepped Frederick W. Taylor, the inventor of high-speed machine tools and the father of scientific management. Taylor analyzed production tasks into their elementary units and determined the best motions and time for each task. Properly applied, his methods often doubled output without tiring the workers (Thompson, 1914/1972).

One effect of the efficiency movement on education was the development of rating systems for teachers that yielded an "efficiency grade." They were used, instead of personal general impressions, for salary increments, retention or dismissal, and teacher improvement (Boyce, 1915). The early instruments, however, lacked both a strong conceptual framework and instructions for the raters. Thus, ratings by different judges often were not comparable.

The other effects of the efficiency movement in education were (1) the collection of data on school promotions, retentions, and costs and (2) investigations into the allocation of time for different subjects. An example: Should the weekly time allocated to handwriting be divided into five 12-minute periods, four 15-minute periods, three 20-minute periods, or two 30-minute periods? (Nifenbecker, 1918). The efficiency priorities of industry had found their way into education. However, such studies did not yield particularly useful information for schools. Factors that influence achievement that were not addressed in these studies include differences in student entry skills and differences in teaching ability.

One early report on schools, the New York inquiry of 1911–1912, set the direction for further studies of educational productivity. In addition to data on costs, promotions, and retentions, the study also reported student performance on the Courtis standardized arithmetic test.

The New York study firmly established the principle that well-designed tests must be used in any study of school operations (Ayres, 1918). Newly established research bureaus began routinely collecting achievement data in addition to other information. In the 1930s, educators expressed concerns that this widespread testing would emphasize memorizing, "freeze" the curriculum, might lead to cramming, and would reduce the teacher to the role of tutor for the examination. Nevertheless, the practice continued and set the stage for later school-by-school comparisons.

The Eight-Year Study

Teachers in several schools that are developing innovative curricula are concerned that a standardized test will be used to evaluate their efforts at the end of the first year. Their goal is to accomplish more than memorization of facts and definitions. Several schools threaten to leave the study (Nowalski, 1983).

The year was 1932; the country was in the throes of the Great Depression. Thirty schools had elected to develop programs designed to serve the large numbers of teenagers who were remaining in school because they could not find work (50 percent as opposed to 10 percent a few years earlier). The schools were allowed to experiment free of both state requirements and college entrance requirements. Ralph W. Tyler was selected to direct the project because his philosophy was that evaluation should be based on the important learnings selected by the school and the teacher.

Under Dr. Tyler's direction, the Eight-Year Study became a unique collaboration between the evaluation staff assigned to the schools and the teachers. Together, they clarified the important abilities, thinking strategies, interests, and attitudes that the teachers hoped to foster in students. Tyler recalled that the teachers often began with trite phrases (Nowalski, 1983). However, the staff probed beneath the surface to uncover goals with which the teachers were not initially aware. The result was sets of comprehensive objectives that addressed modes of critical thinking, critical interpretation, and so on. The teachers and the evaluation staff then devised innovative ways of assessing these goals (see Chapter 2 for an example). Performance on the indicators for the goals was used to revise the curriculum where necessary. Dr. Tyler also introduced the terms "evaluation" and "evaluation instruments" to refer to methods for actually determining student learning. The purpose was to differentiate such methods from the term "test" which, at that time, consisted only of memorization items. In later years, when evaluation began to mean many different things to different people, he began using the term "assessment" (Tyler, in Nowalski, 1983, p. 28).

A follow-up evaluation of students who went to college indicated that academically, they performed as well as or better than their counterparts. They also were more likely to be involved in extracurricular activities than their peers.

The Eight-Year Study demonstrated that (1) a variety of activities could be used to assess educational objectives, (2) evaluators could contribute to teacher expertise in developing meaningful assessments, and (3) continuous monitoring of students is beneficial for both the curriculum and the student. The findings attracted little attention, however. The United States became caught up in World War II and the attention of the nation was focused on the massive effort to win the global conflict.

Schools Become a Focus of National Reform

Governmental leaders and the American public are stunned. The USSR "won" the first lap in the space race by launching the suborbital space capsule Sputnik. Would the United States lose the struggle for world influence to a nondemocratic country? Would the schools be able to produce the needed scientists and scholars to close the perceived technology gap?

The United States emerged from World War II as a country with both national and international priorities. One of these priorities was to protect freedom and democracy in the world by opposing communism. The launch of Sputnik was perceived as a threat to that aim and to national security. Curiously, government leaders and the American public viewed the educational system as part of the problem.

The Sputnik launch in 1957 thrust American education into a new role. No longer were schools simply a local enterprise. Instead, they were to respond to perceived national priorities as well. Congress legislated massive funding for curriculum redesign to produce disciplined thinkers through discovery learning and student interaction with the subject. Mathematics, science, and foreign languages—subjects identified as essential to national security—were targeted first for development.

A few years later, in 1965, another priority emerged for American schools. As already stated, the prevailing view had been that very few students were fit to go on to higher education and tests played a major role in the selection process (Bloom et al., 1971). However, in the 1960s, the educational system was targeted as failing to meet the needs of minorities. Social unrest about school inequality led to the Elementary and Secondary Education Act (ESEA). Billions of dollars were provided to local education agencies to develop compensatory education and other special programs.

A key component of the post-Sputnik and compensatory education efforts was the use of standardized norm-referenced tests to determine the effects of new programs. As stated earlier, these tests sample content from a broad domain and report student performance relative to the performance of typical students in the individual's grade or age level. With the exception of Lee J. Cronbach (1963), evaluators did not question the applicability of norm-referenced tests for determining the effects produced by innovative curricula. However, the tests often were unrelated to the experiences provided by the new curricula (Linn, 1992; Powell & Sigel, 1991). Further, the tests used with the early childhood programs were standardized on a diverse population. Thus, the tests were insensitive to individual differences in disadvantaged children (Clarke-Stewart & Fein, 1983). Despite the problems, the use of norm-referenced tests in efforts to evaluate new programs legitimized their use for group comparisons.

In addition, some measurement experts had long cautioned that the tests were designed only to provide information about an individual relative to a population to which he or she belongs. The tests are not designed to assess the range and variety of the goals and priorities of a particular curriculum (Haertel, 1992). Also, they should be used to report group performance *only* when inputs are also considered (Thorndike & Hagen, 1969). Input consists of the earlier status of the student, the relative emphasis on different goals, and the resources of the classroom or school. This information, however, is rarely provided. Despite these problems, the use of norm-referenced tests to compare groups of students was legitimized in the program evaluations of new curricula in the 1960s. "Tests were being implemented to make keep-or-kill decisions about educational programs. Big dollars were riding on the results of achievement tests . . . the days of penny-ante assessment were over" (Popham, 1983, p. 23).

Program developers and educators, however, were disappointed that norm-referenced tests did not clearly indicate the specific effects of particular programs. The conclusion was that tests designed to assess identified program objectives were needed. Developers then identified the skills and competencies to be acquired by students in particular programs and developed tests to measure those capabilities. Referred to as mastery, criterion-referenced, objectives-referenced, or competency tests, they answer the question, What skills has the student mastered? Development of such tests requires the identification of the capability or competency to be mastered, such as analyzing data presented in bar graphs. Situations representative of the capabilities are then developed and a mastery score is identified for the test. This perspective to developing tests also led to the movement referred to as competency testing.

Perhaps the best known objectives-referenced assessment, the National Assessment of Educational Progress (NAEP), was developed in the late 1960s. Mandated by Congress, NAEP was designed to provide information about the educational achievement of U.S. students at different age levels. Different subject areas were assessed in alternating years on a national sample of students. In 1988, Public Law (PL) 100-297 established the schedule of reading and mathematics as every two years, writing and science every four years, and history/geography and other subjects every six years. Results are reported in terms of the percentages of students that achieve at the basic, proficient, and advanced levels for ages 9, 13, and 17 and grades 4, 8, and 12 (Fitzharris, 1993).

The Era of Accountability and High-Stakes Testing

Fueled by media reports of declining student scores on college entrance examinations in the 1970s, various critics of the schools joined in a revolt against school failures. They became advocates of minimum competency testing (Gray, 1980).

In the 1970s, further concerns about education surfaced. The media reported declines in Scholastic Aptitude Test (SAT) scores, and this decline was interpreted by some as an indicator of major weaknesses in American education. However, participation in the SAT is voluntary, and larger numbers of students from groups who had not previously aspired to college were taking the test. Thus, the pool of test takers was changing. In addition, a 138-item test of verbal and mathematical aptitude is not an adequate measure of curricula that include history, science, the humanities, foreign languages, social studies, the arts, and other school subjects.

Nevertheless, the perceived link between SAT scores and school performance persisted. However, other critics maintained that norm-referenced tests penalized minorities. Some state legislatures responded by enacting laws for minimum competency testing as a requirement for a high school diploma. These criterion-referenced tests assessed the mastery of selected basic skills. (Others have since called for "maximum competency testing" to describe the mastery of knowledge in a subject area [Madaus, 1985]. The New York State Regents Examinations are examples.)

Of interest is that politicians, not educators, were prescribing testing as the mechanism for resolving educational problems. The intent was twofold. Some groups wanted to ensure that students had acquired the necessary skills for survival in society and the tests were expected to restore confidence in the high school diploma.

Others saw such testing as a way to reform education (Baker & Choppin, 1990). This use of testing is a transition from evaluating curricula intended to bring about reform to that of being an instrument of reform itself (Airasian, 1988).

Some problems, however, have arisen in relation to minimal competency tests for high school diplomas. They include (1) the use of multiple-choice items as proxies for writing and mathematics skills, (2) the lack of agreement on ways to establish mastery standards, and (3) court challenges to use of the tests for graduation. One of the legal challenges was that the tests lacked essential test characteristics, defined as validity and reliability. That is, the challengers maintained that inappropriate inferences were being made on the basis of test scores (lack of validity) and the test results were inappropriately discriminating among students (lack of reliability). Other challenges included the identification of the potential for racial or linguistic discrimination, lack of adequate advance notice and phase-in of the testing, lack of correspondence between the curriculum and test, and the extent to which remediation might lead to or reinforce tracking (Anderson, Stiggins, & Gordon, 1980). As a result, in 1988–1989, only 19 states required students to pass minimum competency tests for high school graduation (U.S. Department of Education, 1989).

However, in 1992–1993, approximately 34 states were using criterion-referenced tests as part of their statewide testing programs (Barton & Coley, 1994). Also, in the 1980s, several states passed legislation requiring competency testing of teachers. Tests used for students in schools of education are paper-and-pencil tests on basic communication and mathematical skills and, in some cases, subject-matter and pedagogical knowledge (Jaeger, 1992).

Pressure for accountability continued in the 1980s with the publication of *A Nation at Risk*. The problems described had existed for some years, particularly in inner-city and rural schools (Berlak, 1992). However, the report added to the anxiety brought on by a faltering economy, the trade imbalance, rising unemployment, and concerns about the nation's second-rate status.

Similar to the earlier Sputnik crisis, schools became both the cause and the solution of problems related to political and economic events. Instead of curricular reform, *A Nation at Risk* suggested standardized tests at major transition points in students' education. The purpose was to identify both the need for remediation and opportunities for advanced work. However, the emphasis quickly became that of accountability. Within 8 years of the publication of *A Nation at Risk*, every state was implementing top–down measures to raise educational standards, and the most common mechanism was statewide testing (Berlak, 1992).

The Call for Assessment Reform

> *"Tests should involve students in the actual challenges, standards, and habits needed for success in the academic discipline or in the workplace." (Wiggins, 1989, p. 700) "Multiple-choice items, however, test isolated pieces of information, rules, and procedures. They are typically only exercises in detection and selection." (Wolf, Bixby, Glenn, & Gardner, 1991)*

The advent of mandatory testing led to several effects. Measurement experts continued to point out that standardized tests are useful only within limits. However, when used as the sole indicator of quality, they are poor indicators of teacher quality or for comparing divergent school populations (Rudman, 1993, p. 8). Schools have reacted to the use of standardized testing for comparison purposes by realigning curricula to reflect the focus of the test, selecting easier tests instead of those that most accurately measure their educational goals, and ensuring that class time is spent practicing the skills to be tested (Fredericksen, 1984; Haladyna, Nolen, & Haas, 1991; Linn, 1989; Smith & Rottenberg, 1991).

In addition, some analyses seemed to indicate a decline in performance on complex cognitive tasks. The National Assessment of Educational Progress (1982) reported a decline from 62 to 58 percent on mathematical problem solving, 51 to 41 percent on analysis of reading passages, and 21 to 15 percent on writing analytical essays.

Criticisms of multiple-choice tests also began to increase in the late 1980s. Some educators expressed the view that these tests are unrelated to classroom activities and do not provide information about student progress on complex intellectual goals. (Multiple-choice items can be constructed to measure complex skills [see Chapters 2 and 6]. However, poorly constructed items often address trivial content and/or only the recall of information.)

Alternative forms of assessment were proposed to involve students in the actual challenges and habits required in the real world. Initiated originally in the late 1980s as a means to assess meaningful curricular goals, alternative assessments have begun to capture the attention of policymakers.

Alternative assessments are tasks that measure complex intellectual capabilities, such as developing a persuasive argument or analyzing the effects of an important historical event. In addition, they should focus on important and teachable learning processes and inform teachers about students' strengths and weaknesses (Baker, Freeman, & Clayton, 1991). Examples are portfolios, which are collections of student work over a period of time, and performance assessments, such as conducting an experiment on the absorbency of paper towels.

Among the expectations expressed for alternative assessments are that (1) testing will become productive rather than punitive; (2) the assessments can guide educational reform; and (3) teacher participation in scoring can enhance professional development. At present, some states are implementing performance assessments as a component of statewide testing and schools and districts are implementing both portfolios and performance assessments. However, various issues related to these assessments are as yet unresolved (see Chapters 8 and 9) and the long-term effects are yet to be determined.

Discussion

Assessment in American education has, for the most part, reflected the role of the educational system in the political, economic, and social priorities of the country. Early in the country's history, for example, paper-and-pencil tests of basic reading, writing and computation skills were sufficient for the needs of a largely rural society.

The crude spelling test administered by Joseph Rice marked the beginning of a new approach to making decisions about curricula and students. Instead of discussion or personal opinion, he relied on student performance. In less than 20 years, the Stanford-Binet intelligence test and several broad-range achievement tests were used to make decisions about the placement and selection of students. In addition, the efficiency movement in industry and society led to efficiency ratings of teachers and the reporting of achievement test results in summaries of school operation.

The first formal evaluation of innovative curricula according to curriculum objectives is the Eight-Year Study. The evaluation demonstrated that a variety of activities could be used to assess educational objectives important to the school. In addition, evaluators and teachers collaborated in the development of meaningful assessments.

From a fairly restricted use of test results in the first half of the twentieth century, the 1960s initiated major changes. Public policy began to view testing as a key barometer of the nation's educational health (Rudman, 1993, p. 5). First, norm-referenced tests were used to evaluate innovative curricula developed in the wake of Sputnik and the social unrest of the early 1960s. Disappointment with the findings led to the development of criterion-referenced or mastery tests designed to measure specific skills.

The use of widespread testing as a tool for educational reform began with the competency testing movement in the 1970s. Competency testing was seen as a way to reverse declining college entrance examination scores and restore the worth of a high school diploma. Pressure for accountability continued in the 1980s, fueled by concerns about the nation's economic status and the publication of *A Nation at Risk*. Statewide testing programs were instituted as a way of raising standards.

The chain of reasoning that links lack of economic competitiveness to weaknesses in the educational system relies on highly questionable assumptions about the effects of schooling (Cremin, 1990; Feuer & Fulton, 1994, p. 31). Also, measurement experts continue to point out the limitations of standardized tests. Nevertheless, the public supports statewide testing with associated sanctions and rewards, such as a high school diploma, grade promotion, and so on.

Airasian (1988) offers three reasons for the acceptance of widespread testing. First, tests are symbols of external order and unbiased judgments in a world that is increasingly diverse and unpredictable. Second, tests are viewed as symbols of important values. For example, a so-called survival skills test calls up images of an array of proficiencies that goes beyond the actual 25 vocabulary and 25 basic math items on the test (p. 308). Third, tests are viewed as motivating students to learn. Thus, they symbolize values such as hard work and nose to the grindstone.

In summary, large-scale testing has become the educational parallel to the Dow Jones average (Airasian, 1988). Therefore, despite the effects on the curriculum, students, and teachers, large-scale testing is likely to continue.

✦ Overview of the Text

Large-scale testing impacts students, teachers, and administrators. However, the day-to-day assessment of student accomplishments and strengths and weaknesses rests with the classroom teacher. The purpose of the three remaining chapters in Part One of the text is to provide a knowledge base about the various types of assessment, both informal and formal, two approaches to measurement, the basic requirements for all assessments, and the relationship of assessment to the planning and implementation of instruction. Chapter 2 provides an overview of quantitative methods that yield a numerical score or rating and verbal or qualitative methods that yield descriptive information about students. Included are appropriate uses of each, as well as a discussion of two approaches to measurement, referred to as norm-referenced and criterion-referenced.

Chapter 3 describes and provides examples of the two essential characteristics of assessments—validity and reliability. Examples of each as well as events that can jeopardize these important assessment features are discussed.

Chapter 4 discusses first the possible relationships between teaching and assessment. For example, one approach, prevalent in higher education, is that assessment is outside of and independent of instruction. In contrast, in elementary classrooms in particular, informal and formal assessment are closely integrated with teaching and are important in guiding the direction of instruction. This chapter also describes the role of curriculum goals and frameworks in setting priorities for the classroom and the use of classroom objectives in planning and selecting assessments.

Part Two, Classroom Assessment Tools, describes five types of assessment used to obtain information about student achievement and achievement-related activities. Chapters 5 and 6 discuss the construction of various types of items for classroom tests. Included are true-false, matching, multiple-choice, short-answer, and essay questions. The chapters emphasize ways to construct items to assess the application of knowledge, interpretation of information, and other higher cognitive processes. Chapter 7 discusses observational methods. Included are anecdotal records, interviews, and checklists and rating scales for student performances and products.

Chapter 8 describes performance assessments, their use in both the classroom and large-scale testing, and cautions to observe in constructing performance assessments. Also discussed is the application of rating scales to these assessments.

Portfolio assessment is discussed in Chapter 9. Four major types of portfolios and their roles are described, as well as the types of information that may be included. Evaluating portfolio contents also is discussed.

Part Three of the text focuses on other assessment issues of importance in the classroom. The focus of Chapter 10 is the assessment of attitudes and interests. Discussed are the use of simple interest inventories in the classroom in planning instruction, the use of behavior rating scales, and the role of self-attitudes in current research and the classroom. The types of disabilities defined by federal legislation methods for assessing the special needs of learners and the development of IEPs are discussed in Chapter 11. Included are informal reading inventories, and event and duration recording of behaviors. Developing a grading system, and the relationship of one's grading system to the teacher's model of teaching and assessment are discussed in Chapter 12.

Chapters 13 and 14 address two issues in standardized testing. Chapter 13 discusses the interpretation of standardized tests, an important responsibility of classroom teachers. Chapter 14 discusses legal and ethical issues in implementing standardized tests, including recent court challenges.

Chapter Questions

1. As secondary education developed and became mandatory in the early twentieth century, it began to resemble the factory assembly line. Currently, bells announce the change in "shifts" (class periods), and the "raw material" (students) then move to each "product development area" (classroom). In what ways has testing contributed to or counteracted this image?

2. The early use of norm-referenced tests was to select the brightest students at each educational level who could benefit most from further schooling. This use was consistent with the belief that only 5 percent of the school population could benefit from higher education. Since that time, in what other ways has assessment served as either an instrument or target of public policy?

3. Given the potential for misinformation of test scores from standardized norm-referenced tests, why do you think their extensive use continues?

4. As the country approaches the twenty-first century, terms such as "the information society" and "learning to negotiate the information highway" have surfaced to symbolize the use of computers in communication and knowledge acquisition. What are some of the implications of these changes for assessment?

References

Airasian, P. (1988). Symbolic validation: The case of state-mandated high-stakes testing. *Educational Evaluation and Policy Analysis*, *10*(4), 301–313.

Anderson, B. L., Stiggins, R. J., & Gordon, D. W. (1980). *Educational testing facts and issues: A layperson's guide to testing in the schools*. Portland, OR: Northwest Educational Laboratory and California State Department of Education.

Armstrong, A. (1993). Cognitive-style differences in testing situations. *Educational Measurement: Issues and Practice*, *12*(3), 17–22.

Ayres, F. (1918). History and present status of educational measurements. In G. M. Whipple (Ed.), *The measurement of educational products: The seventeenth yearbook of the National Society for the Study of Education, Part II* (pp. 9–15). Bloomington, IL: Public School Publishing.

Baker, E. L., & Choppin, B. H. (1990). Minimum competency tests. In H. J. Walberg & G. D. Haertel (Eds.), *The international encyclopedia of educational evaluation* (pp. 499–502). Oxford: Pergamon Press.

Baker, E. L., Freeman, M., & Clayton, S. (1991). Cognitive assessment of history for large-scale testing: In M. Wittrock & E. Baker (Eds.), *Testing and cognition* (pp. 131–153). Englewood Cliffs, NJ: Prentice Hall.

Barton, P. E. & Coley, R. J. (1994). *Testing in America's Schools*. Princeton: Educational Testing Service.

Berlak, H. (1992). The need for a new science of assessment. In H. Berlak, F. M. Newmann, E. Adams, D. Archbald, T. Burgess, J. Raven, & T. A. Romberg, *Toward a new science of educational testing and achievement* (pp. 1–21). Albany: State University of New York Press.

Bloom, B., Hastings, J., & Madaus, G. (1971). *Handbook on formative and summative evaluation of student learning*. New York: McGraw-Hill.

Boyce, A. C. (1915). Methods for measuring teachers' efficiency. In S. C. Parker (Ed.), *Methods for measuring teacher efficiency: Fourteenth yearbook of the National Society for the Study of Education: Part II*. Chicago: University of Chicago Press.

Cizek, G. J. (1993). Some thoughts on educational testing: Measurement policy issues into the next millenium. *Educational Measurement: Issues and Practice, 12*, 10–16.

Clarke-Stewart, K., & Fein, G. (1983). Early childhood programs. In M. Haith & J. Compas (Eds.), *Handbook of child psychology: Vol. 2. Infancy and developmental psychology* (pp. 917–999). New York: Wiley.

Cremin, L. (1990). *Popular education and its discontents*. New York: Harper & Row.

Cronbach, L. J. (1963). Course improvement through evaluation. *Teachers College Record, 64*(8), 672–683.

Feuer, M., & Fulton, K. (1994). Educational testing abroad and lessons for the United States. *Educational Measurement: Issues and Practice, 13*(2), 31–39.

Fitzharris, L. H. (1993). An historical review of the National Assessment of Educational Progress from 1963 to 1991. Unpublished doctoral dissertation, University of South Carolina. Columbia, S.C.

Fredericksen, N. (1984). The real test bias: Influences of testing on teaching and learning. *American Psychologist, 39*(3), 193–202.

Gray, D. (1980). *Minimum competency testing: Guidelines for policy makers and citizens*. Washington, DC: Council for Basic Education.

Haertel, E. (1992). *Performance measurement*. In M. C. Alkin (Ed.), *Encyclopedia of educational research* (6th ed.) *Vol. 3* (pp. 984–989). New York: Macmillan.

Haladyna, T. M., Nolen, S. B., & Haas, N. (1991). Raising standardized achievement test scores and the origins of test pollutiore. *Educational Researcher, 20*(5), 2–7.

Jaeger, R. M. (1992). Competency Testing. In M. C. Alkin (Ed.), *Encyclopedia of Educational Research* (6th ed.) *Vol. 3* (pp. 222–232). New York: Macmillan.

Linn, R. L. (1989). *Educational measurement* (3rd ed.). Englewood Cliffs, NJ: Prentice Hall.

Linn, R. L. (1992). Achievement Testing. In M. C. Alkin (Ed.), *Encyclopedia of educational research* (6th ed.) *Vol. 3* (pp. 2–12). New York: Macmillan.

Madaus, G. F. (1985, May). Test scores as administrative mechanisms in educational policy. *Phi Delta Kappan*, 66(9), 611–617.

Melcher, G. (1918). Suggestions for experimental work. In G. M. Whipple (Ed.), *The measurement of educational products: The seventeenth yearbook of the National Society for the Study of Education, Part II* (pp. 139–151). Bloomington, IL: Public School Publishing.

National Assessment of Educational Progress. (1982). Graduates may lack tomorrow's "basics." *NAEP Newsletter, 15*, 8.

Nifenbecker, E. A. (1918). Bureaus of research in city school systems. In G. M. Whipple (Ed.), *The measurement of educational products: The seventeenth yearbook of the National Society for the Study of Education, Part II* (pp. 52–56). Bloomington, IL: Public School Publishing.

Nowalski, J. R. (1983, May). On educational evaluation. A conversation with Ralph Tyler. *Educational Leadership, 40*(9), 24–29.

Popham, W. H. (1983). Measurement as an instructional catalyst. In R. B. Ekstrom (Ed.), *New directions for testing and measurement: Management, technology, and individuality in education*, No. 17 (pp. 19–30). San Francisco: Jossey Bass.

Powell, D., & Sigel, I. (1991). Searches for validity in evaluating young children and early childhood programs. In B. Spodek & O. Saracho (Eds.), *Issues in early childhood curriculum* (pp. 190–212). New York: Teachers College Press.

Rice, J. M. (1897, April and June). The futility of the spelling grind. *The Forum XXIII*, 163–172; 409–19.

Rudman, H. C. (1993). National testing or political testing: Is there a difference? *Educational Measurement: Issues and Practice, 12*(3), 5–9, 30.

Skates, D. E. (1947). Fifty years of objective measurement and research in education. *Journal of Educational Research, 41*, 241–264.

Smith, M. L., & Rottenberg, C. (1991). Unintended consequences of external testing in elementary schools. *Educational Measurement: Issues and Practice, 10*(4), 7–11.

Taylor, G., & Nolen, S. B. (1996). A contextualized approach to teaching teachers about classroom-based assessment. *Educational Psychologist, 31*(1), 77–88.

Thompson, C. B. (1914/1972). The literature of scientific management. In C. B. Thompson (Ed.), *Scientific management* (pp. 3–48). Boston: Hine Publishing.

Thorndike, R., & Hagen, E. (1969). *Measurement and evaluation in psychology and education* (3rd ed). New York: Wiley.

U.S. Department of Education (1989). *The condition of education: Vol. 1*. Washington, DC: U.S. Government Printing Office.

Wiggins, G. (1988, January). Revitalizing classroom assessment: The highest instructional priority. *Phi Delta Kappan, 69*(5), 363–368.

Wiggins, G. (1989, May). A true test: Toward more authentic and equitable assessment. *Phi Delta Kappan, 70*(9), 703–713.

Wolf, D., Bixby, J., Glenn, J., & Gardner, H. (1991). To use their minds well: Investigating new forms of student assessment. In G. Grant (Ed.), *Review of Research in Education, Vol. 17* (pp. 32–73). Washington, DC: American Educational Research Association.

Chapter 2

Assessment Methods

Major Topics

Quantitative Assessments

Tests and Rating Scales

Construction Steps

Strengths and Limitations

Measurement Models

Norm-Referenced

Criterion-Referenced

Qualitative Assessments

Teacher Observations

Teacher Questions

Interviews and Student Reflections

One report indicates that teachers spend 20 to 30% of the time directly involved in assessment-related activities (Wiggins, 1988). Also, most of the assessments developed by teachers are nonmultiple-choice.

–Barton & Coley, 1994

As indicated by the cited report, assessment is a major responsibility of the classroom teacher. In this role, teachers use a variety of methods, both formal and informal, to make decisions about instruction and students. Among the decisions are diagnosing student problems, planning and conducting instruction, placing students in groups, providing feedback to students, and reporting to parents. Important in these decisions is understanding the range and variety of assessments that are available, and the contribution of each to the decision-making process.

Assessment refers to all the systematic methods and procedures that are used to obtain information about behavior. As indicated in Figure 2-1, assessment may be subdivided into broad categories, quantitative and qualitative. Quantitative assessments yield numerical estimates of characteristics or behaviors, whereas qualitative assessments yield verbal descriptions. For example, a fifth-grade teacher's notes (anecdotal records) may indicate that Simon avoids writing by moving frequently in and out of the library while carrying a sheet of paper and a pencil.

In addition to differences in basic characteristics, these two broad types of assessment differ in the decisions for which they are appropriate as well as in their advantages and limitations.

✦ Quantitative Assessments

The two major types of quantitative assessments, also referred to as measurements, are tests and rating scales.

Tests and Rating Scales

A test is a set of tasks or questions that usually is administered to a group of classroom students in a specific time period. Tests typically address the cognitive capabilities learned in a particular course, subject area, or discipline. Included are recalling definitions and important terms, adding two-digit numbers, interpreting concepts and ideas, and solving problems. Tests often consist of essay questions, problems, or structured-response questions, such as matching, multiple-choice, or true-false items.

Unlike tests, rating scales are instruments for obtaining judgments by others or self-judgments of one's capabilities, interests, attitudes, or social skills. (See Table 10-3 for an example.) For example, college students complete evaluations of their courses. Dimensions such as the communication skills of the instructor,

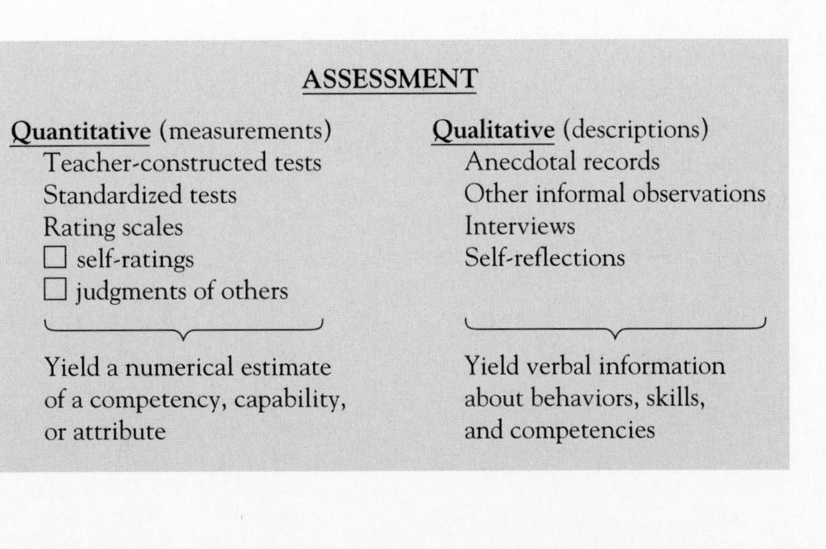

FIGURE 2.1
An overview of assessment methods.

the instructor's knowledge of the subject matter, and relevance of the textbook may each be evaluated on a range such as 1 to 4 or 1 to 7.

Rating scales also are used to evaluate student performances and products that require complex cognitive skills. Examples are delivering a speech or conducting an experiment (performances) and essays, research reports, computer programs, or lesson plans (products). (See Tables 7-4 and 7-5 for examples of product rating scales.)

Basic Steps in Construction

Of importance is that a test or rating scale is not simply a collection of questions or items that occur to the developer. Such an instrument is unlikely to address important capabilities and unlikely to yield dependable information about students. An example is Joseph Rice's compilation of 50 spelling words. Problems included the failure to check word difficulty and appropriateness of the words for the ages of the children.

Measurements, in other words, are carefully selected samples of behavior. From the student's responses to items or tasks in the assessment, inferences are made about the student's performance, beliefs, or attitudes. Therefore, the assessment must be carefully constructed.

Four major steps are involved in developing measurements. First is to identify the capabilities, competencies, attributes, or qualities to be measured. For example, the assessment focus may be a measure of comprehensive achievement in social studies. The framework for the test is a blueprint referred to as a table of specifications. It typically lists common topics and concepts in the major textbooks as column headings, identifies cognitive skills as row headings, and the number of items needed in each cell of the table. In contrast, a test for the certification of respiratory therapists would be based on an analysis of essential diagnoses and prescriptive solutions, whereas a measure of self-esteem requires identification of particular personal characteristics.

The second step is to determine the set of operations that serve as indicators of the capability. For a comprehensive social studies test, multiple-choice and other structured-response items are developed to measure the variety of facts, concepts, and principles identified in the table of specifications. In contrast, a certification examination for respiratory therapists consists of hypothetical medical problems that require the diagnoses and prescriptive solutions essential for competent performance. After the items or tasks are developed, they are carefully reviewed for consistency with the conceptual framework for the test.

The third step is to establish procedures to translate the responses into quantitative estimates of degree or amount (Thorndike & Hagen, 1969). For example, one point may be assigned to each correct answer in an achievement test. In contrast, scoring guides or rubrics that address important aspects of the diagnostic process may be developed to score the decisions of respiratory therapists.

Step four involves the collection of information to determine that the measurement actually functions as it should. This essential characteristic, referred to as validity, is discussed in detail in Chapter 3. Information also is obtained on the consistency of the scoring procedures, known as reliability (discussed in Chapter 3).

Strengths and Limitations

One strength of measurements is that they provide a common basis for discussing or analyzing an educational outcome. In contrast, verbal descriptions of educational outcomes or products will vary because they are influenced by characteristics of the evaluator, such as beliefs, opinions, and powers of observation.

A second strength is that the score or rating is typically easily interpreted by teachers and administrators. For example, a test score of 88 out of 100 on an addition test indicates substantive performance.

A third strength is versatility. Tests and rating scales can assess broad constructs such as verbal reasoning or particular skills such as interpreting tables and graphs. Further, measurements are appropriate for decisions about educational outcomes as well as identified benchmarks during instruction. Finally, tests and rating scales are easy to administer and efficient. That is, they can provide dependable information in a brief time period.

Measurements are structured situations that focus on particular characteristics or behaviors. Therefore, one limitation is that they cannot capture behaviors or interactions as they naturally occur. In addition, several cautions should be observed to avoid the misuse of quantitative assessments. As indicated in Table 2-1, measurements are only samples of characteristics or behaviors and they are not perfect indicators. Further, the measurement should reflect the complexity of the capabilities that are assessed and should be used only as a tool for academic decision-making and not for other purposes.

Summary

Assessment refers to all the systematic methods and procedures that provide information about behavior. The two major types of quantitative assessments or measurements are tests and rating scales. A test is a set of tasks or questions that typically address cognitive capabilities. Rating scales, in contrast, are judgments by others or self-judgments of one's capabilities, interests, attitudes, or social skills. The basic steps in constructing measurements are to (1) identify the capabilities, competencies, attributes, or qualities to be measured; (2) determine the set of operations that serve as indicators; (3) establish procedures to translate

Table 2.1 Cautions in Using Measurements

Cautions	Examples
1. A measurement should not be mistaken for a characteristic or behavior; the measurement is only a sample of behavior.	Ms. Murray, a fourth-grade teacher, patiently explains to David's mother that his grade-equivalent score of fifth grade, second month on language arts does not mean he is a genius. David simply answered more questions correctly on this test than did other students.
2. A numerical score or rating is not a perfect indicator of the characteristic or behavior; it is only an estimate.	Sally scores 83 on a math test in October; on a similar test 3 weeks later, she is tired and distracted and her score is only 71.
3. Educational tasks are often complex and require more than one capability. A complete measurement should address this complexity.	Evaluation of an essay should address characteristics such as clarity of expression, content accuracy, paragraph construction, and grammar.
4. A measurement is only a tool; it is not an end in itself.	Avoid the practice of "It's Friday, so I have to schedule a spelling test."
5. Assessments should not be used as classroom management tools.	Avoid the practice of administering a test because the class has misbehaved.

examinee responses into quantitative estimates; and (4) collect information about the ways the instrument functions. Strengths of measurements are that they provide a common basis for analysis, they are easily interpreted, and they are versatile. However, they are only estimates, should be used only as assessment tools, and should not be mistaken for the characteristic itself.

✦ Two Measurement Models

Two approaches to conceptualizing achievement are norm-referenced and criterion-referenced measurements. Each provides important information about student performance.

Norm-Referenced Measurement

As indicated in Chapter 1, the norm-referenced model originally reflected the measurement of fixed traits, such as adult height. This model was applied in education first to intelligence, viewed as a fixed trait, and then to achievement in broad curriculum areas. The rationale for the development of norm-referenced achievement tests, since achievement is not a trait, was based on quantitative data. Specifically, the data indicated a fairly strong relationship between scores on broad-range achievement tests and intelligence tests and between the achievement test scores and school performance. (Researchers calculated a statistic referred to as a correlation on student scores from both types of tests. Correlations of 0.70 to 0.80 indicated similar performance on both types of tests.)

Characteristics of standardized tests. The defining characteristics of standardized norm-referenced tests are listed in Table 2-2. That is, they assess a broad domain, include items that range in difficulty, and, therefore, produce a range of performance by the examinees.

In addition, standardized tests, such as the Metropolitan Achievement Test and the Iowa Test of Basic Skills, include performance norms with which to derive the individual student's comparison score. These norms typically are established by administering the test items to large numbers of the group(s) identified as the target population for the test. The performance of these students, referred to as the norming or reference group, is the "yardstick" for evaluating the performance of future examinees.

Table 2.2 Characteristics of Standardized Norm-Referenced Tests

1. Assess a broad domain of knowledge
2. Based on a test blueprint that identifies common topics and concepts in the subject-matter textbooks and important cognitive skills
3. Include items on a range of difficulty
4. Answer the question: What is the student's relative standing in a broad domain?
5. Report examinee performance in terms of the performance of a relevant comparison group
6. Provide performance norms with which to derive the examinee's comparison score
7. Report comparison performance in the form of percentiles, grade equivalents, or standard scores

Of major importance is that test norms are only *typical* performance; they do not represent a desirable standard. Also, over the years, typical performance has changed. Linn, Graue, and Sanders (1990) note that student performance on various tests (the California Achievement Test, the Iowa Test of Basic Skills, the Metropolitan Achievement Test, the Stanford Achievement Test, and the Comprehensive Test of Basic Skills) has increased *annually* an average of 1.01 to 2.20 percentile ranks (p. 12). This information is not widely known, because commercial tests are recalibrated approximately every 7 years. That is, new norms are established by adjusting the yardstick for comparisons so that the average score earned by students in the target population is at the midpoint. Thus, the norms with which students are compared on the standardized tests have gradually moved upward. If student performance continues to increase gradually over the years, the norms, which reflect typical performance, will again be adjusted upward.

Scoring. The student's comparison score on a standardized test may be reported in the form of percentiles, grade equivalents, or standard scores. Each indicates the student's performance in comparison to the reference group. A percentile score between 90 and 95, for example, indicates that the student's performance level on the test is higher than 90 to 95 percent of the students in the reference group. (A detailed discussion of the interpretation of standardized test scores is presented in Chapter 13.)

Sometimes norm-referencing is loosely applied in classroom grading, although this practice is not recommended. (Chapter 12 discusses this practice.) Referred to as grading "on the curve," the instructor typically sets an A grade on a test at the level of the highest scores in the class. A B grade is set at the level of 80 percent of the A scores, and so on. One problem with this practice is that the student's grade is dependent in large measure on the performance of others. If an average student is in a class with several very bright students, his or her grade would be lower than if the class consisted of average and below-average students.

Decisions. Two appropriate uses of norm-referenced tests are (1) to compare a student's performance in different subject areas and (2) to inform a teacher of a new student's relative performance in a subject compared to a national sample. For example, a student's score between the 40th and 45th percentile in vocabulary development should alert the teacher to a potential reading problem, particularly if the texts used in the school are difficult to read.

When used with other information, norm-referenced tests can assist in academic decisions about individual students, such as selection for an accelerated program or identifying a possible learning disability. However, low performance on a norm-referenced test is only a red flag to signal that follow-up is needed to determine if a problem exists.

Norm-referenced tests are designed as measures of individual student progress in relation to national peers (Smith, 1991, p. 541). They were not designed to provide comparative information about *groups* of students. Therefore, they should not be used to make decisions about retaining or eliminating educational programs. Moreover, standardized norm-referenced tests do not address the variety of goals in a particular curriculum (Haertel, 1990). Tyler (1990, p. 734) noted that the topics that are not common to tests and school curricula are more numerous than the common topics in these tests. Further, the tests typically do not assess complex cognitive processes. That is, thinking processes such as planning an experiment or eliminating hypotheses are not captured by these measures. To the extent that program goals emphasize the development of complex thinking processes, other assessments are needed.

Finally, standardized norm-referenced tests are not designed for accountability decisions. Aggregate scores can indicate performance differences only if they rule out other reasonable explanations of score differences (Koretz, 1992, p. 19). These explanations include the earlier status of students and differences in school funding. For example, some school districts spend as much as $11,000 per student per year, whereas others spend as little as $3,000 (Kozol, 1991).

Criterion-Referenced Measurement

Criterion-referenced tests are designed to measure particular skills and capabilities, not a broad construct or curriculum area. They emerged in the 1970s primarily to address the particular goals and objectives of new educational programs.

The theoretical basis for criterion referencing is a continuum of knowledge in a specifically defined domain and the goal is to place an individual's performance on the continuum on the basis of proficiency measures (Glaser, 1963).

The knowledge continuum in a domain may be defined in any of several ways (Nitko, 1984). Spelling, for example, may be ordered on difficulty of the subject matter. In contrast, writing narratives, debugging computer programs, and interpreting X-rays can be organized on quality of performance from novice to expert (see Chi, Glaser, & Farr, 1988). In other words, an expert's performance is both qualitatively and quantitatively different from that of a novice.

In developing a test for the classroom, evaluation of a program, or certification of competencies, the continuum may or may not be fully developed in advance. However, the type of domain and a general sense of placement of the particular skills is important.

Some writings on criterion-referenced assessment have interpreted the term *criterion* to mean "standard of performance." However, the term does not refer to the cut-off score or performance standard of the test. Instead, it refers to the tasks or behaviors that are the basis for the test (Hambleton, 1990; Nitko, 1984). Examples are making inferences from tables or graphs of data and evaluating the logic of a persuasive argument (see the example in the following section).

Characteristics. The characteristics of criterion-referenced assessments, also referred to as mastery, objectives-referenced, or competency tests, are listed in Table 2-3. Tasks or items are developed to reflect particular skills or competencies and performance is reported in terms of skills mastery. That is, the yardstick for student performance is a preestablished level of proficiency.

Two approaches to the development of criterion-referenced assessments are objectives referencing and the continuum or levels-of-proficiency approach. (A third type is minimum competency testing, used by several states to test basic skills.)

The earliest example of the objectives-referenced approach is the Eight-Year Study in which teachers developed assessments for broadly stated end-of-course objectives. The study produced measures for critical thinking, appreciation of literature, and social sensitivity (Coffman, 1993, p. 6). An example is the objective of interpreting data; Table 2-4 illustrates the assessment task for junior high school students. Because the objectives were general statements, the aspects of the skill to be tested were first specified, and then testing situations were developed.

A similar testing format for higher cognitive skills is the multiple-rating item (Scriven, 1994). For example, the test may present a prose passage and five summaries of the passage. The student grades the summaries and also selects a ratio-

Table 2.3 Characteristics of Criterion-Referenced Tests

1. Assess particular skills or competencies on an identified continuum of knowledge
2. Based on objectives that state particular capabilities or a continuum of performance in a domain
3. Do *not* include items or tasks on a range of difficulty
4. Answer the question: What skills has the student mastered?
5. Report examinee performance in terms of the objectives or the skills continuum that is the basis for the test
6. Provide a mastery standard or identified levels of proficiency on a novice/expert continuum with which to grade the examinee's performance
7. Report examinee performance as (a) mastery or nonmastery or (b) a level of competency on a novice/expert continuum

Table 2.4 Description of Test Situations for Making Inferences from Data

Objective:	The ability to make inferences from data
Skills involved:	Making comparisons, identifying elements common to several items of data, recognizing prevailing tendencies or trends in the data, and recognizing the limitations of given data
Content:	Data pertinent to topics such as heredity, crop rotation, immigration, government expenditures, and health
Test items:	Data presented in various forms, including tables, charts, and different kinds of graphs. Each set of data is followed by 15 statements that purport to be interpretations. The student is asked to place the statement in one of three categories as follows: (1) true; (2) insufficient data; and (c) false.

Source: Summarized from Smith and Tyler (1942).

nale for each grade from a set of rationales provided on the test. Such items assess higher-order cognitive skills; are resistant to multiple guessing (efforts to eliminate the wrong answer); and avoid the problem of verbal fluency, which may mask deficiencies in subject-area knowledge (Scriven, 1994).

Skills that are ordered on a continuum require definitions of the different proficiency levels and the development of tasks and/or scoring guides (rubrics) that represent increasing levels of expertise. Examples of such skills are writing evaluative essays and interpreting x-rays.

Scoring. Objectives-referenced tests that are scored for mastery require the prior identification of a proficiency level that represents competent performance. The student receives a pass (mastery) for performance that is equal to or exceeds the cut-off score established for the skill (Hambleton, 1990).

Considerations in setting the cut-off score include the criticalness of the skill (e.g., spelling or medical diagnosis) and the extent of error that is likely in the test. For a classroom test that uses 12 graphs and tables for student inferences about data, the mastery level may be nine correct interpretations. This level does not penalize the student for random errors, and also does not permit the student to pass by chance. If the test has been carefully calibrated to ensure that all 12 situations are of equal difficulty, the mastery requirement may be set at 10 out of 12.

For domains ordered from novice to expert performance, examinees may be evaluated on a continuum. An example is the Kentucky performance assessment in writing. The four levels of proficiency are novice, apprentice, proficient, and distinguished. Novice writing is characterized by a limited awareness of audience or purpose, minimal idea development, weak organization, ineffective (or incorrect) sentence structure and language, and numerous punctuation and spelling errors. Proficient writing, in contrast, is focused, communicates with an audience, develops elaborated ideas, is organized coherently, uses language and sentence structure effectively, and has few spelling or punctuation errors (Neill et al., 1995).

Sometimes an expectation for a course or program may be expressed in a statement such as, 80 percent of the students will master 80 percent of the curriculum concepts. The problem with this approach is that it obscures the different levels and patterns of performance in the classroom (Tyler, 1990). Instead, the concepts or skills that the students are to achieve should be stated. Then, for a class in writing composition, for example, the report should indicate that 15 percent are in the top level for clarity of expression, 50 percent at the middle level, and 25 percent at the low level. The same information can be reported for other writing criteria.

Decisions. Criterion-referenced assessment is appropriate for decisions about the mastery of basic skills and the identification of proficiency level for complex capabilities. Performance assessments in many school districts and states currently use the continuum model to assess student skills in writing and other areas.

Summary

Two approaches to conceptualizing achievement are norm-referenced and criterion-referenced measurement. Standardized norm-referenced tests assess a broad domain of knowledge, include items on a range of difficulty, and report student performance in comparison to the performance of others. Scores may be percentiles, grade equivalents, or standard scores. Although norm referencing is sometimes applied to classroom grading, this practice is not recommended.

Standardized norm-referenced tests, when used with other information, are appropriate for academic decisions about selection or placement. The tests were not designed to provide comparative information about groups and they do not address the variety of goals in different curricula. They can indicate performance differences across schools only if other reasonable explanations for differences, such as funding level, are ruled out.

Criterion-referenced tests, in contrast, measure particular skills and capabilities, not a broad construct or curriculum area. Also referred to as objectives-referenced, mastery, or competency tests, the purpose of criterion-referenced measurements is to establish the student's level of proficiency on particular skills or competencies. The student's performance is scored as (1) either mastery or nonmastery or (2) is a level of competency on a novice/expert continuum. For mastery tests, considerations in setting the mastery level are the criticalness of the skill and the likely extent of error in the test. Criterion-referenced assessment is appropriate for decisions about the mastery of basic skills and the identification of proficiency levels for complex capabilities.

Qualitative Assessments

In contrast to measurements, qualitative data consist of verbal information. For example, qualitative research methods are used by cultural anthropologists and ethnographers to discover the beliefs, customs, and social life of different cultures and communities. Educational ethnographers interpret classroom events through weeks of intensive observation, recording classroom interactions minute by minute, and analyzing the data according to prescribed methods. In one study, for example, analysis of verbal and nonverbal communications in four classrooms indicated that the communications structure differed significantly from that of the Native American culture of some of the students. The requirement to answer teacher-controlled questions for which the answer had already been found was foreign to the children's culture. They reacted with silence, nervous giggling, and failure to answer the questions (Erickson & Mohatt, 1982, p. 140).

Qualitative data collection methods are also useful to the teacher in the daily life of the classroom. Among them are teacher observations, classroom questions, interviews, and student self-reflections.

Teacher Observations

Teacher observations of student actions and reactions in the classroom are important in planning, implementing, and revising instruction. The two general categories of teacher observations are informal observations and anecdotal records. Informal observations are spontaneous, unstructured, and typically are covert. That is, they are not verbalized in oral or written form. A typical example is noting the puzzlement on students' faces during instruction and restructuring the explanation.

In many situations, such as gauging the effectiveness of an explanation, informal observations are an asset to the teacher. However, they have some serious limitations. Observations about students' personal development and other characteristics often are inaccurate. The problem is that these inferences are based on a small sample of behavior, are influenced by the observer's beliefs and attitudes, and are uncorroborated by other types of evidence. Further, they can lead to teacher actions that negatively influence students. For example, Good (1980) lists 11 ways that students perceived as low achievers are treated differently in the classroom. Among them are seating low achievers farther from the teacher, asking them fewer questions, requiring less work of them, and providing less detailed feedback (p. 88).

Teacher perceptions of low ability also can lead to teacher reactions of sympathy or pity for the student. Such reactions, however, typically convey to the student that he or she cannot succeed (Graham, 1984; Graham & Weiner, 1983; Weiner, Graham, Stern, & Lawson, 1982).

Another problem with early inferences about students based on observations is that subsequent disconfirming information may not be noticed (Sadler 1981). In a discussion of the information-processing limitations of humans, he cites research indicating that people tend not to process information that conflicts with a prior hypothesis. The issue is not that individuals deliberately ignore disconfirming instances. Instead, these instances are simply not perceived (p. 28). Strategies for addressing this problem and for increasing the accuracy of informal observations are discussed in Chapter 3.

One mechanism for enhancing the utility of informal observations is the use of anecdotal records. Briefly, an anecdotal record is a factual description of actions and events observed by the teacher (see Chapter 7 for a discussion). The entries are brief, concrete notes that may be placed later in a folder or notebook. The notes, usually sequential, focus on one student at a time. The purpose is to document (1) behavior patterns that may require action or (2) teacher and student responses to a problem.

Teacher Questions

Teacher questions play an important role during instruction in both facilitating student learning and assessing the extent of student understanding. Much of classroom instruction is teacher-directed, and teachers use both lower- and higher-order questions during this process. Lower-order questions, such as "How many sides does a triangle have?" are oriented to predetermined right answers. Higher-order questions, in contrast, require student thinking and decisions about information. Examples are "Explain the main idea in your own words" and "Predict the course of World War II if Japan had not attacked the U.S. fleet at Pearl Harbor in December 1941."

The emergence of performance assessments for complex capabilities has introduced a new role for teacher questioning. The emphasis in mathematics, for example, is developing students' capacity to engage in the processes of mathematical thinking. That is, students are expected to search for patterns, develop hypotheses, make inferences from data, and explain and justify their thinking (Schoenfeld, 1992). Instruction is organized around tasks that may be solved in more than one way and that require student thinking and exploration. An important aspect of the teacher's role, in addition to the careful selection of tasks, is to press for justification by students, explanations, and connections to major concepts through questioning (Stein, Grover, & Henningsen, 1996, p. 467). This factor, along with teacher comments and feedback, was found to be essential in 64 percent of the cognitive tasks that were implemented at a high level in four middle schools (p. 481). In other words, lack of thoughtful teacher questions contributed to the routinized solving of some tasks and a focus on only getting the right answer.

Interviews and Student Reflections

The emergence of portfolio assessment also has contributed to the a focus on student thinking processes. Questions that assessment should assist the teacher in answering are: "Does the student have a grasp of the kinds of thinking processes it takes to sustain long-term serious work?" "Can the student pose interesting questions or solve problems outside the comforting, familiar structure of school assignments?" and "Can the student step back and reflect on his or her own work?" (Wolf, 1987/1988, p. 24).

Two mechanisms that can assist the teacher in answering these questions are interviews and student reflections. Interviews (discussed in Chapter 7) may be conducted three to four times yearly while the other students are engaged in individual or group projects. One approach is to begin with a cognitive task and then to elicit information about the processes used by the student.

Student reflections, in contrast, are an integral component of portfolios as advocated by several educators (Archbald & Newman, 1992; Wolf, 1989; Wolf, Bixby, Glenn, & Gardner, 1991). Two or three times during the semester, students describe characteristics of their work, recent changes, and the progress that has occurred (Wolf, 1989, p. 37). The teacher and the student then discuss the portfolio, the student's analysis, and together they establish new goals, if necessary.

Summary

Qualitative data, unlike measurements, yield verbal information about events, perceptions, beliefs, and other aspects of social life. Qualitative methods useful for the teacher are teacher observations, classroom questions, interviews, and student reflections. Informal observations are spontaneous, unstructured, and, typically, covert. In many situations, such as gauging the effectiveness of an explanation, informal observations can be very useful. However, they may be inaccurate, often lack credibility, and can lead to inappropriate teacher actions. Further, observations made early in the year tend not be altered by subsequent events. One mechanism for enhancing both the accuracy and usefulness of teacher observations is the format referred to as anecdotal records. They are notes about concrete actions that either document behavior patterns or teacher and student responses to problems.

Teacher questions are useful in facilitating student learning, evaluating student understanding, and in developing students' capacities to engage in thinking. Both lower- and higher-level questions are used in teacher-directed instruction to assess initial learning. When students are engaged in complex cognitive tasks, asking them to explain their strategies and to support their methods is essential to facilitating student thinking.

Two classroom mechanisms associated with portfolio assessment are interviews and student self-reflections. Both can provide the teacher with information about the depth of student understanding of the subject matter and their understanding of their own learning.

Chapter Questions

1. A curriculum team has developed eight situations (two to three sentences each) for a criterion-referenced assessment of interpreting map symbols. What is a logical cut-off score for the mastery test? Why?

2. A new student enters Mrs. Gallagher's fifth grade in November. She needs information on his language arts and mathematics performance. Which assessment method/methods discussed in Chapter 2 is/are most appropriate for obtaining this information? Why?

3. Name two skills that are appropriate for the continuum model of criterion-referenced assessment. Discuss the rationale for your choice.

4. Conducting an experiment on the absorbency of different kinds of paper towels is a complex task. In your view, what are the important skills that should be demonstrated by students in this task and should be included in an evaluation of their performance?

5. What are some likely negative effects of administering a "pop quiz" because of class misbehavior?

References

Archbald, D., & Newman, F. (1992). Beyond standardized testing: Assessing authentic academic achievement in the secondary school. In H. Berlak, F. W. Newman, E. Adams, D. Archbald, T. Burgess, J. Raven, & T. A. Romberg. *Toward a new science of educational testing and assessment* (pp. 139–180). Albany: State University of New York Press.

Barton, P. E., & Coley, R. J. (1994). *Testing in America's schools*. Princeton: Educational Testing Service.

Chi, M., Glaser, R., & Farr, M. (1988). *The nature of expertise*. Hillsdale, NJ: Erlbaum.

Coffman, W. E. (1993). A king over Egypt, which knew not Joseph. *Educational Measurement: Issues and Practice, 12*(2), 5–8.

Erickson, P., & Mohatt, G. (1982). Cultural organization of participant structures in two classrooms of Indian students. In G. Spindler (Ed.), *Doing the ethnography of schooling* (pp. 132–174). New York: Holt, Rinehart, & Winston.

Glaser, R. (1963). Instructional technology and the measurement of learning outcomes. *American Psychologist, 18*(8), 519–521.

Good, T. (1980). Classroom expectations: Teacher-pupil interactions. In J. H. McMillan (Ed.), *The social psychology of school learning* (pp. 70–122). New York: Academic Press.

Graham, S. (1984). Communicating sympathy and anger to black and white children: The cognitive attributional consequences of affective cues. *Journal of Personality and Social Psychology, 47*(1), 40–54.

Graham, S., & Weiner, B. (1983). Some educational implications of sympathy and anger from an attributional perspective. In R. Snow & M. Farr (Eds.), *Aptitude learning and instruction: Vol. 3. Conative and affective policy analysis* (pp. 199–221). Hillsdale, NJ: Erlbaum.

Haertel, E. H. (1990). Achievement tests. In H. J. Walberg & G. D. Haertel (Eds.), *The international encyclopedia of educational evaluation* (pp. 485–489). Oxford: Pergamon Press.

Hambleton, R. K. (1990). Criterion-referenced assessment in evaluation. In H. J. Walbert & G. D. Haertel (Eds.), *The international encyclopedia of educational evaluation* (pp. 13–118). Oxford: Pergamon Press.

Koretz, D. (1992). What happened to test scores and why? *Educational Measurement: Issues and Practice, 11*(4), 7–10.

Kozol, J. (1991). *Savage inequalities: Children in America's schools*. New York: Crown.

Linn, R. L., Graue, M. E., & Sanders, N. M. (1990). Comparing state and district test results to national norms: The validity of claims that "everyone is above average." *Educational Measurement: Issues and Practice, 10*(3), 5–14.

Neill, M., Bursh, P., Schaeffer, B., Thall, C., Yohe, M., & Zappardino, P. (1995). *Implementing performance assessments*. Cambridge, MA: Fairtest.

Nitko, A. (1984). Defining criterion-referenced test. In R. Berk (Ed.), *A guide to criterion-referenced test construction*. Baltimore: The Johns Hopkins University Press.

Sadler, R. (1981). Intuitive data processing as a potential source of bias in naturalistic evaluations. *Educational Evaluation and Policy Analysis, 3*(4), 25–31.

Schoenfeld, A. (1992). Learning to think mathematically: Problem solving, cognition, and sense making in mathematics. In D. A. Grouws (Ed.), *Handbook of research on mathematics teaching and learning* (pp. 334–370). New York: Macmillan.

Scriven, M. (1994, April). Death of a paradigm: Replacing multiple-choice with multiple ratings. Invited address, American Educational Research Association, New Orleans.

Smith, E. R., & Tyler, R. W. (1942). *Appraising and recording student progress*. New York: Harper Brothers.

Smith, M. L. (1991). Meanings of test preparation. *American Educational Research Journal, 28*(3), 521–542.

Stein, M. K., Grover, B. W., & Henningsen, M. (1996). Building student capacity for mathematical thinking and reasoning: An analysis of mathematical tasks used in reform classrooms. *American Educational Research Journal, 33*(2), 455–488.

Thorndike, R., & Hagen, E. (1969). *Measurement and evaluation in psychology and education* (3rd ed.). New York: Wiley.

Tyler, R. (1990). Reporting evaluations of learning outcomes. In H. J. Walberg & G. D. Haertel (Eds.), *The international encyclopedia of educational evaluation* (pp. 733–738). Oxford: Pergamon Press.

Weiner, B., Graham, S., Stern, P., & Lawson, M. (1982). Using affective cues to infer causal thoughts. *Developmental Psychology, 18*(2), 278–286.

Wiggins, G. (1988, January). Revitalizing classroom assessment: The highest instructional priority. *Phi Delta Kappan,* 69(5), 363–368.

Wolf, D. (1987, December/1988, January). Opening up assessment. *Educational Leadership, 45*(4), 24–29.

Wolf, D. (1989). Portfolio assessment: Sampling student work. *Educational Leadership, 46*(7), 35–39.

Wolf, D., Bixby, J., Glenn, J., & Gardner, H. (1991). To use their minds well: Investigating new forms of student assessment. In G. Grant (Ed.), *Review of Research in Education, Vol. 17* (pp. 32–73). Washington, DC: American Educational Research Association.

Chapter 3

Validity and Reliability

Major Topics

Validity

Conceptions of Validity

Developing Valid Measurements

Other Validity Concerns

Qualitative Assessments

Aspects of Reliability

Reliability

Methods of Establishing Reliability

A small school system in Tennessee used a rating scale to select children who were to be promoted to first grade. The purpose of the scale was to identify those children who were ready to learn to read and, therefore, could benefit from instruction in first grade. However, the instrument was heavily weighted with items on motor skills such as "ability of the child to tie his shoes." The problem is that shoe tying and other motor skills are not related to reading or other measures of first-grade success.

—Gredler, 1992

The rating scale in the preceding example is deficient because its use denies children entry into first grade on the basis of inappropriate criteria. Specifically, the rationale that shoe tying and other motor skills are indicators of reading readiness is unsound. The instrument, therefore, is said to lack validity because the inferences that are made (a child is not ready to learn to read and should not be in first grade) are inaccurate. In other words, in the school setting, validity refers to the inferences that are made from student data.

Validity is an essential property of all assessments from tests and rating scales to teacher questions and anecdotal records. Also important in an assessment is reliability, which refers to the consistency of assessment results.

✦ Validity

Discussed in this section are the broadening of the concept of validity in recent years, methods for developing valid measures, and other validity concerns. Particularly important are the social consequences of an assessment that lacks validity.

Conceptions of Validity

From a fairly limited concept, validity has evolved to include a variety of factors that can contribute to inaccurate inferences about student characteristics and capabilities.

Early views. At the beginning of the twentieth century, developmental psychology viewed human dispositions and abilities as becoming fixed in early childhood. The characteristics also were considered to remain generally unchanged even into old age (Clarke, 1978). Given this view, verifying that a measure of intelligence or achievement was reasonably accurate was a relatively straightforward task. Researchers simply administered the instrument at one point in time, then measured academic performance at a later point in time, and determined the relationship between the two sets of scores. If the high scorers later performed well and the low scorers subsequently were not high performers, then the instrument was viewed as an acceptably accurate measure of intelligence or achievement. In other words, the instrument was considered to be valid because student performance was similar on the two administrations.

In the 1950s, professional standards were developed for tests and diagnostic techniques. Revised in 1966, the standards described three types of validity. They are content, criterion, and construct validity, and they were viewed as relatively independent of each other. Content validity addresses the adequacy with which items on an achievement test sample the particular subject area or domain. Content validity is established primarily through review of the items. Criterion validity investigates the relationship between the scores on a particular test or rating scale and some predicted performance (the criterion). An example is obtaining data about the similarity of student performance on a standardized norm-referenced achievement test and later academic achievement. The third type, construct validity, was typically used when the assessment addressed a theoretical trait, such as self-concept or self-esteem. Although three types of validity were identified, test validity through the 1970s was primarily addressed through data in the form of correlation coefficients provided by the test publisher (Angoff, 1988; Geisinger, 1992).

The current perspective. Over the years, changing social priorities for education and research on human characteristics and educational interventions has contributed to an expanded view of validity. First, public education is no longer viewed as an inflexible system in which only a few students can attain the highest levels, and research studies have indicated the importance of environment in influencing achievement. In addition, the increased use of tests for high-stakes decisions, such as promotion to the next grade and a high school diploma, has also led to court challenges of some of these tests. The events have contributed to a current focus on the meaning of test scores.

The 1985 standards for tests reflect the altered focus by defining validity as the "appropriateness, meaningfulness, and usefulness of the specific inferences made from test scores" (American Educational Research Association et al., 1985, p. 9). In other words, the role of validity in relation to testing is to explain the behavior that the test score summarizes (Moss, 1995).

The current conception of validity has three major features, which are summarized in Table 3-1. First, the 30-year-old idea of three separate types of validity cannot address current requirements for tests. Instead, content and criterion validity are strands within a cable of the validity argument (Cronbach, 1988, p. 4).

Second, validity is an integrative process (not a procedure) (Angoff, 1988; Cole & Moss, 1989; Cronbach, 1988; Messick, 1988, 1989; Moss, 1995). Further,

Table 3.1 Features of the Current Conception of Validity

1. Validity is a unitary concept, referred to as construct validity, and it incorporates both content and criterion validity.
2. Development of a valid test requires multiple procedures that address the test rationale, the performance of different groups of students on the test, and the inferences that are made from the test scores.
3. Validity is a dynamic rather than a static concept. It begins with the basis for the test and continues through development to subsequent use by various groups.

the multiple procedures that are used are implemented at different phases of the assessment construction process (Anastasi, 1986, p. 3). Applying this perspective to the development of a readiness scale for first grade, for example, means first asking, "Are there specific behaviors or skills that can reflect the capability to benefit from instruction in first grade?" and "What theoretical and/or research evidence supports the selection of these behaviors?" If these questions are answered satisfactorily and a test is developed, two other important questions should be asked. They are: "What is the subsequent performance in first grade of both high and low scorers on the test?" and "What are the effects of denying some children entry to first grade?" Third, as illustrated by the prior readiness example (and in the following section of this chapter), validity is a dynamic rather than a static concept.

Developing Valid Measurements

Validating a measurement involves a comprehensive strategy that may be applied to both standardized and teacher-developed measures.

Basic steps. A program for establishing validity requires information about both the internal structure of the assessment and external relationships of the assessment to other behaviors, tests, and situations (Shepard, 1993, p. 417). As indicated in Table 3-2, this approach requires three major steps. They involve the basis for the assessment, likely rival explanations for performance, and the collection of data to refute, if possible, the alternative explanations. Implementation of these steps is discussed in the following pages.

Application to standardized tests. If the focus of the assessment is comprehensive achievement in a subject area, development of the test begins with a blueprint referred to as a table of specifications. This blueprint, which identifies the major concepts and skill levels to be assessed, should be compared to a map of the subject domain to ensure that important concepts and subconcepts are included on the test. In contrast, the framework for a criterion-referenced test should include (1) a statement of test purpose, (2) an example of test directions and a model test item, and (3) a description of the structure and content of the pool of tasks or items (Hambleton, 1990).

The conceptual framework for the assessment provides a mechanism for identifying tasks or items that are unrelated to the competency or capability that is being assessed or predicted. Otherwise, irrelevant items may be included in the test. The rating scale at the beginning of this chapter is an example. Another is an instrument (challenged in a court case) that was developed to screen candidates for employment as firemen. Applicants who would otherwise be eligible

Table 3.2 Requirements for Establishing the Validity of Quantitative Assessments

Requirement	Purpose
1. Establish an explicit conceptual framework for the assessment.	1. Provides a frame of reference for reviewing assessment tasks or items and for placing the test within the subject domain.
2. Identify rival explanations for performance on the assessment.	2. Identifies possible weaknesses in the rationale or conceptual framework for the assessment and provides a basis for data collection on student performance.
3. Collect multiple types of evidence on the rival explanations of assessment performance.	3. Provides a basis for refuting alternative explanations for performance or for revising the assessment, if necessary.

Sources: Summarized from Cronbach (1988) and Moss (1995).

were blocked by two items on physics (Cronbach, 1980). Because this knowledge is not relevant to the skills needed by firemen, the test lacked validity for screening job applicants.

Other potential explanations for erratic or poor performance are (1) the test is too difficult for the students, (2) the directions are vague or confusing, and (3) the assessment is measuring other constructs or skills. The performance assessment in Table 3-3 is an example.

Procedures for addressing validity should be implemented until the developers can verify that the inferences made from the assessment are sound. Then the findings should be reported in the form of an evaluative argument that integrates the evidence for the validity of the assessment (Cronbach, 1988).

Example. The comprehensive approach to obtaining evidence about validity also may be applied to existing assessments. An example is the Gesell School Readiness Test. The assessment claims to measure "developmental maturity" or "behavioral age" (Shepard, 1993, p. 422) and is intended as a screening test for entry into first grade.

Developers maintained that the test measures a construct that differs from intelligence. Proponents cite the similarity of performance between test scores on the Gesell and scores on a test of Piagetian developmental tasks (a correlation of 0.64) as evidence that the test measures "developmental maturity" (Kaufman, 1971; Shepard, 1993).

Table 3.3 Examples of Procedures for Establishing the Validity of Standardized Assessments

Requirement	Examples
1. Establish an explicit conceptual framework for the assessment.	1. For a broad-range, norm-referenced test, map the domain and compare this charting with the test blueprint. Then determine how effectively the test approximates the domain and the table of specifications (Geisinger, 1992, p. 208).
2. Identify rival explanations for performance on the assessment.	2. Reading ability may account for scores on performance assessments in mathematics that pose complex situations to be interpreted.
3. Collect multiple types of evidence on the alternative explanations for performance.	3. If reading ability is posed as a possible explanation for scores on mathematics assessment: (a) calculate the relationship between mathematics and reading scores; (b) administer the situations orally to students who are poor readers and compare their performance to that of poor readers who completed the written test; (c) compare students' scores on the performance assessment with other data on their mathematics achievement.

However, children's scores on the Gesell and on the Lorge-Thorndike Intelligence Test are also similar (a correlation of 0.61). In addition, a conceptual analysis of the tasks on the Gesell test indicates that they are identical or highly similar to items on preschool intelligence tests (Shepard & Graue, 1993). In other words, analyses indicate that the test cannot be shown to assess constructs other than intelligence. Therefore, it is not a measure of developmental maturity.

Teacher-developed measurements. At least three major differences may be identified between teacher-constructed measurements and standardized tests.

First, the tests and rating scales developed by teachers do not undergo the lengthy development that is applied to standardized tests. Therefore, the teacher must anticipate, as much as is possible, the ways that a measurement may fail to assess student learning in a valid way and ensure that these shortcomings are avoided. Second, a key focus of teachers' tests (and scoring criteria for student products) is the assessment of learning over a short time span, from 1 week to a semester. Third, they also are directly (rather than indirectly) related to instruction.

A similarity between teacher-developed and standardized measurements is that both should be derived from a sound conceptual framework. For the teacher, the framework typically consists of objectives that reflect the key learnings in the unit of instruction, a period of 6 weeks or a semester. (Chapter 4 discusses the development of objectives.) Once the items or tasks are selected or developed, they should be reviewed carefully prior to implementation.

Questions suggested by Taylor and Nolen (1996) for the review of the assessment are listed in Table 3-4. Questions 1(a) and 1(b) examine the relationship between the test items or tasks and the conceptual framework. Questions 1(c), 2, and 3 address potential alternative explanations for student performance. Specifically, students should not be unsuccessful on the test because (1) they were not taught particular methods or skills the test requires, (2) the test is not congruent with class objectives, or (3) the students may understand the concepts, but not the method of assessment. In 1(c), for example, if the teacher has not taught the ways to compare and contrast ideas, then such items are not informing the teacher about student learning in his or her class.

The teacher also reviews the assessment to ensure that the directions are clear and easily understood and that sufficient items or tasks are included for students to demonstrate their skills. A mathematics test of one or two problems, for example, is inadequate. (This issue and other validity concerns specific to performance and portfolio assessments are discussed in Chapters 8 and 9, respectively.)

Following administration and scoring of classroom measurements, the teacher should conduct other activities that address validity (Step 3 in Table 3-2). First, examine the relationships among student responses to different tasks or items and the assessment. This review can provide clues to (1) processes and concepts that received insufficient attention during instruction (if many students miss the same items) or (2) tasks to which different groups respond differently.

Also important is to note relations between teacher-developed assessments and other assessments and to trace the social consequences of interpreting and using test scores in particular ways, noting unintended as well as intended outcomes (Taylor & Nolen, 1996, p. 81). Research indicates, for example, that class-

Table 3.4 Suggested Review Questions for Teacher-Developed Measurements

Review questions	Examples
1. Item or task: (a) Can it draw out the student's learning related to the particular objective(s) it is intended to assess?	1. (a) A unit objective states that students should be able to view the American Revolution and its effects from several perspectives. An essay assessment that asks students to discuss the American Revolution from only one perspective is not valid because it does not address the intended learning (Taylor & Nolen, 1996, p. 82).
(b) Does it reflect key concepts, skills, and/or processes in the discipline?	(b) A history assessment that only requires students to recognize definitions of some terms does not measure their understanding of the concepts.
(c) Is it congruent with the instructional methods used?	(c) If instruction has not provided students opportunities to compare and contrast ideas and receive feedback, then items that ask students to demonstrate this skill are testing either intelligence or instruction in some other course.
2. Do the scoring criteria relate directly to the particular objective(s) that the task or item is intended to measure?	2. A course objective states that students should be able to represent problems in mathematics clearly and to demonstrate more than one way to solve them. However, points are awarded only for correct answers.
3. Can all students who understand the concepts demonstrate their knowledge in the selected mode of assessment?	3. Children are able to demonstrate place value orally with stacks of pennies, but are unable to demonstrate their understanding if asked to produce a written description.

Source: Summarized from Taylor and Nolen (1996, p. 83).

rooms that focus on learning goals (also referred to as task involvement or mastery goals), in contrast to classrooms that focus on performance, foster greater use of learning strategies by students and more positive student perceptions of competence (Ames & Archer, 1988; Ames, 1992; Dweck, 1986; Elliott & Dweck, 1988; Jagacinski, 1992). That is, classrooms that make use of comparisons of students' scores lead to a student focus on outperforming others (performance goals).

Other Validity Concerns in Measurement

The prior sections discussed some of the assessment characteristics that contribute to invalid inferences. Other validity concerns include the consequences of the use of an assessment, school practices related to assessment, and student characteristics that can jeopardize validity.

The role of consequences in determining validity. In addition to examining the evidence supporting the interpretations and uses of measurements, several researchers (e.g., Cronbach, 1988; Linn, 1997; Messick, 1995; Moss, 1992; Shepard, interview 1991, 1993, 1997) maintain that the consequences of the assessment (both positive and negative) also should be examined. An analogy to this view is the approach to drug testing undertaken by the Federal Drug Administration. That is, both anticipated effects and any side effects must be carefully researched before the product is considered "safe and effective" for widespread use (Shepard, 1993, p. 426).

Attention to assessment consequences involves answering two questions. They are "What does the assessment claim to do?" and "What are the effects on the system of using the assessment other than what the assessment claims?" (Shepard, 1993, p. 429). An effect of district or statewide testing, for example, is the application of labels to certain groups of students (Geisinger, 1992, p. 210).

Consequences are particularly important when an assessment is a key source of information about promotion or educational placement. In many cases, research data are already available that can provide information about the placement decisions resulting from the use of tests. For example, most screening or readiness tests for first grade lack the predictive accuracy to support their use in making decisions that affect children's school careers (Shepard, 1993). An analysis of research studies of 12 well-known screening tests conducted by Gredler (1992) indicates that 34 to 85 percent of the children who were predicted to fail did not develop learning problems (p. 44).

Shepard (1993) argues that when a test is used for placement, validity evidence also should include the effects of the program or the different instruction that the students receive. For example, one analysis of 63 controlled studies indicates that only 9 showed positive effects for kindergarten retention. In addition, in subsequent years, retained children lagged behind promoted control-group children in both achievement and self-esteem. Moreover, many parents of retained children reported negative emotional reactions associated with retention (Gredler, 1992; Shepard, 1993). In other words, Shepard (interview, 1991) maintains that research data indicate the lack of validity of screening tests for placement in a second year of schooling prior to first grade because the placements themselves are invalid (p. 23).

School practices related to use of the assessment. Several school practices can contribute to inaccurate conclusions about student performance. First, assessments that are used for key decisions should not be administered during the first or last few weeks of the school year or the week before Christmas. Students' performance at these times is likely to be unrepresentative of their capabilities.

The use of standardized achievement tests for high-stakes decisions (the assignment of positive and negative consequences based on test scores) has led to administrative practices in some schools that lead to invalid inferences about student achievement. Among these practices are hints to students during the assessment, altering the wording in the directions when reading them to students, and increasing the testing time specified for the assessment (Haladyna, Nolen, & Haas, 1991; Mehrens & Kaminski, 1989). Other inappropriate practices are a classroom focus on drill-and-practice exercises to the neglect of other activities, using commercial test preparation materials that teach or review the skills to be tested, teaching items from the current year's test, and dismissing low-achieving students on test days (Haladyna et al., 1991; Mehrens & Kaminski, 1989; Shepard, interview 1991; Smith & Rottenberg, 1991). The effects of these practices on test results are referred to as test score pollution. Scores are increased or decreased with no connection to the concepts or capabilities represented by the test (Haladyna et al., 1991, p. 2).

Characteristics of students. One student characteristic that is an issue particularly for assessments of young children is the instability of the behavior that is being assessed. Children who do not have long-term behavioral problems typically require from 1 to 4 months to adjust to the demands of the school environment. Testing that is conducted too early in the school year is likely to indicate behavioral problems that may not be present later in the year (Gredler, 1992, p. 23).

Anxiety and lack of motivation are two student reactions to tests that can depress student performance. Also, factors in the student's educational and cultural background as well as age and experience can interact with the assessment in various ways. For example, a test that may involve science reasoning for a group of fifth graders may be simply a test of knowledge facts for eighth graders.

Prior cultural experiences or practices may also influence the performance of particular groups on assessments. For example, a reading test in English as a measure of the learning potential of Spanish-speaking fourth graders lacks validity for this group. In other words, a test score that has implications for a relevant subgroup of test takers that are different from the meanings or implications for the remainder of the test takers has differential validity (Cole &

Moss, 1989). A related but less frequent example is that of the school psychologist faced with administering an I.Q. test to a child from a culture in which adults do not ask children known-answer questions or where verbal exchanges with a strange adult are unknown (Miller-Jones, 1989). In such situations, lack of response or poor performance cannot be confidently attributed to lack of knowledge.

Qualitative Assessments

Validity also is an essential property of informal teacher observations, anecdotal records, interviews, and other qualitative data. However, the teacher, like the cultural anthropologist and the ethnographer, faces two particular problems in collecting qualitative data. One is that the teacher (or researcher) is the data collection instrument. The data collection process, therefore, is largely dependent on the insights and conceptual capabilities of the individual. That is, a teacher's prior beliefs and attitudes and such factors as teacher fatigue and stress level are likely to influence the observations.

The second problem is that the observations are relatively unstructured, and they attempt to capture behavior as it is occurring. A particular sample of behavior is only a fragment of a student's daily actions, and the potential exists for misinterpretation and distortion of its meaning.

Some of the strategies used by researchers to ensure the validity of their qualitative data are also useful to the classroom teacher (see Table 3-5). The first strategy is to restrict observations to concrete actions and to avoid global impressions. The reason is that global impressions are intuitive inferences and they are influenced by the observer's beliefs, attitudes, and other factors. Thus, they are often inaccurate.

Next, obtain evidence from multiple data sources and multiple methods. Checking information in this way is referred to by anthropologists as triangulation (Webb, Campbell, Schwartz, & Sechrest, 1966; Denzin, 1978). Specifically, informal observations should be accompanied by more systematic observations during other classroom activities and by other assessment methods as in the examples in Table 3-5.

Further, as indicated in Chapter 2, individuals tend not to notice events and actions that conflict with previously developed inferences. The two techniques for addressing this concern are to test rival hypotheses and search for negative cases. That is, test alternative explanations for the behavior and look for instances of appropriate behavior when inappropriate behavior is observed. These methods sensitize the teacher to be consciously aware of information that does not fit with his or her tentative inferences about student behavior. Observed behaviors, as indicated in Table 3-5, may reflect any of several situations, and test-

Table 3.5 Strategies for Enhancing the Validity of Qualitative Data

Strategy	Example
1. Limit observations to concrete behavior not global impressions.	Note concrete actions such as staring out the window rather than arriving at a global impression, such as the student is unmotivated.
2. Consult multiple data sources.	During instruction, observe several students, not three or four, for signs of understanding or confusion.
3. Use multiple methods to obtain information.	Implement a classroom game followed by homework exercises to gauge understanding; an ungraded weekly test provides additional data.
4. Test rival hypotheses.	If the observed behavior seems to indicate lack of motivation, obtain data, where possible, about fatigue, depression, or other possible explanations.
5. Search for negative cases.	When instances of misbehavior are observed, search for examples of appropriate behavior.
6. Limit inferences to the context of the observation.	Sally follows directions promptly and keeps her desk neatly organized. However, this information does not mean that she will be a high achiever.

ing rival hypotheses broadens the types of information to be considered. Searching for negative cases, in contrast, alerts the teacher to notice, for example, when a student who has been uncooperative a couple of times is helpful and cooperative. Noticing the positive behavior also provides the teacher an opportunity to react positively to the student. Also important is not to generalize observations to inappropriate situations or settings. Neatness does not indicate achievement level, for example.

Summary

When human dispositions were viewed as fixed in early childhood, researchers determined instrument validity by comparing performance at two different points in time. Subsequently, professional standards for tests and diagnostic measures identified three types of validity. Now defined as construct validity, the concept incorporates both content and criterion validity.

Establishing validity involves multiple procedures implemented during both test development and use. The three basic steps are (1) define a conceptual framework for test development, (2) identify rival explanations for assessment performance, and (3) collect multiple types of evidence on the alternative explanations. For classroom tests, teachers should review tasks and items for congruence with their objectives and methods, and review the mode of assessment and scoring criteria. Then the relationships between student scores and other classroom measures and assessments should be reviewed.

In addition to the social consequences of interpreting scores for particular decisions, other validity concerns include school practices related to assessments and the influence of student characteristics. Practices that lead to invalid inferences include teaching items from the current test. Student characteristics that contribute to invalid inferences include instability of the behavior to be assessed and anxiety.

Validity is also an essential property of teacher observations. Two particular validity concerns are the influence of the observer's beliefs and attitudes and the sampling of behavior. Methods of ensuring validity include restricting observations to concrete actions, use of multiple data sources and methods, testing rival explanations for the behavior, searching for negative cases, and restricting inferences to the observed context.

✦ Reliability

Validity refers to the appropriateness and meaningfulness of the test scores or the inferences that are made from observations of students. Reliability addresses another important yet related dimension of assessment. Reliability refers to the consistency of scores (quantitative assessments) or observations (qualitative assessments) obtained about students. For example, if a student earns a high score on a social studies test this week, he or she also should earn a high score if the test is administered to the class a month or so later. Also, if the student completes another test on the same social studies content, his or her score should be similar.

Aspects of Reliability

The features of reliability and the relationship of reliability to validity are important issues in assessment.

Features of reliability. The term reliability refers to the results of an assessment and not the assessment itself. Assessment results cannot be exactly consistent because temporary conditions, such as the student's physical well-being, his or her motivation and/or anxiety, and testing conditions, such as an overheated classroom, can affect performance. However, assessment results should be reasonably consistent if obtained on different occasions, obtained on different tasks or items, or determined by different scorers or observers. For example, a test that is too difficult for students will lead to guessing and the results will fluctuate from one administration to another. Such a test is not reliable (nor is it a valid measure of student capabilities).

Different assessments on the same topics, drawn from the same domain, or intended to measure the same complex skills, also should yield similar results. One method of assessing the reliability of criterion-referenced assessments, for example, is to administer two equivalent tests or sets of tasks and note the similarity of masters/nonmasters classification of students (Thorndike, 1990).

Particularly important is that too few tasks or items on an assessment prevent the scores from being reliable. Suppose, for example, that one word problem was used to measure problem solving in arithmetic. A difficult problem would result in few students scored as proficient, whereas an easy problem would lead to a large number of passing scores. Including more problems that are representative of the course content makes possible a more consistent assessment of student competencies. Similarly, too few observations of behavior in the classroom setting are also likely to be highly unreliable. The classroom teacher or other observers should obtain observations of a student over several days before making an inference about the behavior.

Possible differences in scoring are not a problem in tests composed of multiple-choice and matching items. The correct answers are determined in advance and even a clerk (or a computer when scan answer sheets are used) can consistently score the tests. In contrast, open-ended assessments, such as essay tests and performance assessments, require judgments by the scorers. The key to enhancing reliability involves developing specific scoring procedures and training the scorers. (These methods are discussed further in Chapters 8 and 9.)

Relationship to validity. First, a test or observation that lacks reliability also lacks validity. For example, confusing or ambiguous test directions lead to guessing and inconsistent student scores (lack of reliability). Also, because of the high rate of guessing, the assessment does not tap the student's actual capabilities and so is not a valid measure. Similarly, an observation of a student's work habits and persistence when he or she is ill or upset will not be consistent with observations made at other times, and it is not an accurate (valid) assessment of the student's approach to tasks.

Of importance is that a test that is highly reliable may not be valid. An example is the multiple-choice test for applicants for the job of fireman mentioned earlier. Scores were highly consistent, but because the test included items on physics, it lacked validity as a screening instrument. In other words, verifying that test scores are reliable is not evidence of test validity.

Methods of Estimating Reliability

Five methods that involve the calculation of a reliability index are used with formal assessments. These methods are illustrated in Table 3-6. The index calculated for methods one through three is a correlation coefficient. When used to measure test reliability, it indicates the extent of similarity between two sets of scores. (An example of calculating a reliability index from two sets of scores is presented in the appendix.)

As indicated in Table 3-6, these methods provide information about different types of consistency. The test-retest method provides an estimate of stability, which is particularly important for standardized achievement and intelligence tests. The test-retest method is appropriate if (1) all the test exercises are so similar in content or function that any particular sample of exercises is equivalent to any other, and (2) the number of exercises or their nondescript nature leads to little or no recall of one's initial responses to them (Thorndike, 1990, p. 271). One problem with the test-retest method is that the longer the time interval between assessments, the greater the impact of the students' experience or differential rates of growth on the scores.

An important requirement for the equivalent forms method is that both tests should be constructed from the same set of specifications. Although this approach does not provide information about test stability, it can be combined with the test-retest approach and provide maximum information about reliability. That is, one form of the test is administered a few weeks later. Thorndike (1990) also suggests the use of equivalent forms with criterion-referenced tests. Visual examination of the data on the consistency of masters/nonmasters classifications between the two tests provides information about reliability.

Although easy to implement, the reliability methods that rely on a single test administration (split-half and the formula methods) do not provide information on changes in student performance from one occasion to another (Thorndike, 1990). Thus, the coefficients calculated from these methods are likely to be higher than those based on two test administrations. Also, the formula methods (KR-20 and coefficient alpha) are not appropriate for speeded tests.

The use of performance and portfolio assessments has increased the use of raters to score student products. Appropriate indices of reliability for these ratings are percentage agreement between pairs of raters and the correlation between two sets of scorers. Factors that can influence the reliability of performance and portfolio assessments are further discussed in Chapters 8 and 9, respectively.

Table 3.6 Methods of Calculating a Reliability Index

Method	Description	Role
Tests that yield a range of scores:		
1. Test-retest	Administer the same test to a group a few weeks apart. Calculate a correlation between the two sets of scores.	Provides an estimate of test stability.
2. Equivalent (parallel) forms	Administer two very similar tests (with a brief interval) to a group. Calculate a correlation between the two sets of scores.	Provides an index of the short-term constancy of student responses.
3. Split-half	Administer a test that is somewhat longer than you plan to use. Then divide the test into two parts (typically, odd- and even-numbered items). Calculate a correlation between the two sets of scores.	Provides an index of internal consistency.
4. (a) Kuder-Richardson (KR-20)	Administer a test with items scored right/wrong to a group. Use computer software to calculate the index using the KR-20 formula.	Provides an index of internal consistency.
(b) Coefficient alpha	Administer a rating scale to a group (each response is one of several values on a range, such as 1 to 5 or 1 to 7). Use computer software to calculate the index using the formula.	Provides an index of internal consistency.
Ratings of student performance:		
5. Interrater consistency	Calculate percent agreement between two raters of the ratings assigned to essay examinations, performance assessments and portfolio entries or calculate a correlation between the two sets of scores.	Provides an index of the consistency between raters.

Summary

Reliability refers to the consistency of scores or observations of students. Although temporary conditions may influence individual student performance, assessment results should be reasonably consistent if obtained on different occasions, on different tasks or items, or determined by different scorers or observers. Particularly important for both teacher observations and quantitative assessments is the inclusion of adequate samples of behavior.

Reliability is related to validity in two ways. First, a test that lacks reliability also lacks validity. Second, evidence on the consistency of test scores (reliability) is not evidence that the assessment is adequately measuring the capability of interest. That is, evidence of reliability is not an indicator of validity.

The methods used for estimating the reliability of quantitative assessments include test-retest, equivalent forms, split-half, two formula methods (KR-20 and coefficient alpha), and interrater consistency. The reliability of scores assigned to student performance by judges is determined by calculating an index of interrater consistency. The other methods are used with assessments that yield a range of student scores.

Chapter Questions

1. A test purports to measure Star Trek trivia and the developers maintain that this test predicts those who will excel in courses that require memorization of unrelated details. What evidence would you collect to test this assertion? Why?

2. A college course focuses on teaching students hypercard and strategies for designing computer-delivered instruction. What do you think would be valid assessments for such a course? Why?

3. A teacher notices that David always greets other students in the morning, smiles, and frequently initiates conversations with them. She concludes that he will make a natural class leader. Discuss her reasoning.

4. Eric's teacher has tentatively hypothesized that he will be the class bully because he pushed Don on the playground one day and hit him in the back the next day. What rival hypotheses might the teacher test in this situation?

5. Discuss the issue of reliability in the example in question 4.

References

American Educational Research Association, American Psychological Association, & National Council on Measurement in Education (1985). *Standards for educational and psychological testing.* Washington, DC: American Psychological Association.

Ames, C. (1992). Classrooms: Goals, structures, and student motivation. *Journal of Educational Psychology*, *84*(3), 261–271.

Ames, C., & Archer, J. (1988). Achievement goals in the classroom: Students' learning strategies and motivational processes. *Journal of Educational Psychology*, *80*(3), 260–267.

Anastasi, A. (1986). Evolving concepts of test validation. In M. R. Rosenzwieg & L. W. Porter (Eds.), *Annual Review of Psychology*, *37*, 1–15.

Angoff, W. H. (1988). Validity: An evolving concept. In H. Wainer & H. Braun (Eds.), *Test validity* (pp. 19–32). Hillsdale, NJ: Erlbaum.

Clarke, A. D. B. (1978). Predicting human development: Problems, evidence, implications. *Bulletin of the British Psychological Society*, *31*, 249–258.

Cole, N. S., & Moss, P. A. (1989). Bias in test use. In R. Linn (Ed.), *Educational measurement* (3rd ed., pp. 201–219). Washington, DC: American Council on Education & National Council on Measurement in Education.

Cronbach, L. J. (1980). Validity on parole: How can we go straight? In S. Schrader (Ed.), *Measuring achievement over a decade: New Directions for Testing and Measurement*, *5*, 99–108.

Cronbach, L. J. (1988). Five perspectives on validity argument. In H. Wainer (Ed.), *Test validity* (pp. 3–17). Hillsdale, NJ: Erlbaum.

Denzin, N. (1978). *Sociological methods*. New York: McGraw-Hill.

Dweck, C. S. (1986). Motivational processes affecting learning. *American Psychologist*, *41*(10), 1040–1048.

Elliott, E. E., & Dweck, C. S. (1988). Goals: An approach to motivation and achievement. *Journal of Personality and Social Psychology*, *54*(1), 5–12.

Geisinger, K. F. (1992). The metamorphosis in test validation. *Educational Psychologist*, *27*(2), 197–222.

Gredler, G. R. (1992). *School readiness: Assessment and educational issues*. Brandon, VT: Clinical Psychology Publishing.

Haladyna, T. M., Nolen, S. B., & Haas, N. S. (1991). Raising standardized achievement test scores and the origins of test score pollution. *Educational Researcher*, *20*(5), 2–7.

Hambleton, R. K. (1990). Criterion-referenced assessment in evaluation. In H. J. Walberg & G. D. Haertel (Eds.)., *The international encyclopedia of educational evaluation* (pp. 113–118). Oxford: Pergamon Press.

Jaqacinski, C. M. (1991). Interview on assessment issues with Lorrie Shepard. *Educational Researcher*, *20*(2), 21–23, 27.

Kaufman, A. S. (1971). Piaget and Gesell: A psychometric analysis of tests built from their tasks. *Child Development*, *42*(5), 1341–1360.

Linn, R. L. (1997). Evaluating the validity of assessments: The consequences of use. *Educational Measurement: Issues and Practice*, *16*(2), 14–16.

Mehrens, W. A., & Kaminski, J. (1989). Methods for improving standardized test scores: Fruitful, fruitless, or fraudulent? *Educational Measurement: Issues and Practice*, *8*(1), 14–22.

Messick, S. (1988). The once and future issues of validity: Assessing the meaning and consequences of measurement. In H. Wainer (Ed.), *Test validity* (pp. 33–45). Hillsdale, NJ: Erlbaum.

Messick, S. (1989). Validity. In R. L. Linn (Ed.), *Educational measurement* (3rd ed., pp. 13–103). Washington, DC: American Council on Education & National Council on Measurement in Education.

Miller-Jones, D. (1989). Culture and testing. *American Psychologist, 44*(2), 360–366.

Moss, P. A. (1995). Themes and variations in validity theory. *Educational Measurement: Issues and Practice, 14*(5), 5–13.

Shepard, L. A. (1989). A review of research on kindergarten retention. In L. A. Shepard & M. L. Smith (Eds.), *Flunking grades: Research and policies on retention* (pp. 64–78). London: The Falmer Press.

Shepard, L. A. (1993). Evaluating test validity. In L. Darling-Hammond (Ed.), *Review of Research in Education, 19* (pp. 405–450). Washington, DC: American Educational Research Association.

Shepard, L. A. (1997). The centrality of test use and consequences for test validity. *Educational Measurement: Issues and Practice, 16*(2), 5–8, 13, 24.

Shepard, L. A., & Graue, M. E. (1993). The morass of school readiness screening: Research on test use and test validity. In B. Spodek (Ed.), *Handbook of research on the education of young children* (2nd ed., pp. 293–305). New York: Macmillan.

Taylor, C. S., & Nolen, S. B. (1996). A contextualized approach to teaching teachers about classroom-based assessment. *Educational Psychologist, 31*(1), 77–88.

Thorndike, R. L. (1990). Reliability. In H. J. Walberg & G. D. Haertel (Eds.), *The international encyclopedia of educational evaluation* (pp. 260–273). Oxford: Pergamon Press.

Webb, E. J., Campbell, D. T., Schwartz, R., & Sechrest, L. (1966). *Unobtrusive measures: Nonreactive research in the social sciences*. Chicago: Rand McNally.

Chapter 4

Teaching and Assessment

Major Topics

Models of Teaching-Assessment Relationships

- The Teaching/Summative-Assessment Model
- The Formative Evaluation Model
- The Integrated Teaching-Assessment Model

Goals and Curriculum Frameworks

Classroom Objectives

- Characteristics
- Classification Systems
- Developing Instructional Objectives

> *"Teachers create the classroom environment by the assessment choices they make about format, frequency, instructional function, and feedback. These choices reflect the teachers' knowledge of the subject, students, and assessment principles, their instructional practices, and their relationships with students."*
>
> —Brookhart, 1997

The classroom environment created by the nature and use of assessments sends students a variety of messages. In the 1970s, for example, children's early exposure to mathematics often meant solving sets of computation or word problems for right answers. The messages conveyed by such assessments include the following: (1) only one correct approach can solve a given problem (the method in the text or the one given by the teacher), (2) one should have a ready method to solve a given problem, and (3) the method should produce the correct answer quickly (Schoenfield, 1992).

Students also view this form of mathematical problem solving as unrelated to real life (Schoenfield, 1985).

Several issues are important in understanding the ways that assessments contribute to the messages students receive about themselves and the nature of the subject area. Among them are (1) the teacher's model of the relationships between teaching and assessment, (2) the goals and curriculum frameworks in the discipline, and (3) the teacher's classroom objectives.

✦ Models of Teaching-Assessment Relationships

The teacher's model of the relationships between teaching and assessment sets the broad framework for planning both instruction and classroom assessments. At present, three models of the relationship between teaching and assessment may be identified. They are the teaching/summative-assessment model, the formative evaluation model, and the integrated teaching-assessment model. The following sections present these perspectives in order, from the least to the greatest role for assessment in the teaching process.

The Teaching/Summative-Assessment Model

The teaching/summative-assessment model prevails in higher education, and variations are found at other levels of schooling, particularly at the high school level.

Characteristics. The key feature of the teaching/summative-assessment model is that assessment is outside of or after instruction (see Figure 4-1). Many preservice teachers often view assessment in this way based on their experiences as students when assessments were used primarily for grading (Taylor & Nolen, 1996).

An assumption of this model is that teachers function as tellers, knowledge consists of facts, and learners are passive accumulators of information (Cole, 1990, p. 5). Thus, the teacher's primary role is to transmit course content. Assessments typically are broad-range tests that sample definitions, concepts, and principles in a variety of course topics.

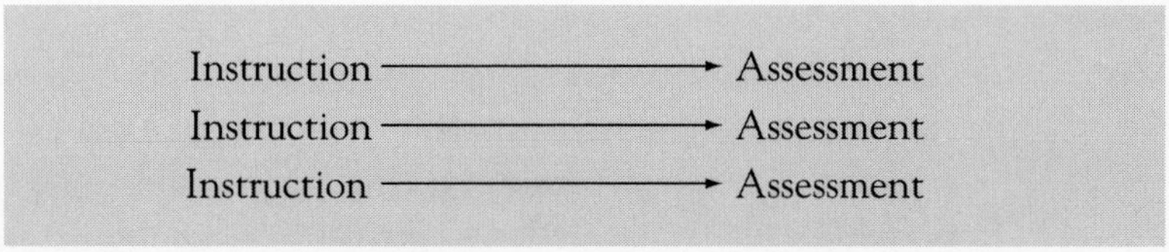

Instruction ⟶ Assessment
Instruction ⟶ Assessment
Instruction ⟶ Assessment

FIGURE 4.1
The teaching/summative-assessment model.

Some public school classrooms have also implemented variations of this model. The focus on learning basic mathematical procedures in the 1970s is an example. The teacher illustrated basic concepts and demonstrated the procedure for solving a particular type of problem. The students then completed worksheets and/or homework problems. At the beginning of the next class period, the teacher reviewed the worksheet and/or homework problems and the cycle began again. Assessments were administered periodically to determine the extent to which students were able to apply the different procedures to particular problems.

Function of assessment. The original function of assessment in this model was to categorize and select students. It originated in the early years of public education when a primary role of the school was to identify the 5 percent of the student body who could benefit from higher education (Bloom, Hastings, & Madaus, 1971).

Currently, classroom assessments document the extent of the students' acquisition of knowledge, and scores serve as the basis for computing grades. The assessments provide some limited feedback to the individual student if the teacher reviews the examinations in class. The student learns which items he or she missed and is informed of the correct answers. However, this information may be of minimal assistance in learning when subsequent instruction and assessments address different content.

Advantages and disadvantages. The advantage of this model is that it is cost-efficient in terms of the time allocated to implementing assessments. However, the tests often assess a range of content, including both major concepts and minor facts and details. Two major disadvantages of this approach to assessment identified by Crooks (1988) are that it leads to fragmented views of a discipline and surface approaches to learning. Specifically, surface approaches rely primarily on efforts to memorize course materials as though the various topics and facts are unrelated. A third disadvantage is that the model provides little opportunity for reteaching.

The Formative Assessment Model

The formative assessment model is an outgrowth of Benjamin Bloom's (1968) mastery learning model. His model is based on the principle that most students could master the subject matter in public schools if given additional time to learn.

Bloom's model. An original contribution of the model is that it identifies two types of assessment: formative and summative. Formative assessments are not included in the student's grade; their function is to provide feedback to teachers and students about students' errors and misunderstandings. Students who do not achieve mastery on the unit test receive targeted instruction on missed concepts and principles and then take another test on the unit. Summative assessments, administered every 2 to 3 units or weeks during the marking period, are used for grading.

Implementation of Bloom's model requires the following steps: (1) setting a mastery standard for each unit (typically, performance that equals a grade of B), (2) treating each unit test as a mechanism for feedback only, (3) providing targeted instruction to the students who do not achieve mastery on the unit test and retesting them on missed concepts, and (4) administering only two to four tests in the course for grading purposes.

Variations. Classes that develop ways to assess student errors frequently prior to a summative assessment are variations of Bloom's model. An example is using a 20-minute exercise in which small groups of students apply difficult concepts (see Figure 4-2). Discussion of each group's efforts in class identifies students' misunderstandings. Such classes also typically determine student grades on the basis of the levels-of-proficiency model introduced in Chapter 2.

The key differences from Bloom's model are (1) the implementation of formative assessments in the form of frequent, relatively brief exercises prior to graded tests and (2) the avoidance of delay in instruction on subsequent units while students who did not master a unit receive assistance.

Function of assessment. The function of formative assessments is to provide feedback to teachers and students ideally about student misunderstandings. They are administered frequently so that errors may be corrected prior to graded tests.

Advantages and disadvantages. A disadvantage of Bloom's model is that it requires extensive investment in test development. Included are two tests for each unit (one for the formative test and the other for tasks to retest the nonmastery students) and summative tests. Another disadvantage is the delay in beginning instruction on a new unit while the nonmastery students are retaught missed

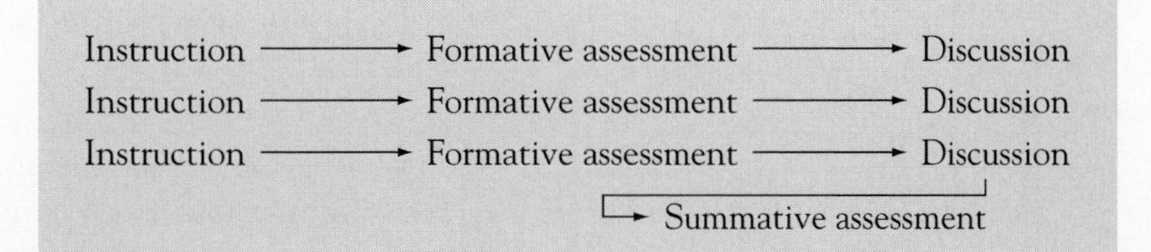

FIGURE 4.2
The formative assessment model.

concepts. A third disadvantage is that this model tends to narrow the focus of instruction to minimal competencies (Crooks, 1988).

The flexible variations of the model maintain most of the advantages of Bloom's original concept while eliminating the disadvantages. Specifically, a review of research on Bloom's model conducted in actual classrooms (Kulik & Kulik, 1988) indicates that substantial gains in achievement are primarily the result of frequent assessment with detailed feedback on a regular basis. Frequent formative assessment also reduced the anxiety associated with one-shot testing.

Another advantage of the assessment evaluation model is that it expands the role of assessment to include assisting students to learn (Kulik & Kulik, 1988). In addition, encouraging understanding and the application of key concepts and principles fosters deep learning as opposed to surface memorization.

The Integrated Teaching-Assessment Model

Curriculum reform initiated in the 1980s introduced a new model of teaching and learning. The model grew out of a body of research that indicated that students were able to repeat facts and principles, but were unable to explain events using the principles or to apply them in solving problems (Cole, 1990; Wood, Cobb, & Yackel, 1991). The purpose of the reform is to redesign curriculum and instruction to focus on meaningful learning and thinking.

Characteristics. The model describes a changed role for teachers and students. The teacher's role is that of coach, guide, and facilitator of student learning. The student's role is that of a learner and thinker in the discipline. This broad role involves using concepts and principles in the subject area to solve real-world tasks.

The changed teacher role from that of transmitter of information to facilitator reduces the amount of large-group instruction. Instead, the teacher or students may introduce questions or issues to be addressed and students may work in pairs or small groups to develop solutions. For example, one first grader was curious about how much older a book published in 1968 was than the children in the class. Working in small groups, some children stacked and moved counters to solve the problem while others counted up by tens and then ones from 1968. When the groups finished, they shared their approaches with the class (Fennema, Franke, Carpenter, & Carey, 1993). The teacher recorded the strategies used by each group in order to identify the children who were ready to move on to more sophisticated strategies.

Function of assessment. Changes in the focus of instruction also require changes in assessments. First, assessments should focus on the students' capabilities to apply their skills to real-world tasks. In language arts, for example, assess-

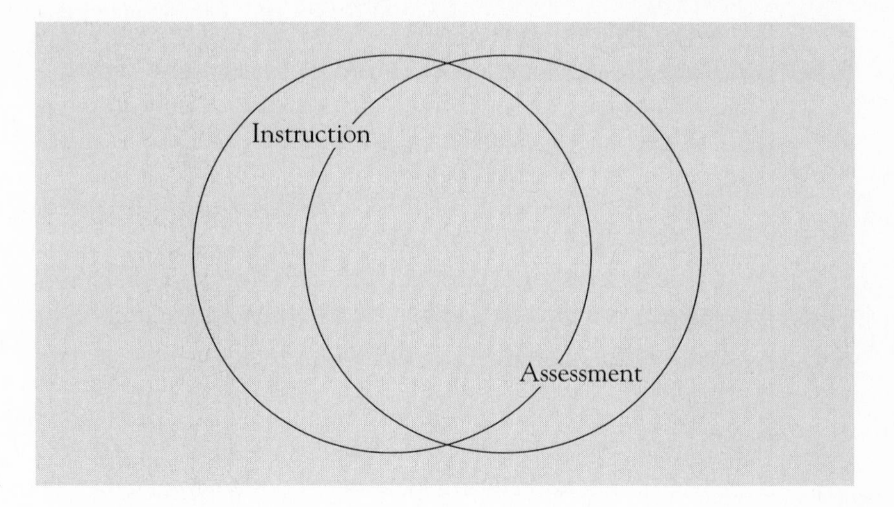

FIGURE 4.3
The integrated teaching-assessment model.

ments should inform teachers about student capabilities to communicate orally and in writing and to construct meaning from text materials.

Second, assessment should be closely intertwined with instruction (see Figure 4-3). In reading, for example, an assessment may require children to relate an event in a story they are reading from the viewpoint of another character or to write about an event they considered most important in the story. One problem-based curriculum in science, for example, designed an assessment referred to as the assessment conversation. It is a specially formatted instructional dialogue that imbeds assessment into the activity structure of the classroom (Duschl & Gitomer, 1977, p. 39). The intent is to engage students in the consideration of a diversity of ideas, to discuss the supporting evidence for their ideas, and then to determine which line of reasoning they have identified is most consistent with the evidence. The teacher then uses this information to select the next problem-based activity.

Third, a variety of activities and formats can be used to inform teachers of student strengths and weaknesses as instruction is progressing. Examples include checklists and both product and observational rating scales of student work, as well as structured teacher-student interviews. Performance assessment and portfolio assessment (discussed in Chapters 8 and 9, respectively) are also consistent with the integrated teaching-assessment model.

Summary

Three models of the relationship between teaching and assessment are (1) the teaching/summative-assessment model, (2) the formative assessment model, and (3) the integrated teaching-assessment model. Characteristics of the summative model are that (1) teachers function as tellers and students are passive recipients of knowledge and (2) the function of classroom assessments is to document the acquisition of knowledge. Although cost-efficient, the model can foster fragmented views of the subject and may encourage surface approaches to learning.

The formative assessment model began with the mastery learning perspective. Each unit test is a formative test for feedback only. Students who do not achieve mastery receive targeted instruction on their understandings and then complete another unit test. Summative tests for grading purposes are administered periodically. Disadvantages of the mastery model are (1) the number of tests involved, (2) the delay in beginning a new unit, and (3) the tendency to narrow instruction. However, the practice of implementing frequent, informal formative assessments followed by discussion preserves the feedback advantage of Bloom's model without some of the disadvantages.

The roles of both the teacher and the student are altered in the integrated teaching-assessment model. The teacher's role is to guide and facilitate student learning. This role requires less emphasis on large-class instruction and more on student pairs and small groups. Instruction also focuses on the application of new learning to real-world tasks. The student's role is that of learning to think in the discipline. In this model, assessment is integrated with instruction. Included are teacher observations of students, and students interacting with instructional materials in new ways. An advantage of the model is the emphasis on meaningful student learning. A disadvantage is that new skills are required of teachers. If districts do not provide in-service training, these changes can be difficult for the teachers.

✦ Goals and Curriculum Frameworks

Two mechanisms for establishing priorities for the curriculum in a subject area are goals and curriculum frameworks. They differ primarily in the amount of information that is provided for planning.

Goals

Goals are statements of ultimate outcomes that represent the idealized outcomes of a student's education. Thus, goals specify neither the time nor the criteria for achievement. Examples are "The student appreciates human achievement in the arts" and "The student can communicate effectively."

The two major functions of goals are to (1) express the learning priorities for the curriculum based on an identified philosophy and (2) assist teachers in planning the curriculum and assessments. An early example of the use of goals for these functions is the Eight-Year Study. Teachers clarified the important abilities, thinking strategies, interests, and attitudes they hoped to foster in students and stated them in the form of broad goals. Examples are "application of principles in science," "sensitivity to art values," and "ability to make inferences from data" (Smith & Tyler, 1942). Teachers then identified the skills involved in these curriculum goals and developed assessments for the skills.

A more recent example is the refocus of mathematics on sense making by the National Council of Teachers of Mathematics (1989). The goals of mathematics instruction shifted away from learning established procedures for textbook problems. Instead, current goals include (1) understanding structure and structural relationships, (2) developing analytical skills, and (3) developing the ability to reason and to logically support one's problem approaches and methods (Schoenfield, 1992). The purpose is for students to acquire a sense of the scope and power of mathematics and to develop confidence in their ability "to do math" (p. 349). These goals require a shift in both the nature of classroom activities and the methods of assessment. The focus becomes that of conceptual understanding and opportunities to address real-world situations involving mathematics with flexibility and resourcefulness.

The National Council of Teachers of English (1989) identified language arts goals as (students) (1) using language with increasing fluency, (2) experiencing and understanding the wide range of genres and functions available to them through language, and (3) developing ownership of their own literacy and their ability to use that literacy in any context. One purpose is to refocus classroom activities away from worksheets, drills, and contrived reading passages. Instead, the focus is on the use of stories, developing writing skills through writing for real purposes, and using language to present the results of student projects and inquiries.

On occasion, public agencies and committees suggest statements as goals that are, instead, performance statements, specific content items, or management objectives for the teacher. The problem with such statements is that they do not serve as useful guidelines for planning the curriculum. Examples are "the students' performance on the Metropolitan Achievement Test will increase one grade level" (performance statement) and "The student will understand that water flows uphill" (content item). Examples of management objectives are "to increase reading rate" and "to improve the student's self-concept." These statements do not describe the broad capabilities that the student is to acquire in the curriculum.

Curriculum Frameworks

In the 1990s, some states began to develop curriculum guides or frameworks as a basis for curriculum and assessment. Like goals, frameworks are based on basic beliefs about the nature of the subject and its role in the student's life. For example, English language arts may be described as a set of complex interrelated processes—listening, speaking, reading, and writing—and should be taught as interrelated processes. Further, the curriculum should provide students the opportunity to know themselves and their many worlds through these processes, particularly reading (South Carolina English Language Arts Framework, 1996).

Curriculum guides and frameworks differ from goals in that they provide information in addition to broad priorities for the curriculum. They may include, for example, priorities for each grade level, key topics, cognitive processes (such as relating ideas), and/or sample activities for each broad priority. One approach used for English language arts organizes standards according to curriculum strands and includes sample instructional activities. Table 4-1 illustrates the strands and associated standards. As the table indicates, the standards identified for the curriculum are, in practical terms, goal statements.

The capabilities reflected in the strands are developed at different levels in different grades. For example, for standard 2, the curriculum framework indicates that first-grade children may be expected to use context and picture clues as well as letter/sound relationships to identify new words in meaningful text, dramatize or retell stories to demonstrate understanding, and relate story events to their own lives. Middle school students, in contrast, may be expected to investigate current issues and problems by formulating research questions, evaluating different perspectives, and gathering additional information as needed.

In summary, both goals and curriculum guides and frameworks can provide information about learning priorities for the curriculum. Goals are idealized outcomes that do not specify time or criteria for achievement. Statements that describe content items, the teacher's actions, or test performance are not goals. Similarly, statements that refer to improving test performance are not goals because they do not describe the learning or capabilities to be acquired by the student.

Curriculum guides and frameworks, unlike goals, provide some information about the scope and sequence of the curriculum. In addition to standards, they may include suggested classroom activities or expected accomplishments at different grade levels.

✦ Classroom Objectives

The purpose of classroom objectives is to translate the broad capabilities identified in curriculum goal statements into key focal points for instruction. That is, objectives should reflect the particular capabilities that students should achieve at the end of a unit of instruction.

In addition to goals for the curriculum, the Eight-Year Study introduced end-of-course objectives to describe the capabilities that students should acquire at the conclusion of each course in the curriculum. An example in science is the objective that the student will be able to make inferences from data.

An emphasis on accountability and identification of the particular skills mastered by students contributed to the introduction of specific instructional objec-

Table 4.1 An Example of Strands and Standards for English Language Arts in One Curriculum Framework

Strand: Using language to learn

Standards:

1. Use language processes and strategies for continuous learning.
2. Use personal experience, the printed word, and information gained from observation as a basis for constructing meaning.
3. Use language to clarify thought.
4. Synthesize information from a variety of sources.
5. Critically analyze and evaluate language.

Strand: Using the conventions and forms of language

Standards:

6. Demonstrate competency in standard English.
7. Use language in a variety of forms.

Strand: Using language to communicate

Standards:

8. Use language processes and strategies effectively to communicate.
9. Use language for a variety of real purposes and audiences.
10. Communicate effectively in various ways.

Strand: Appreciating language

Standards:

11. Select and read from a wide range of literature.
12. Demonstrate an understanding of the aesthetics of language.

Source: Summarized from *South Carolina English Language Arts Framework* (1996).

tives for classroom use in the 1970s. In many cases, these efforts resulted in trivial statements of outcomes, because they often consisted of narrow behaviors accompanied by somewhat artificial performance standards. An example is "The student can identify 10 state capitals with 80% accuracy." Instead, as discussed in the following sections, objectives should identify the meaningful capabilities that students should acquire in a unit of instruction. Examples include summarizing the main points in stories one has read and developing public awareness programs on major diseases.

Characteristics

Goals are idealized expectations for schooling that may be interpreted in more than one way. In contrast, objectives for instruction are unambiguous statements of particular capabilities the student is to develop. Instructional objectives clarify, in specific terms, the intent of goals. For example, one of the language arts goals in Table 4-1 is "using language to learn." In an elementary school classroom, one six-weeks objective is "summarize the main points in stories one has read." Subobjectives for the unit, which are prerequisite skills to the end-of-unit objective, are "identify the beginning, middle, and end of stories" and "differentiate main ideas from supporting details."

Of importance is that objectives describe what the learner will be able to do after instruction. Statements that describe the teacher's actions, specific content items, or activities that the student will engage in are not useful as objectives. Examples that should not be used are "provide a variety of problem-solving activities" (a reminder to the teacher), "retell the plot of *Moby Dick*" (a content item), and "identify the parts of a microscope after reading the text" (student activity). Instead, objectives state the capabilities that are not restricted to a particular situation (*Moby Dick*) or activity (reading the textbook).

The role of instructional objectives is twofold. One function is to translate educational goals into focal points for classroom instruction. Of importance is that objectives are not written for each activity that is implemented in the classroom. Instead, as indicated by the example in language arts, objectives identify major checkpoints of student learning during instruction.

The second function of objectives is to serve as a guide for developing assessments. Stating the complex achievements that are the focus of instruction can assist the teacher in avoiding trivial assessments. In the language arts example, children are assessed after classroom instruction on the subobjectives and some work on summarizing brief stories. They use tape recorders placed at the back of the class to begin recording their summaries of stories read during free reading time. The teacher evaluates the summaries using a checklist.

Classification Systems

Classification systems used in the 1970s to develop instructional objectives for the classroom were based on the view of learning as composed of discrete skills that were hierarchical and learned in a linear fashion. That is, specific lower-level skills are prerequisite and essential to the learning of more complex skills.

Table 4.2 Levels of Learning in the Cognitive Domain in Bloom's Taxonomy

Types of learning	Definition	Sample verbs
Knowledge	Recall of (1) specific universals such as structures and generalizations that dominate a subject field and (2) methods and processes	State, name, define, label, describe
Comprehension		
translation	Restatement by paraphrasing a communication	Paraphrase
interpretation	Explanation or summarization of a communication	Summarize, explain
extrapolation	Extension of trends or tendencies beyond the given data that are in accordance with the original communication	Extrapolate
Application	The use of abstractions (ideas, procedures, generalized methods, or technical principle[s]) in particular concrete situations	Demonstrate, apply, compute
Analysis	The deconstruction of a communication into its elements or parts so that the relations among ideas are made explicit	Deduce, relate (one part to another)
Synthesis	Arrangement and combination of elements and parts to form a pattern or structure not clearly evident before	Design, create
Evaluation	Use of a standard appraisal to develop judgments about the value of material and methods for stated purposes	Judge, evaluate, appraise, critique

Source: Summarized from Bloom et al. (1971).

Bloom's taxonomy. One well-known classification system is the *Taxonomy of Educational Objectives: Cognitive Domain* (Bloom, Engelhart, First, Hill, & Krathwohl, 1956). The six categories of cognitive skills listed in Table 4-2 are knowledge, comprehension, application, analysis, synthesis, and evaluation. This taxonomy was originally developed to describe and categorize discrete test items. That is, each item on a test may be reviewed for the particular cognitive process that the item requires.

The taxonomy also has been used to write objectives for instruction. However, Kulik and Kulik (1988) report that many researchers and educators have experienced difficulties in applying the six levels of the taxonomy in practice. For example, the purpose of a unit may be to develop student expertise in problem solving. However, the taxonomy does not include problem solving but two separate components of problem solving—analysis and synthesis. Kulik and Kulik (1988) note that some educators have used a simplified version of the taxonomy consisting of three levels—knowledge, comprehension/routine application, and problem solving (see Table 4-3).

Gagné's domains of learning. Unlike Bloom's taxonomy, the purpose of Robert Gagné's domains was to identify distinct categories of learning that meet at least three criteria:

1. Each category reflects a formal and unique class of performance that occurs through learning.
2. Each category applies to a diverse set of human activities and is independent of intelligence, age, socioeconomic status, classroom, grade level, and so on.
3. Each category requires different instructional treatments, prerequisites, and processing requirements by the learner (Gagné, 1984, p. 2).

The five domains of learning are verbal information, intellectual skills, motor skills, attitudes, and cognitive strategies (Gagné, 1972, 1985). Three of the domains (verbal information, intellectual skills, cognitive strategies) address cognitive capabilities (see Table 4-4). Verbal information refers to the recall of information, whereas intellectual skills represent the various ways of applying information to different types of situations. Included are such capabilities as discriminating between different geometric shapes (discrimination learning) and calculating the amount of wallpaper needed to repaper a room with particular dimensions (problem solving).

Table 4.3 Adaptations to the Taxonomy of the Cognitive Domains

Level	Example
Knowledge	Describe the characteristics of goal statements.
Comprehension application	Identify the errors in proposed statements of goals.
Problem solving	Evaluate proposed goal statements in your curriculum area for their utility in planning curriculum and assessments.

Table 4-4 Overview of three domains of cognitive learning

Category of learning	Description	Sample verbs
Verbal information	Stating or communicating the information in some way	State, label, define
Intellectual skills	Interacting with the environment using symbols	
Discrimination learning	Responding differently to characteristics that distinguish objects, such as shape, size, color	Differentiate between
Concept learning	Classifying objects or events as members of a concept class	Classify (typical and atypical objects and events)
Rule learning	Demonstrating or applying a rule or relationship	Apply, demonstrate (a rule)
Problem solving	Combining subordinate rules in order to solve a problem (most effective learning strategy is guided discovery)	Solve, generate (a solution)
Cognitive strategies	Efficiently managing one's remembering, thinking, and learning	Organize (one's learning), self-test (oneself on learning)

The four specific capabilities in intellectual skills form a hierarchy. That is, each skill is essential to the learning of the next higher skill. For example, learning a concept, such as triangle, depends on learning to differentiate triangles from other geometric figures. These capabilities are prerequisite to learning to apply rules about the properties of triangles, such as the relationship between the base and altitude, and to solving problems involving triangles.

The domain of cognitive strategies refers to the development of how-to-learn skills. This category includes the capabilities that control one's management of learning, remembering, and thinking. Unlike verbal information and intellectual skills, which relate to the curriculum, the object of cognitive strategies is the learner's own thought processes. Examples of cognitive strategies include summarizing the main points in a text and generating questions about the material as a self-test of one's comprehension.

An example of cognitive strategies is the strand "using language to learn" in Table 4-1. A capability in the language arts strand for grades Pre-K–3 is "use phonics to decode words; use phonics, prior knowledge and context to construct meaning" (*South Carolina English Language Arts Framework*, 1996, p. 18). For grades 9–12, the level of that capability is "apply reading and vocabulary strategies fluently and automatically as appropriate for text and purpose" (p. 19). As with the broad objective of making inferences from data, discussed in Chapter 2, the teacher's task is that of identifying the skills involved in these capabilities that are to be taught.

Developing Instructional Objectives

An assumption of Bloom's taxonomy and Gagné's intellectual skills is that learning is both linear and hierarchical. Some school learning may proceed in this way. For example, the child may first learn to discriminate different geometric shapes (discrimination learning), then to identify typical and atypical examples of triangles in different contexts, such as mosaics and textile designs (concept learning). The next objective may be to deduce the similarities and differences in complex patterns composed of triangles from those composed of other figures, such as rectangles and pentagons (rule learning).

The current emphasis in curriculum is to establish a balance between learning important concepts and principles in the subject area, learning to use one's capabilities in real-world situations, and developing skills in managing and directing one's own thinking. As indicated in the prior section, the strands in language arts include communicating effectively and using language to learn, in addition to learning to use the conventions and forms of language. In planning instruction, the priorities of developing knowledge, learning to apply new capabilities in real-world tasks, and developing cognitive strategies are weighted differently in different schools and classes and at different levels of education. Also, becoming proficient in cognitive strategies requires an extended period of time and the teaching of the desired strategies. One approach, therefore, is to identify the types of cognitive strategies that the learner should develop by the end of the year and to write year-end objectives for those capabilities. The teacher assists students by teaching the strategies and informally assesses their use during the year. Near the end of the school year, the teacher formally assesses these strategies. An example for first grade is to sound out the letters in new words.

Some sources suggest that teachers should consult textbooks and other published materials as sources of objectives. However, textbook objectives typically do not represent major checkpoints in a unit and they often focus on narrow behaviors. For example, the two objectives for the topic of viruses in a published textbook for middle school science are to list the parts of a virus and to describe how a virus reproduces and causes disease (both verbal information). In addition, Taylor and Nolen (1996) note that students in their assessment course were faced with textbooks that listed as many as 10 objectives for 1 day's reading, most of which were at the knowledge or verbal information level (p. 82).

Information that is learned at the recall level is quickly forgotten. Therefore, the primary focus of objectives should not be the recognition or recall of information. Instead, the focus should be on developing a coherent knowledge base and higher levels of cognitive capabilities. The science goals in the prior section stated the importance of student reasoning and problem solving in addition to building a knowledge base. Given these goals, a unit on viruses may have as an end-point objective "to organize the information essential for a public awareness program" (problem solving). This objective requires that students (possibly in pairs or small groups) identify the essential points to be conveyed about viruses. This requirement, particularly if students are required to justify their choices, also can contribute to the objective of developing logical supporting arguments.

Logical subobjectives for this unit are "contrast viruses with cells" and "identify common diseases caused by viruses." In contrasting cells and viruses, the students will be addressing the way that viruses reproduce as well as their minute size. Common diseases caused by viruses include smallpox, polio (which is virtually nonexistent now), AIDS, and new diseases such as the hanta and ebola viruses. Student learning on the subobjectives may be evaluated first informally during class discussions. Then, if this information is crucial in the course, it may be included on a unit test. Student learning on the unit objective—organizing information for a public awareness program—may be evaluated through student projects.

The recommended steps for developing classroom objectives are presented in Table 4-5. As indicated in the prior example, objectives are written only for the essential learnings in a unit. When objectives are written to address major disciplinary understandings, a maximum of four to five objectives for a 2- to 4-week unit is sufficient (Taylor & Nolen, 1996).

Table 4.5 Suggested Steps for Developing Classroom Objectives

1. Review curriculum goals, guides, and framework for priorities.
2. Beginning with the first unit of instruction, identify the essential learnings for that unit.
3. Write objectives for the one or two complex capabilities that are end points of the unit.
4. Identify supporting or prerequisite capabilities that are essential to learning the complex skills in the end-of-unit objectives.
5. Write a subobjective for each supporting capability.
6. Review the objectives to ensure that the higher levels of cognitive learning are addressed.
7. Complete objectives for the other units in the same way.
8. Revise the objectives as needed based on teaching the unit.

Also, a unit may be addressed in more than one way. For example, the unit objective for viruses may be to design a research program (problem solving). This objective may require students to develop other concepts in addition to those named in the preceding subobjectives.

An elementary school teacher in language arts, in contrast, may determine the sound/symbol principles to be taught and interweave those objectives with skills in verbal communication.

The completed objectives and subobjectives should not be viewed as cast in concrete. For example, some objectives may require more time to teach and adequately assess than originally planned (Taylor & Nolen, 1996). Also, as teaching proceeds, some of the objectives originally planned may not be addressing curriculum priorities and may be deleted. Finally, after teaching a particular unit, the teacher should make notes about needed changes and revisions for the next year.

Summary

Unlike goals, objectives are unambiguous statements of the capabilities the student is to learn in the classroom. Objectives do not describe the teacher's actions, specific content items, or classroom activities. Objectives express focal points for instruction and they serve as a guide for developing assessments.

Two classification systems that may be used as a reference for instructional objectives are Bloom's taxonomy and Gagné's domains of learning. Bloom's taxonomy identifies the particular cognitive processes required to address different test items. Gagné's domains identify categories of human capabilities that differ from each other and are the outcomes of learning. Also, Gagné's classification includes cognitive strategies that address learning-to-learn skills. Their utility from the current perspective of curricular reform is to serve as a reference point to ensure that complex capabilities are included in instructional objectives.

Developing objectives for the classroom begins with the analysis of curriculum goals and frameworks for classroom priorities. Then the one or two most complex capabilities for each unit and the supporting subobjectives are identified. This approach is implemented in different ways depending on the age of the student and the nature of the subject matter.

Chapter Questions

1. Suggested social studies goals include environmental/ecological awareness and preservation. What are some different ways this goal may be translated into instructional objectives for a middle school class?

2. One of the national educational goals in Goals 2000 states that U.S. students will be first in the world in science and mathematics. What problems does this type of statement create for curriculum planning?

3. One of the curriculum goals in the Eight-Year Study was the ability to make inferences from data. Choose three grade levels separated in time, such as second, sixth, and tenth grades. What are logical end-of-course objectives for this goal for each grade level?

4. Identify the appropriate domain of learning in Gagné's system for the two following objectives. Support your choice.

(a) The student can develop a strategy to improve the growth of unhealthy plants with particular symptoms.

(b) The student uses context clues to determine likely word meaning of new terms in the text.

References

Bloom, B. S. (1968). Learning for mastery. *Evaluation Comment, 1*(2). University of California, Los Angeles Center for the Study of Evaluation of Instructional Programs.

Bloom, B. S., Engelhart, M., First, E., Hill, W., & Krathwohl, D. (1956). *Taxonomy of educational objectives: Handbook I: Cognitive domain*. New York: David McKay.

Bloom, B. S., Hastings, J., & Madaus, G. (1971). *Handbook on formative and summative evaluation of student learning*. New York: McGraw-Hill.

Brookhart, S. M. (1997). A theoretical framework for the role of classroom assessment in motivating student effort and achievement. *Applied Measurement in Education, 10*(2), 161–180.

Cole, N. S. (1990). Conceptions of educational achievement. *Educational Researcher, 19*(3), 2–7.

Crooks, J. T. (1988). Impact of classroom evaluation on students. *Review of Educational Research*, 58(4), 438–481.

Duschl, R. A., & Gitomer, D. H. (1997). Strategies and challenges to changing the focus of assessment and instruction in science classrooms. *Educational Assessment*, 4(1), 37–73.

Fennema, E., Franke, M. L., Carpenter, T. P., & Carey, D. A. (1993). Using children's mathematical knowledge in instruction. *American Education Research Journal*, 30(3), 555–563.

Gagné, R. M. (1972). Domains of learning. *Interchange*, 3(1), 1–8.

Gagné, R. M. (1984). Learning outcomes and their effects: Useful categories of human performance. *American Psychologist*, *37*(4), 377–385.

Gagné, R. M. (1985). *The conditions of learning* (4th ed.). New York: Holt, Rinehart, & Winston.

Kulik, J. A., & Kulik, C. C. (1988). Timing of feedback and verbal learning. *Review of Educational Research*, 58(1), 79–97.

National Council of Teachers of Mathematics (1989). *Curriculum and evaluation standards for school mathematics*. Reston, VA: Author.

Schoenfield, A. H. (1985). Metacognition and epistemological issues in mathematical understanding. In E. A. Silver (Ed.), *Teaching and learning mathematical problem solving: Multiple research perspectives* (pp. 361–379). Hillsdale, NJ: Erlbaum.

Schoenfield, A. H. (1992). Learning to think mathematically. Problem solving, cognition, and sense making in mathematics. In D. A. Grouws (Ed.), *Handbook of research on mathematics teaching and learning* (pp. 334–370). New York: Macmillan.

Smith, E. R., & Tyler, R. W. (1942). *Appraising and recording student progress*. New York: Harper Brothers.

South Carolina English Language Arts Framework. (1996). Columbia: South Carolina State Department of Education.

Taylor, C., & Nolen, S., (1996). A contextualized approach to teaching students about assessment. *Educational Psychologist, 37*(1), 77–88.

Wood, T., Cobb, P., & Yackel, E. (1991). Change in teaching mathematics: A case study. *American Educational Research Journal, 28*(3), 587–616.

PART TWO

CLASSROOM ASSESSMENT TOOLS

Chapter 5

Structured-Response Items

Chapter 6

Constructed-Response Questions

Chapter 7

Observational Techniques

Chapter 8

Performance Assessment

Chapter 9

Portfolio Assessment

Chapter 5

Structured-Response Items

Major Topics

"Regardless of quality, assessments tell students about themselves as learners, create representations of what is important to learn, and convey ideas about the structure of the various subject disciplines."

—Taylor & Nolen, 1996, p. 78

As students progress through the grades to middle and high school, many of the assessments they face are subject-matter tests. Items used in these tests consist of true-false, matching, and multiple-choice items (referred to as structured-response items) and short answer and essay questions (discussed in Chapter 6).

General Guidelines

Structured-response items require the student to choose an answer from the options provided; the student does not construct a response. These items are sometimes referred to as "objective" because each item has a single correct answer and any clerk can score the test accurately with an answer key. That is, the judgment of the scorer does not influence the students' scores. Nevertheless, to the extent that the development or selection of items is influenced by the teacher's opinions, attitudes, or beliefs, they are not objective.

Planning the Test and Constructing Items

A common failing in developing tests in a subject area is that the items often address only the recall of trivial information, such as the number of smallpox cases in the United States in 1950. Such tests are sometimes referred to as "regurgitation" type because they require only the surface memorization of many facts and other items of information in order to be prepared for the test.

Any of several factors may contribute to the development of such tests. First, items that require only recall are much easier to write than items that require inference, analysis, interpretation, or application of a principle (Aiken, 1982; Fredericksen, 1984). Second, items that accompany textbooks are sometimes used. They are usually recall items (and have other problems that are discussed in this chapter) (Frisbie, Miranda, & Baker, 1993). Other factors that contribute to the development of only recall items are that the teacher or instructor may lack a systematic approach to developing classroom tests and/or constructs the test at the last minute.

General guidelines. Several general guidelines apply to the planning and construction of tests and items (see Table 5-1). Guidelines 1 and 2 are related and

Table 5.1 General Guidelines for Structured-Response Items

1. The test should be carefully planned so that it does not convey a fragmented view of the domain.
2. The test should reflect the classroom goals and objectives.
3. The reading difficulty and vocabulary of each item should be kept as simple as possible.
4. Items should not be statements or phrases lifted from the text.
5. Each item should address important concepts and principles, not trivia.
6. Each item should clearly pose an unambiguous problem.
7. The test should not include trick or catch questions, such as a true-false question that is true except for one obscure term.
8. Each item type (true-false, matching, multiple-choice) should assess an important cognitive skill in the subject.

their purpose is to focus the test on key cognitive capabilities in the discipline, not on trivia. Developing classroom objectives at the level of application of knowledge, from identifying examples of important concepts to analyzing cause-and-effect relationships and solving problems is the first step. As indicated in Chapter 4, objectives serve as the conceptual framework for the test. Also important is to develop test questions according to good models of the particular item types. Then, after completion of the items, review the test using the criteria presented earlier in Table 3-4. Specifically: Do the items draw out student learning related to the particular objectives they assess? Are they congruent with instructional methods in the class? Can students who understand the concepts demonstrate their knowledge on the test?

Important for developing items that allow students to demonstrate their knowledge is to keep the reading level and vocabulary at the appropriate level for the students. As indicated in Chapter 3, a test that is a measure of reading ability as well as knowledge in the subject area lacks validity. When developing items, however, do not take phrases or sentences from the text. Such items measure only the student's capability to identify words and phrases previously read.

As each item is developed, it should be designed to pose an unambiguous question or problem and should address important concepts or principles in the material.

Another problem in item construction is that, in an effort to write items that assess complex thinking, the test developer may inadvertently write catch or trick questions. Trick questions are those that depend on the recognition of a particular word or number in a sentence that appears to focus on another issue. An example is the true-false item: "The use of diphtheria vaccine contributed to the decline in deaths between 1900 and 1968" (Thorndike & Hagen, 1969). The item appears, at first glance, to focus on the period in history when diphtheria deaths declined. A student who knows that this decline occurred between 1900 and 1968 would mark the statement true. However, the statement uses the term "vaccine" early in the sentence instead of the term "antitoxin" as the responsible agent. (Vaccines immunize individuals against viruses such as smallpox and influenza.) Although the basic fact of the decline of deaths is true, the item writer has rendered the item false by the use of the term "vaccine." Thus, answering the item correctly depends only on recognizing that vaccine is an inappropriate term in reference to diphtheria. If the purpose of an item is to test the student's understanding of the differences between vaccines and antitoxins, then the item should directly focus on those terms. Answering this question correctly depends on recognizing that either a toxin or antitoxin is the immunizing material for diphtheria. Finally, as discussed in the following paragraphs, each item should address a cognitive skill that is important in the subject area.

Types of cognitive skills appropriate for structured-response items. Three types of cognitive skills can be assessed with structured-response items. The lowest-level skill is the recall of previously learned information (referred to as knowledge in Bloom's taxonomy and verbal information in Gagné's domains of learning).

Two application skills also may be assessed—specifically, concept learning and rule learning (two of the intellectual skills identified by Gagné). The definition of concept learning is the acquisition of a label and the defining criteria of the concept so that the learner can correctly classify new situations or new objects as examples or nonexamples of the concept (Gagné, 1985). Therefore, an adequate assessment of concept learning requires the student to identify *previously unencountered* examples or situations as examples of the particular concept. Assessment of rule learning requires that the student apply a principle or rule to previously unencountered situations. An example is reviewing the food consumed by an individual in a 24-hour period and identifying the nutritional deficiencies.

Some texts state that true-false items can be used only for recall of information and that matching items can address only recall and classification of examples (concept learning). However, if properly constructed, true-false, matching, and multiple-choice items can address concept learning and rule learning in addition to testing the recall of information.

Some developers maintain that multiple-choice items can also measure problem solving. However, two difficulties occur if teachers rely on this format. First, multiple-choice items cannot obtain information about the ways students internally represent problems and make use of strategies (Fredericksen, 1984). Second, if the purpose is to solve a problem and select the correct answer from the response options, some students will first select a likely correct answer and work backward to the problem.

Problems with textbook tests. Most textbook series in mathematics, science, and social studies used in the elementary and middle school grades include unit or chapter tests. Because the tests are published as part of the textbook materials, quality of the items has generally been assumed to be high. However, an examination of items in textbook tests by this author indicates that the focus is primarily on the recall of information.

In addition, a systematic analysis of textbook tests in social studies and science for grades 2 to 7 indicates other problems. Frisbie, Miranda, and Baker (1993) analyzed 42 textbook tests in social studies and 49 in science from five publishers. The tests were analyzed for (1) content match between items and objectives, (2) taxonomic level required by items and objectives, and (3) extent of phrase matching between each test item and the textbook readings. The taxonomic levels used were knowledge, comprehension, and application from Bloom's system.

Table 5.2 Results of the Analysis of 91 Textbook Tests in Social Studies and Science from Five Publishers (Grades 2 to 7)

1. In science, half of the tests matched 50% or less of their unit objectives.
2. In social studies, half of the tests matched 50% or less of their unit objectives.
3. In three-fourths of all tests, 50% of the items matched the wording in the text, and in half the tests, 65% or more of the items matched text material.
4. On all tests, 90% of the items were at the knowledge level. In one-fourth of the tests, *all* the items were at the knowledge level.

Source: Summarized from Frisbie et al. (1993).

Study findings are summarized in Table 5-2. As indicated in results 1 and 2, the content match between items and unit objectives was very poor. That is, overall, for a typical unit, half of the objectives were not covered by the unit test at all (Frisbie et al., 1993, p. 30). Further, the extent of phrase matching with the text was extremely high. Finally, 90 percent of the items were at the knowledge level.

Because the researchers sampled both a range of publishers and grade levels, they state that the findings of their research generalize to textbook tests in science and social studies throughout the intermediate grades. Therefore, the three major problems that they identified may be found in other textbook tests in science and social studies. First, student scores will misrepresent the nature of student achievement because of the lack of coverage of unit objectives and the high amount of extraneous information that is addressed. Misalignment, in other words, seriously weakens the validity of inferences that may be made from the scores (Frisbie et al., 1993, p. 34).

Second, the skill that is most needed to perform well on these tests is simply the recall of word strings that were read in the text. That is, the tests do not address learning beyond the identification of phrases previously read. This problem is particularly serious given the emphasis in the last few years on curriculum reform to address higher cognitive skills.

Third, the tests convey the message to students that memorization of facts and terms is the key to doing well in these two subject areas (Frisbie et al., 1993, p. 33). They contribute to the learning of habits that are not productive for future learning.

Therefore, the researchers recommend that classroom teachers should thoroughly evaluate textbook tests. Teachers should select only those items that match their unit objectives that also are not phrase matches to words and sentences in the textbook.

In summary, although structured-response items are objective, this term does not describe their development. Ways to reduce the subjectivity of the item-development process include basing items on classroom objectives, assessing important cognitive skills, avoiding trick or catch questions, and keeping the vocabulary level and reading level at the appropriate level for the students.

Assembling the Test

Items should be arranged on a test according to type with adequate space between the items so that they are easy to read. Also important is that an item should not be split between the bottom of one page and the top of the next page. Instead, place the entire item on the next page. Turning back and forth for a question introduces confusion.

Although every type of item will not appear on every test, the rule of thumb for item arrangement is true-false, matching, short-answer, multiple-choice, and essay, if one or two questions are included. The rationale is that the more complex or time-consuming items are not placed at the beginning of the test. Otherwise, some students may not get to the less complex items. Essay questions also should include the number of points allocated to each and the approximate amount of time to be spent on each (discussed in Chapter 6). Also important is to allow adequate spaces for student answers for short-answer and essay items and to provide a clear set of directions for each item type.

✦ True-False Items

True-false items are examples of the type referred to as alternate-response items. Specifically, they provide only two answer choices for the student. An example is the following item that assesses knowledge of verb forms:

Neither Mary nor Susan _________ red hair.
(a) has
(b) have

True-false items, however, are the most used type of the alternate-response format. Although sometimes described as very easy to write, developing true-false items that are not superficial requires some planning and thought.

Implementation

True-false items are appropriate for assessing facts, definitions (knowledge or verbal information), and simple applications (rule learning). The answer choices are T or F or, for children, Y for "yes" and N for "no."

A major problem in the use of true-false items is that they often address trivial information or nonessential facts or details. A test peppered with items of this nature conveys an unconnected fragmented view of the subject matter. Instead, the items should address the most important knowledge items in a unit that can be unequivocally categorized as true or not true. They should not be used for isolated details.

Recall the objective in Chapter 4 that the student can identify diseases caused by viruses. Table 5-3 illustrates the appropriate format of a true-false question to test this objective. Referred to as a cluster true-false item, this format enables the teacher to assess part of a topic in depth.

If the objective had stated that the student can identify diseases caused by viruses and monerans (bacteria), the identifiers Y and N in the question may be replaced with M for monerans and V for viruses. The directions then would ask

Table 5.3 Examples of Cluster Alternate-Response Items that Assess the Recall of Knowledge

True-false item

1.B. Using the letters "Y" for "yes" and "N" for "no," identify which of the following diseases are caused by viruses.

(Y)	1. AIDS	(Y)	5. measles
(Y)	2. chickenpox	(Y)	6. mumps
(Y)	3. influenza	(N)	7. tuberculosis
(N)	4. malaria	(N)	8. typhoid fever

Identification item

1.B. Using the letters "M" for "monerans" and "V" for "viruses," identify the causes of the following diseases.

(V)	1. AIDS	(V)	5. measles
(V)	2. chickenpox	(V)	6. mumps
(V)	3. influenza	(M)	7. tuberculosis
(M)	4. malaria	(M)	8. typhoid fever

the student to identify the diseases caused by each. An alternate format for the identification item is to list the two choices (virus and moneran) beside each item and ask the student to circle the correct answer.

To use true-false or other alternate-response items to assess applications or simple inferences, the question must provide some stimulus material to which the student reacts. Table 5-4 illustrates an example of this type. The student

Table 5.4 Example of an Alternate-Response Item to Assess Application of Rules

Directions: Review the food consumed by a 12-year-old girl in 1 day. Then identify the nutritional deficiencies from the following list, using the words "adequate" or "deficient."

Breakfast	*Lunch*
1 cup black coffee	1 8-oz glass of Sprite
	1 8-oz hamburger with mayonnaise & mustard
	25 French fries

Dinner

3 smoked ham slices

1 cup sweet potatoes

1 glass of Sprite

1 piece of apple pie with one scoop of ice cream

Using the words "adequate" and "deficient" listed below, identify which of the following are deficiencies in her diet. Circle the term that applies to each of the following dietary essentials in the girl's meals.

adequate	deficient	1. Calcium
adequate	deficient	2. Calories
adequate	deficient	3. Carbohydrates
adequate	deficient	4. Iron
adequate	deficient	5. Niacin
adequate	deficient	6. Protein
adequate	deficient	7. Vitamin A
adequate	deficient	8. Vitamin C

Source: Adapted from Thorndike and Hagen (1979).

reviews the girl's meals for the day, determines the nutritional deficiencies, and selects them from the list provided.

Other stimulus materials that are appropriate for the cluster true-false item are maps, charts, and graphs. For example, a classroom objective may state that the student can interpret map symbols. A small map, for example, may be followed by a set of interpretive statements that the student identifies as true or false.

Some texts discuss the use of statements as true-false questions and present several cautions in writing such statements. Included are avoid ambiguous, vague sentences; do not use sentences stated in the negative; do not use sentences that are half true and half false; and do not use words such as always, never, frequently, and usually. The position taken by this text is that, even if well-written, several such sentences on a test are likely to be assessing the recall of fragmented bits of information about a topic or subject. Instead, if true-false items are to be used in a classroom test, they should probe depth of learning in an identified key topic in the cluster format.

Guidelines for Development

The first step, as indicated in Table 5-5, is to review the lesson objectives to identify the essential facts and definitions the student should know. Then develop a cluster item with directions for the true-false identification. For example, a course in teacher education may identify the teaching principles derived from Jean Piaget's cognitive-development theory as important. A cluster item may ask the students which of a set of statements about teaching is supported by Piaget's theory. For example, the statement "The teacher demonstrates the use of Cuisenaire rods" should be marked false because the focus of the theory is student exploration and discovery using various materials.

Table 5.5 Guidelines for Developing Cluster True-False Items

1. Review lesson objectives to identify the essential facts and definitions for key concepts.
2. Review lesson objectives to identify key rules or principles that the student can apply in a true-false format.
3. Arrange the situations or examples into clusters according to the common fact they represent (e.g., caused by viruses) or the rule to be applied (e.g., nutritional deficiencies).
4. Ensure that the terms, statements, or situations in the questions are either clearly true or clearly false.
5. Ensure that the false options are plausible.

In assessing rule learning, select situations that the student can evaluate by judging a set of terms or statements. An example is the question about nutritional deficiencies in a set of meals.

Selection of terms or statements to be evaluated is also important. The options that are false should be plausible and the terms or statements used should be clearly true or clearly false. Avoid any statements that are only true some of the time.

Advantages and Limitations

Properly constructed, alternate-response items are useful for assessing the recall of information as in the examples in Table 5-3 and the application of information (Table 5-4). They are also efficient test items; that is, they assess knowledge with fewer words than do multiple-choice items.

The limitation of two-choice items, however, is that they are subject to guessing. That is, the student has a 50–50 chance of answering a particular item correctly in the absence of knowledge about the topic. However, if the student knows little or nothing about the topic, guessing will not earn the student an adequate score on a cluster of 8 to 12 items.

Summary

True-false items, the most used type of alternate-response question, are appropriate for assessing facts, definitions, and rule learning. To probe student depth of understanding, the cluster format should be used. This format consists of a set of brief statements or words and the directions that state the common fact they represent or the rule to be applied.

Development begins with the review of lesson objectives to identify the facts, definitions, and applications of rules that may be assessed with the cluster true-false format. Of importance is that the words or sentences to be evaluated by the student should be either clearly true or clearly false and the false examples should be plausible. An advantage of the cluster format is that it is efficient and can probe student knowledge in depth about a topic. A limitation is that true-false items are subject to guessing.

✦ Matching Items

The distinguishing characteristic of matching items is that they present several problems accompanied by a single list of possible answers. The item typically consists of two parallel columns of information. The task for the student is to identify the pairs that are related on the basis of the association described in the directions.

Implementation

Matching items are appropriate for factual associations such as persons and achievements, authors and books, terms and definitions, and symbols and concepts. Matching items are also useful in conjunction with diagrams and charts. For example, the parts of a cell may be numbered in a diagram. The task is to match the numbers to the names of the cell parts that are provided in a list.

The typical format for matching items is the parallel columns arrangement. The first question in Table 5-6 is an example of this type. The item asks students to determine the particular early learning theory that the proposed research projects represent.

The application of knowledge can be measured also by the matching format referred to as the classification type or master list (Thorndike & Hagen, 1969, p. 118). This format is appropriate for high school or college classes. The categories or principles to be tested are identified first. Then a set of situations is devised that reflect the selected categories or principles. Item (b) in Table 5-6, from a course in educational research, is an example. The categories are 3 threats to the validity of a research study; that is, they are problems that can render the findings of a research study uninterpretable. Examples appropriate for high school students include identifying different types of weather patterns and different architectural styles.

Guidelines for Development

The purpose of the matching item is for the student to make fine discriminations in order to select the correct answer. Therefore, the set of statements, or situations should be homogeneous. If individuals, for example, they should all be inventors, U.S. statesmen, or some other category.

This requirement and four other essential characteristics are listed in Table 5-7. The list of items to be matched should be brief for two reasons. One is to minimize the reading requirement. The other is that a lengthy list can be confusing and lead to errors when the student knows the correct answers. Also important to minimize confusion is to state clearly the basis for the matching in the directions and arrange the items in a logical order. For example, names of individuals should be arranged in alphabetical order and dates should be in chronological order. An unequal number of situations or statements and response choices ensures that the last item cannot be answered by a process of elimination. For the master list format, first identify three to five related concepts. Then develop situations that represent them.

Table 5.6 Examples of Matching Items that Measure Complex Learning

(a) Topic: Early learning theories

1-4. Match each of the research projects on the left with the appropriate theory from the list on the right. Options may be used more than once or not at all, but each question has only one answer.

Research projects	*Theories*
__(C)__ 1. The computer gives children a clue in a treasure hunt for each question they answer correctly.	(A) Classical conditioning
__(A)__ 2. A small toy is held out to each toddler as the doctor places the stethoscope on his/her chest.	(B) Gestalt theory
__(B)__ 3. Students are given a candle and a box of thumbtacks. The task is to mount the candles on the wall.	(C) Operant conditioning
__(B)__ 4. Students from different cultures are given pictures of paint spatters and asked to name them.	

(b) Topic: Threats to internal validity in research

1-6. Match the situations in the list with the appropriate threat to internal validity, using the letters A through C. Only one letter is correct for each situation; the answer choices may be used more than once.

__(B)__ 1. The posttest in a study of thinking skills is administered on the day the school band members are participating in a state competition.	A. Effects of history
__(C)__ 2. Mrs. Jones is judged to be an efficient secretary because she conveys an impression of neatness and willingness to work.	B. Subject mortality
__(B)__ 3. Students participating in a peer counseling study drop out of school.	C. Halo effect
__(C)__ 4. In addition to the experimental teaching method, students in the experimental group received new textbooks with colored illustrations and study guides.	
__(A)__ 5. A social studies unit on the Supreme Court is begun 2 days before a controversial national debate over a new nomination to the court.	
__(B)__ 6. Thirty percent of the student teachers in a study fail to return their questionnaires.	

Table 5.7 Guidelines for Matching Test Items

1. Develop a set of statements, names, or situations that are homogeneous.
2. Keep the set of statements relatively short.
3. Clearly state the basis for matching in the directions.
4. Arrange the statements or situations and the response choices in a logical order.
5. Provide an unequal number of statements or situations and response choices.

Advantages and Limitations

The master list format of the matching items is particularly powerful in assessing concept learning and rule learning. As indicated in Table 5-6, they can require that the student make careful judgments in applying the criteria for concept membership. A disadvantage is that developing situations that are brief and clearly meet essential concept criteria requires practice. That is, choosing situations that do not overlap in their characteristics requires careful selection of situations and review prior to implementing the test.

Summary

Matching items present several problems accompanied by a single list of items, typically in two parallel columns. The student's task is to identify the related pairs. These items are appropriate for associations such as persons and achievements and authors and books. The format referred to as the classification or master list format is appropriate for assessing concepts and rule learning.

Requirements for developing the parallel columns format include ensuring that the set of items is homogeneous, brief, and arranged in a logical order. The directions should clearly state the basis for matching. Developing an item in the master list format requires first identifying two or three related concepts and then constructing situations that reflect them. An advantage of the master list format is that it is particularly powerful in assessing concepts and rule learning. A limitation is that developing situations that clearly meet concept criteria requires practice.

✦ Multiple-Choice Items

The multiple-choice item consists of two parts: (1) the stem, which poses the question or problem, and (2) the response choices. The stem may be written as either an incomplete statement or as a question. One response choice of the three to five options is the correct answer that completes the sentence or answers the question. The other options are referred to as foils or distractors.

Implementation

Multiple-choice items are useful for assessing the recall of knowledge (verbal information) and the application of knowledge, both concept learning and rule learning. The limitation with using multiple-choice items for measuring knowledge recall is that they are not efficient. That is, a stem and three to five responses are required for an item that requires a simple cognitive process, recognition of the correct answer. (True-false or short-answer items are more efficient for testing recall.)

Table 5-8 illustrates multiple-choice items that measure concept learning and rule learning. Item (a) requires the student to review the criteria for each type of rehearsal and then to determine that the situation meets the criteria for elaborative rehearsal. Item (b) requires the student to first recall information about test reliability and validity and then apply that knowledge to the described situations. Example (c) involves the application of the definition of reinforcement, that is, any event that strengthens or increases performance.

Of importance is that the situations in these three examples include only those that have not been previously discussed in class or described in the textbook. If the student has previously learned the examples that are in the test item, then the item is merely assessing the recall of previously learned information, not the student's skill in applying concept criteria or rules.

Example (b) in Table 5-8 illustrates a variation of the typical multiple-choice format that may be used in high school or college classes. However, this format is not appropriate for younger students, because it may be confusing. In this arrangement, the student must choose which combination of statements is the correct answer. It is particularly useful in assessing the application of concept criteria in the identification of examples and the application of rules.

The format illustrated in example (b) should be used instead of the format that lists three answer choices followed by a fourth choice that is "all of the above" or "none of the above." When "none of the above" is used, it usually means the item writer could not think of a plausible fourth option. In such a situation, the phrase is simply a place filler. When "all of the above" is used, it is typically the correct answer. Testwise students will choose this answer. In contrast, the format illustrated in Table 5-8 allows for a more flexible combination of possible answers and does not contain clues to the correct combination.

Like the true-false items illustrated in Table 5-4, multiple-choice items also may be used to evaluate a set of statements about a particular situation, as well as analyzing charts and graphs. The test items for the objective "The ability to make

Table 5.8 Examples of Multiple-Choice Items that Assess Concept Learning and Rule Learning

(a) Concept learning

Asking children to draw pictures about a story they have just read is an example of

A. elaborative rehearsal

B. primary rehearsal

C. maintenance rehearsal

D. selective rehearsal

(b) Rule learning[1]

A multiple-choice test has a reliability coefficient of 0.30. Which of the following do we know about the test?

I. The test scores are invalid.

II. The test scores are unreliable.

III. The test scoring is subjective.

A. I only

B. II only

C. I and II

D. II and III

E. I, II, and III

(c) Rule learning

Some research studies indicate that certain students learn more under mild criticism. This finding indicates that

A. reinforcement is ineffective.

B. generalized reinforcers are needed.

C. praise should be used sparingly.

D. criticism is a reinforcer.

Note: These items assess concept learning and rule learning, respectively, only if the situations presented in the items have not been previously discussed and identified in class or in the textbook.

[1]This format should not be used with students below the high school level.

inferences from data" illustrated in Table 2-4 is an example. The student evaluates a set of statements for each graph or chart as true, insufficient data, or false. Graphs, charts, maps, and descriptive paragraphs also may be followed by a series of specific multiple-choice questions about the material. Of importance is to avoid questions in which a paragraph is followed by only one question. Such an item is not efficient because of the reading time, and it is assessing reading ability as well.

Guidelines for Development

The first step in developing multiple-choice questions is to review the lesson objectives that address key concepts and principles. Then develop examples and situations that require the application of the defining criteria for the concepts and the particular rules.

Several guidelines that should be observed in the construction of each item are illustrated in Table 5-9. Particularly important is that the stem or question should pose a specific issue or problem to be addressed by the student and should not be cluttered with irrelevant information. The stem also should not contain clues to the correct answer. For example, if the stem asks students to make choices about a set of statements, the stem should say, "Which of the following is/are true?" This format avoids signaling whether one or more than one statement is correct.

Table 5.9 Guidelines for the Development of Multiple-Choice Items

1. Review lesson objectives that address key concepts and principles.
2. Develop situations that require the application of defining criteria for the concepts and the selected rules.
3. Develop response options, set aside the questions for a day or so, and then review them.
4. Ensure that the stem poses a specific problem or issue and excludes irrelevant information.
5. Do not state the stem in the negative.
6. Avoid including clues to the correct answer in the stem or in the options.
7. Write concise options that are approximately the same length.
8. Ensure that only one option is the correct answer.
9. Do not use multiple-choice questions to split hairs about a minor point or fact.

The options should be as concise as possible and all should be approximately the same length. Typically, a response option that is longer than the other choices signals that it is the correct answer. Other clues that signal the correct answer are that all wrong answers begin with the same letter or share other features, such as terminology.

Also important is that each response option should be plausible. If one of the choices in a set of four, for example, is not plausible, then the decision for the student is effectively reduced to three choices, not four.

Finally, do not use multiple-choice questions to split hairs about a minor point or fact in the material. Instead, thought-provoking questions that are fair can be devised by testing concepts and rule learning, as illustrated previously in Table 5-8.

Advantages and Limitations

An advantage of multiple-choice items is that they can assess students' skills in identifying examples of key concepts in the lesson and in applying important principles. They may also be used to assess knowledge, particularly when the item asks the student to select the correct combination of statements.

A limitation is that constructing multiple-choice items requires practice. The best time for the teacher to get ideas for questions is during preparation time for teaching the lesson, when various approaches to the subject matter are being explored.

Summary

The multiple-choice item consists of a stem, which may be an incomplete statement or a question, and three to five response choices. Although the items can assess the recall of knowledge, this use is not efficient. However, multiple-choice items are very useful in assessing concept learning and rule learning.

A variation of the basic format appropriate for high school or college classes consists of a question, three statements, and four to five response options that combine the statements in different ways. This format eliminates the need for the options "none of the above" and "all of the above."

In constructing multiple-choice items, care should be taken to ensure that the stem or question poses a specific problem to be addressed by the student and also does not contain grammatical or other clues about the correct answer. Also important is that the options should be concise, approximately the same length, and plausible.

An advantage of multiple-choice items is that they can assess student mastery of key concepts and principles in the subject area. A limitation is that constructing multiple-choice items requires practice.

Chapter Questions

Identify the errors in the following test items.

1. *Directions:* Place the correct letter to the left of each number. Use each letter only once.

1. Number of permanent teeth	A. Sunshine
2. Vitamin D	B. Cleaning advice
3. Bleeding gums	C. Decay
4. Acid	D. 32
5. Dental floss	E. Gingivitis

2. Penicillin is obtained from a

A. bacteria
B. particular type of mold
C. coal-tars
D. tropical tree

3. Microscopic particles made up of either a DNA or RNA core covered by a protein coat are

A. nitrogen-fixing bacteria
B. bacterial cells
C. cyanobacteria
D. viruses

4. The cell or organism on which a virus depends is a

A. host
B. infection
C. interferon
D. parasite

5. Vaccines made from virus particles or from weakened viruses can cure certain viral diseases. (True or False?)

References

Aiken, L. R. (1982). Writing multiple-choice items to measure higher-order educational objectives. *Educational and Psychological Measurement*, *42*(3), 803–806.

Fredericksen, N. (1984). The real test bias: Influences of testing on teaching and learning. *American Psychologist*, *39*(3), 193–202.

Frisbie, D. A., Miranda, D. U., & Baker, K. K. (1993). An evaluation of elementary textbook tests as classroom assessment tools. *Applied Measurement in Education*, *6*(1), 21–36.

Gagné, R. (1985). *The conditions of learning* (4th ed.). New York: Holt, Rinehart, & Winston.

Taylor, G., & Nolen, S. B. (1996). A contextualized approach to teaching teachers about classroom-based assessment. *Educational Psychologist, 31*(1), 77–88.

Thorndike, R. W., & Hagen, E. (1969). *Measurement and evaluation in psychology and education* (3rd ed.). New York: Wiley.

Chapter 6

Constructed-Response Questions

The hypotheses generated by students for brief descriptions of research studies were used to construct a multiple-choice test of possible hypotheses. Scores on the number, unusual nature, and quality of ideas from the student-generated hypotheses were related to separate measures of the fluency of their ideas. However, scores from the multiple-choice form were not related to fluency scores.

—Fredericksen, 1984

Major Topics

Short-Answer Questions

Implementation

Scoring

Advantages and Limitations

Essay Questions

Implementation

Guidelines for Scoring

Advantages and Limitations

The researcher concluded from the preceding study that the open-ended format required a broad search of memory for relevant ideas and information. In contrast, the multiple-choice format precipitated only narrow memory searches in which students reviewed each test choice specifically in terms of information they were able to recall about it.

One advantage of constructed-response questions is that the possibilities for the search for ideas are not restricted by a preestablished set of choices provided by the test writer. In contrast, true-false, matching, and multiple-choice items present a limited choice of response options for the student to consider.

The two types of constructed-response questions are short-answer and extended writing tasks, which include essay questions and performance tasks such as writing a letter of application for a job or writing to a fictitious pen pal. Discussed in this chapter is the construction and scoring of essay questions for subject areas such as social studies, history, geography, economics, and literature. The unique contribution of essay questions to assessment is that they can assess the student's organization of ideas, skills in marshaling evidence to support an idea or conclusion, and communication skills.

✦ Short-Answer Questions

To be considered a short-answer exercise, the item should require a number, a phrase, or, at most, two sentences as an answer to a specific problem (Thorndike & Hagen, 1969). Examples are the following.

1. What is the process of preparing information for storage in long-term memory called? (encoding).
2. Asking children to draw pictures about a story they have just read is referred to as (elaborative rehearsal).
3. Name the most serious problem with punishment, according to B. F. Skinner. (Punishment only informs the individual of what not to do; it does not inform the person of the appropriate behavior).

As indicated in the prior examples, short-answer questions may be either in the form of a question or a sentence-completion exercise. Generally, these two forms are interchangeable; however, the question format is sometimes easier to construct so that it poses a direct problem for the student.

Implementation

Short-answer questions are appropriate for assessing knowledge of facts, definitions, and terminology and for simple applications, including simple word problems. They are also appropriate for the identification of examples of concepts.

A short-answer item should be used when demonstrating understanding in one's own words is important. It also should be used when the options in a matching or multiple-choice item may help the student guess the correct answer. An example is multiple-choice example (a) in Table 5-8. The answer "elaborative rehearsal" is provided. In the short-answer version (item 1), the student must supply the answer.

A similar situation is the multiple-choice question that poses a simple mathematical word problem. As stated in Chapter 5, a student may select a likely answer and work backward to the problem. However, in the short-answer format, the student must complete the calculations and produce an answer.

Guidelines for Development

Similar to structured-response items, each short-answer exercise should deal with essential and important knowledge in the lesson objectives. Table 6-1 illustrates this requirement and other guidelines for the development of these exercises. Perhaps most difficult is to write the item so that only certain content is plausible and correct. For example, the question "What does the tobacco leaf contain?" will generate a variety of answers. Among them are chlorophyll, veins, pigments, moisture, cells, and poison. Instead, the question should be rephrased to read "What is the poisonous substance found in tobacco leaves?" The one and only correct response is nicotine.

Questions should be constructed to elicit brief answers. One reason is that the possibilities for spelling errors and irrelevant information in the student's answers increase with the amount of information required to answer a question. These problems generate scoring difficulties for the teacher.

Table 6.1 Guidelines for the Development of Short-Answer Items

1. Be sure that each item deals with important content and skills.
2. Construct each item so that one and only one answer is plausible and correct.
3. Construct the question so that the answer is brief.
4. Do not use statements from the textbook.
5. Be sure that the blank in the statement requires an important, not a trivial term to complete the sentence.
6. If several questions are used, answer blanks should be equal in length.
7. For numerical items, indicate the unit of measure for the answer.
8. Do not place blanks at the beginning or in the middle of the sentence.
9. Group items of the same type (short-answer, completion) according to type.
10. Write clear, complete directions for each type.

Statements from the textbook should not be used as short-answer items. First, the statement is taken out of context and, therefore, is highly likely to be ambiguous. Second, many textbook statements are details, rather than key summary descriptions of concepts and principles.

The blank in the statement also should elicit important information, not a trivial term. For example, the items "the liver __________ (stores) excess glucose as glycogen" (Thorndike & Hagen, 1969, p. 90) should be rewritten to omit either glucose or glycogen.

Items also should not provide inappropriate cues to the student and the arrangement of the item should assist the student in processing the basic question. Therefore, the length of the answer blanks for a set of questions should be equal. Otherwise, a short blank signals a one-word answer and a longer blank signals a phrase. The space for the answer also should be generous to allow for different printing or handwriting styles. Further, any item that requires a numerical response should include the required metric at the end of the blank. An example is

A member of the U.S. House of Representatives is elected for a term of ______________ years.

Finally, blanks should not be placed at the beginning or middle of the sentence. Such an arrangement requires the student to read through the item to grasp the meaning and then go back to fill in the blank. Instead, with the placement at the end of the sentence to the right, the student can read through the sentence, enter the response, and move on.

If both short-answer and completion types are used on the same test, do not scatter them throughout the test. Instead, group items of the same type together and, as much as possible, group items on the same content together.

The directions for short-answer items are also important to ensure that students are certain of what they are to do. If complete sentences are required, the directions should state this information. If needed, problems requiring a numerical answer should state if the student's answer should be carried out to the nearest tenth or to the nearest hundredth, and if it is to be rounded up.

Scoring

Constructed-response items introduce issues into scoring that are not found with true-false, matching, or multiple-choice items. Scoring guidelines that address these issues are listed in Table 6-2.

Two issues are spelling and sentence structure. If these components of student-generated responses are to be evaluated, then the score should be separate

Table 6.2 Guidelines for Scoring Short-Answer Items

1. If spelling and sentence structure are to be scored, provide a separate score for each.
2. Assign equal weight to each question.
3. Score the content of each answer either right or wrong.
4. Check the answer key against a few papers first, to identify any consistent student answers that differ from the key.
5. Provide the correct answers and comments on the students' papers or provide a complete set of the correct answers when the papers are returned.

Source: Summarized from Thorndike and Hagen (1969).

from the content score. Also, students should be told at the beginning of instruction that these components will be scored on tests.

Suppose the test includes six short-answer items that require one- or two-word answers. One point for a correct answer for each is a total of 6 points for content. However, allowing 1 point per item for spelling is not appropriate. If some students miss several of the items, the teacher is faced with a dilemma. Either points must be assigned for the correct spelling of incorrect answers or the students are placed in double jeopardy by losing several points for spelling simply because they did not get the content correct. In this situation, one solution is to assign 3 points for spelling for the six short-answer items. If all the student's correct answers are spelled correctly, he or she earns 3 points. If two-thirds of them are spelled correctly, the student earns 2 points. Similarly, if one-half of the student's correct answers are correctly spelled, then he or she earns only 1 point.

Also important is to assign equal weight to each question. One or more items should not be assigned more points because the teacher believes that the content in those questions is more important. If it is, then write more questions on those concepts or principles, and assign the same number of points to each item. In addition, each answer should be scored either right or wrong; assigning partial credit confuses the issue about how much the student has actually learned (Thorndike & Hagen, 1969).

Finally, before scoring the students' answers, check the answer key against a few papers first for consistently incorrect answers. If several students, particularly the good students in the class, do not write the response indicated in the answer key, the key may have a clerical error. Another explanation is that the item did not communicate as the teacher intended and the item should be eliminated from the test before assigning final scores to the students.

When scoring the students' answers, provide the correct answers and comments about the reasons for their correctness. This feedback assists students in addressing these types of questions.

Advantages and Limitations

Four advantages may be identified for short-answer exercises. First, they permit a memory search for a correct answer, instead of a limited evaluation of a brief set of provided choices. Second, they reduce guessing because the student must provide the answer. In addition, items are fairly easy to write and they are efficient. With a minimum number of words, they can probe students' knowledge of important terminology, concepts, and dates.

One limitation of short-answer exercises is that they are ill-suited for situations that require complex evaluations by the student. Consider the matching exercise on threats to internal validity in Table 5-6. Translated into short-answer questions that ask the student to state the particular threat to internal validity represented by each situation will generate a variety of answers. For example, the statement "Students participating in a peer counseling study drop out" may generate responses such as, "insufficient sample size"; "not enough students for the study"; and so on. However, such answers do not address the issue of loss of research subjects from the sample.

A second limitation, discussed in the prior section, is that short-answer items are more difficult to score than structured-response items. For example, suppose that the correct answer to a question is the phrase "thyroid gland." The teacher must decide the point at which a misspelling becomes so garbled that the content cannot be counted as correct.

A third limitation is that, unless carefully phrased, the item may generate many answers of varying correctness. In other words, the stem or question must be both complete and concise to prevent misinterpretations by students.

Summary

Short-answer exercises, either in the form of a question or an incomplete sentence, are appropriate for assessing facts, definitions, terminology, and simple applications. The item may require a number, a phrase, or no more than two sentences. Short-answer questions should be used when demonstrating understanding in the student's own words is important or when the options in a structured-response question may clue the correct answer.

Care should be taken in developing the items to ensure that only one answer is plausible and correct, the expected answer is brief, the directions are clear, and the blank is at the end of the sentence. Statements from the textbook should not be used because they often are trivial details and a particular sentence often lacks the context essential for a logical answer.

If spelling and sentence structure are to be evaluated in addition to content, a separate score for the set of answers for language mechanics should be used. This score should be assigned to the group of questions.

The advantages of short-answer items are that they provide for a memory search for answers, reduce guessing, are fairly easy to write, and are efficient. The limitations are that they are not suited to assessing complex cognitive skills and they are not as easy to score as constructed-response items.

✦ Essay Questions

An essay question poses a problem that requires the student (1) to identify relevant information essential to addressing the problem and (2) to select, organize, and integrate the information in a composed response of one to several paragraphs. The student's answer is then evaluated according to a set of scoring criteria.

Implementation

Currently, essay questions are used in two ways in classroom assessment. One is that of one form of performance assessment, discussed in Chapter 8. That use of essay questions focuses on developing tasks related to real-world situations, such as writing to a pen pal in another country. Also, the primary purpose of essay questions in performance assessment often is the demonstration of writing and communication skills. The other use of essay questions is that of a component of classroom tests on the content of a particular subject area, such as geography, English, and history.

Unfortunately, when used as a component of classroom tests, essay questions are sometimes used to assess the recall of information. They often begin with "describe," "discuss," or "summarize." This use is inappropriate for two reasons. One is that essay questions, because of the time required for student responses, can sample only a limited range of the information in the lesson or unit. A test composed of structured-response items provides much more complete content coverage. The second reason is that using essay questions to measure recall does not come close to their potential.

The uniqueness of essay questions is that, properly constructed, they can assess students' skills (1) to analyze and evaluate assumptions, data, and ideas; and (2) to develop original solutions to novel problems. For example, a question may present the stimulus information illustrated in Table 5-4, the food consumed in 1 day by a 12-year-old girl. Instead of true-false statements, an essay question may ask the student to evaluate the selections for nutritional deficiencies, recommend changes, and provide a rationale for the recommendations.

Table 6.3 Complex Cognitive Tasks Appropriate for Essay Questions

Tasks	Examples
1. Formulate valid generalizations from data and support one's inferences.	1. Review the graph showing crop productivity, climate and economic conditions for 1985–1990. Suggest two plausible generalizations and support your choices.
2. Predict effects of a policy, proposed law, situation, and so on, and support the predictions.	2. The county council is proposing a 12% tax on hotel room rates to fund new roads and new county libraries. Predict two positive and two possible negative effects of this proposal and support your choices.
3. Evaluate situations, policies, or courses of action according to given criteria.	3. Evaluate the following description of a new teaching method according to the theory developed by Jean Piaget.
4. Take a position on an issue and support it with evidence.	4. A leading historian maintains that slavery was not the major issue that led to the War Between the States. Take a position for or against his view and support it with evidence.

Table 6-3 lists four types of tasks that are appropriate for essay questions. Addressing tasks of this nature requires the cognitive skills of analysis, synthesis, and evaluation (Bloom's taxonomy) and problem solving (Gagné's domain of intellectual skills).

Guidelines for Development

Essay questions may initially appear to be easy to construct because they consist of a few sentences and are open-ended. However, to be effective, they require thought and planning. Two essential preliminary steps to writing the questions are to review (1) the lesson objectives and (2) the types of mental tasks listed in Table 6-3 that may be appropriate for the particular lesson.

These steps and other important considerations in developing essay questions are listed in Table 6-4. A key purpose of essay questions is to assess the student's capability to use information, not simply to reproduce information. Therefore, the task should include novel material or a novel organization of material. For example, for task 2 in Table 6-3, the teacher may use a brief paragraph synopsis of

Table 6.4 Guidelines for the Development of Essay Questions

Guidelines	Examples
1. Review the lesson objectives and types of complex cognitive tasks for the skills to be assessed by essay questions.	1. Analysis, synthesis, evaluation, problem solving.
2. Use novel material or novel organization of material in developing each question.	2. Current city council issues in social studies; new discoveries from the Science section of the *New York Times*.
3. Write each question so that the task is clearly and unambiguously defined for each student.	3. See examples in Table 6-3.
4. Be sure the question asks for the behaviors that the student is to demonstrate.	4. Use phrases such as "Identify the strengths and weaknesses of the proposed policy and support your conclusions."
5. Questions dealing with controversial issues should focus on and be evaluated on the presentation of evidence, not the position taken.	5. For question 4, Table 6-3, evaluate the historical evidence cited by the student, such as citations from well-known documents, nineteenth-century papers, and writings of historians.
6. Gear the length and complexity of the question to the maturity level of the students.	6. Middle school students can write a brief paragraph on the outcome of a simple experiment; high school students can write two to three paragraphs on a complex experiment, including hypotheses suggested by their results.
7. Indicate an approximate time limit for each question and the number of points assigned to the question. Provide this information for students alongside each question on the test.	7. A question with two or three components may be designated as 0.5 hour (20 points). In contrast, a less complex question may be assigned 20 minutes (15 points).

Source: Summarized from Thorndike and Hagen (1969).

the first part of a story the students have not read. In social studies, for task 4, an issue currently before the county council or the state legislature may serve as a stimulus.

The purpose of the essay question is to assess how well a student can address a particular task, not how well he or she can figure out the task (Thorndike & Hagen, 1969, p. 80). An example is the problems with the question "Discuss the organizations that contribute to the health of the community." First, the word "discuss" should not be used because it does not refer to a cognitive process (unlike "solve" or "analyze"). When used by inexperienced test developers, it often means "Tell me all you know." Second, the word "organizations" and the phrase "contribute to the health of the community" are vague and unclear (Thorndike & Hagen, 1969).

In contrast, the question "Evaluate the following description of a new teaching method according to the theory developed by Jean Piaget" states the cognitive process the student is to demonstrate. The question also includes specific stimulus material and it references the criteria the student is to use in his or her response.

Equally important is to avoid phrases such as "What do you think about . . ." and "Give your opinion of. . . ." Usually, the item writer is not interested in what the student thinks or the student's opinion. Instead, these phrases are used when the intent is to determine whether the student knows the factual information about the topic. In other words, these phrases do not state the behavior the student is to demonstrate (Thorndike & Hagen, 1969).

Task 4 in Table 6-3 presents a different issue to the test developer from that of the other tasks. Specifically, the purpose of asking a student to take a position on an issue is to determine the extent to which he or she can marshall evidence to support the position taken. The purpose is not to critique the particular perspective selected by the student, which is a value judgment.

When completed, the essay questions should be reviewed for appropriateness for the intended age and grade level of the students. On occasion, as a question is refined, it becomes more elaborated and more sophisticated. At that point, the length and complexity of the question may require adaptation for the students.

Finally, the approximate length of time to answer the questions and the number of points each question is worth should be determined (see the following section). This information also should be included on the test for the students. It will help students to organize the time available for the test. If the entire test is to be an essay examination, it should include questions that represent a range of complexity and difficulty. The purpose is to ensure opportunities for all students in the class to demonstrate their skills.

Guidelines for Scoring

The development of writing tasks for performance assessments led to the introduction of a scoring method referred to as scoring rubrics. This method, discussed in Chapters 8 and 9, established a continuum of performance from no or inadequate response to commendable or excellent. Descriptions of the characteristics of the written response at each level of performance are provided. This scoring method is used extensively at the elementary and middle school levels where developing communication skills is an important goal. For this goal, a scoring mechanism is needed that can show growth over time in writing and communication skills.

When used in a subject area to assess the student's ideas and thinking on important problems or issues, each question is usually assigned a total number of points. The decision as to the number of points per question depends on several factors. Among them are (1) the scope of the question, (2) the importance of the topic or issue, and (3) the number of key points the answer is to include. In addition, the number of those points assigned to relevance of the student's ideas, application of subject-matter concepts, and language usage is determined.

Two particular difficulties can occur in the scoring of essay questions. One is that a student's response that is exceptionally fluent may influence the teacher in the scoring of the other responses. The second is the influence of a student's vocabulary, sentence structure, and fluency on decisions about the student's cognitive skills. Other situations to be aware of in scoring are the use of general phrases and terms that may fit several situations and writing to fit the statements to the question.

Several steps may be taken that guard against these problems (see Table 6-5). First, develop an outline of a model answer that includes the major points and the supporting evidence (or arguments), both major and minor, for the key points. For example, the teacher may identify four key assertions and three major supporting arguments that the answer should include. This procedure provides a mechanism for preventing several types of weaknesses in the answer to be mistaken for subject-matter expertise or fluency. Among them are (1) using glib phrases, such as "this development was significant" without providing supporting documentation; (2) agreeing with the teacher's views; and (3) attempting to fit a related topic to the subject of the question.

Next, as already stated, the weight to be assigned in the scoring to English usage, spelling, and organization is determined. For example, depending on the emphasis during instruction, the teacher may allocate 10 percent of the scoring points to English usage and spelling and 10 percent to organization. Then the total number of points assigned to the question is distributed proportionally to the subject-matter issues, technical use of the language, and organization. For a 60-point question with percentages of 80, 10, and 10, the scoring points for each are 48, 6, and 6, respectively.

Table 6.5 Guidelines for Scoring Essay Questions

1. Develop a model answer to the question.
2. When essay questions are used in particular subject areas, determine the scoring emphasis to be assigned to English usage, grammar, and organization of the answer.
3. Allocate scoring points proportionally to subject-matter issues, technical use of the language, and organization.
4. When scoring student answers, score the papers as nearly anonymously as possible.
5. If the test includes more than one answer, score all the answers to one question before going on to the next question.
6. Shuffle the papers after scoring each question.
7. Do not score the papers when fatigued or rushed.
8. Write comments, including both strengths and weaknesses, on the papers and cor-

This approach to developing a scoring key is appropriate for classes and courses in which (1) the focus is on a particular subject area other than writing or communication and (2) the majority of the assessments are not writing assignments.

The essay responses of students should be scored as nearly anonymously as possible. That is, the students' names should be obscured, perhaps by folding down the corner of the page, and the papers shuffled before grading. If the test includes more than one essay question, score all the answers to one question before going on to the next one. This procedure prevents the problem referred to as "halo effect." That is, a student may write an exceptionally good or exceptionally poor answer to the first question, and this performance influences the teacher's judgment in scoring subsequent answers by the student. Shuffling or rearranging the papers after scoring the first question also contributes to preventing this problem. Also, do not score papers when fatigued or rushed as these factors influence the application of the criteria. Some teachers score more stringently when they are tired and others are more lax.

Write comments and correct errors on each answer. Include both strengths and weaknesses in the comments. This practice is informative, provides valuable information to the teacher, and provides a basis for improving student performance.

Advantages and Limitations

The advantage of essay questions is that they can assess the types of cognitive tasks listed in Table 6-3. Proponents of performance and portfolio assessments assign a major role to writing assignments related to real-world situations because they address cognitive skills that other assessments do not. In addition, essay questions are appropriate for classes that focus on developing skills in analysis, synthesis, evaluation, and problem solving.

Two limitations of essay questions are that development requires thought and planning and scoring is laborious. Further, unless the steps in the prior section are followed, the scoring will be unreliable.

Summary

Essay questions in particular subject areas pose problems that require the student to identify, organize, and integrate relevant information in the solution. Appropriate tasks for essay questions are formulating valid generalizations from data and supporting them, predicting effects and supporting one's choices, evaluating situations or policies, and taking a position on an issue and supporting it with evidence.

Constructing essay questions involves the choice of appropriate tasks, including novel material or a novel organization of material, writing the questions clearly, and stating the behaviors the student is to demonstrate. Questions dealing with controversial issues should focus on the student's capabilities in marshaling evidence, not the particular position taken. When the essay questions are completed, they should be reviewed and revised if necessary for the maturity level of the students. Also, approximate time limits as well as the number of points for each questions should be attached.

Prior to scoring, the teacher should develop a model answer for each question, and determine the weight of writing mechanics in scoring the answers. Then the points for each question should be assigned proportionately according to the established emphases. During scoring, papers should be scored without knowledge of the student's name, each answer to a question should be scored before moving on to the next question, and the papers should be shuffled after each question. Also, do not score papers when fatigued or rushed, and take the time to write both strengths and weaknesses on the answers.

The advantage of essay questions is that they assess complex cognitive tasks that are not measured by structured-response questions. The disadvantages are that development and scoring are time-consuming and, unless proper steps are followed, scoring is unreliable.

Chapter Questions

Identify the problems with each of the following items.

1. ____________ and ____________ are examples of important plant processes.

2. Viruses have many ______________.

3. The kind of nucleic acid, the ______________, and the kind of organism infected are used to classify viruses.

4. Why do bears hibernate?

5. Summarize the characteristics of viruses.

References

Fredericksen, N. (1984). The real test bias: Influences of testing on teaching and learning. *American Psychologist*, 39(3), 193–202.

Thorndike, R. L., & Hagen, E. (1969). *Measurement and evaluation in psychology and education* (3rd ed.). New York: Wiley.

Chapter 7

Observational Methods

Major Topics

Qualitative Methods

Anecdotal Records

Interviews

Observational Instruments

Checklists

Rating Scales

> *"Keeping observational records helped teachers look at the positive; they also saw far more than they had previously about the ways that individual students learned."*
>
> —Lamme & Hysmith, 1991, p. 634

Research on cognitive processes in the 1980s has led to new understandings about learning and thinking. Among them are that successful learners understand the goals of instruction, actively monitor and evaluate their own learning, and redirect their actions, if necessary. In contrast, some young children believe that the goal of seatwork is to finish on time, and others perceive that the goal of reading is to pronounce all the words correctly (Alexander, Schallert, & Hare, 1991). In other classrooms, children in a Title I program for disadvantaged children reported that they simply skipped the words and sentences in reading passages they did not understand. In mathematics, a typical student belief identified by Schoenfeld (1985) was that problems are solved in 10 minutes if they are solved at all (p. 43).

The research on learner knowledge about cognition and concerns about the development of students as thinkers have led to two new classroom initiatives. One is the current emphasis on portfolio and performance assessments as mechanisms for evaluating students' thinking processes. Briefly, a portfolio is a particular type of collection of student work. Portfolio items may consist of, for example, reading-response journals, reading logs, reports, poems, narratives, sketches, drawings, tape recordings, and self-reflections. Performance assessments are evaluations of a student product, such as an analysis of local traffic problems, or the execution of a task, such as delivering a speech.

The other recent classroom focus involves teaching students to be active self-monitoring learners. In addition to teaching students learning strategies, such as deducing word meaning from context, this effort includes when to use particular strategies and many opportunities to apply them.

These classroom initiatives require less direct instruction by the teacher to the whole class and a greater reliance on small groups, pairs, and individual work. They also require that teachers develop information about students' thinking and learning processes.

In addition to observations of student interactions and performances, another use of observational methods is the continuing assessment of students with physical or mental disabilities. Students' adjustment to the classroom setting, work habits, interactions with peers, and other data may be relevant, given the particular disability.

Assessment methods appropriate for these purposes that were introduced in Chapter 2 are informal observations, anecdotal records, rating scales, and teacher questions. Three other methods used for classroom observations are event and duration recording (used for discrete behaviors), checklists, and interactive coding systems. However, the focus of interactive coding systems is to record all the actions of a teacher and/or student (Stallings & Mohlman, 1990, p. 642). They are typically used by researchers who are studying classroom processes.

This chapter discusses four assessment methods that are appropriate for developing information about the ways that students approach and address classroom tasks, their thinking processes, and the products of their learning. These methods are anecdotal records, interviews of students, checklists, and rating scales. Two of these methods are open-ended qualitative methods and two (checklists and rating scales) are structured instruments. Event and duration recording are discussed in Chapter 11.

✦ Qualitative Methods

Among the roles of qualitative methods in collecting information is to identify the behaviors, thoughts, and feelings of individuals as they occur in the natural setting. Two open-ended methods for accomplishing this purpose in the classroom are anecdotal records and interviews.

Anecdotal Records

The original use of anecdotal records was to develop information related to the social and personal development of students. However, anecdotal records are appropriate for documenting the kinds of activities in which students engage, and the kinds of interactions they have with learning materials and with each other.

Characteristics. An anecdotal record is a brief written description of events and actions observed by the teacher (or other observer). Anecdotal records are concrete, factual descriptions of one student's actions over several days. For example, one fifth-grade teacher observes that Bart and Jack, who have previously been unengaged in writing, have begun to work together on writing stories. She writes on the card for Jack, "Nuclear War, using story to collaborate, sees value of audience, tests ideas" (Gomez, Graue, & Block, 1991, p. 620).

A particularly useful application of anecdotal records is to observe students' work habits, such as the amount of time a child focuses on a task or activity. For example, the teacher may observe that Leslie works very quickly on tasks and does not reflect on her work. Michael, in contrast, spends most of his seatwork time in writing, erasing, and rewriting his words (Hunt & Marshall, 1994). These and other observations help the teacher identify specific areas for intervention (p. 214).

As indicated by the preceding examples, anecdotal records should be reserved for those processes that cannot be addressed by other methods. Also, the observations should inform instruction or assess progress.

Role in observing students with special needs. Federal legislation mandates that, whenever possible, students with physical or mental disabilities should be placed in the least restrictive educational environment, which is often the classroom (see Chapter 11). Important in the continuing assessment of these students is documentation by the teacher about their interactions with others and with school tasks. For example, some questions to be answered about a student with speech and language problems include: "What is the extent of attention to and compliance with oral directions?" "Does the student begin to respond to directions or look around to see what other students are doing?" and

"Is uncompleted work associated with these behaviors?" (Moran, 1996, p. 301).

Guidelines for implementation. The teacher is free to note any behaviors that he or she believes are important. An initial difficulty faced by teachers in using anecdotal statements is what to record. In addition, the validity concerns described in Chapter 2 apply to anecdotal records. Of particular importance is that the teacher should guard against statements that are judgments of behavior as good or bad, evaluations derived from a single fact, or general characteristics of the student. Examples of statements to be avoided are Eddie looks out the window when he's not busy, he's such a daydreamer, and Tommy showed a bad attitude when told to stop talking.

Table 7-1 summarizes the general guidelines for using anecdotal records. Guidelines 1 through 4 assist the teacher in identifying the focus of the observations, and guidelines 5 and 6 address validity and reliability concerns. Implementing anecdotal records does require practice. However, teachers have

Table 7.1 Guidelines for Implementation of Anecdotal Records

Guidelines	Examples
1. Record information on processes that are not easily available by other means (such as checklists).	1. Spontaneous interactions with children; see no. 3, which follows
2. Concentrate on one area at a time.	2. Independent writing; small group math activities
3. Decide in advance what to observe.	3. How students are approaching writing activities; how a child selects a topic for writing; strategies used to spell words
4. Be selective so that observation notes will inform instruction and/or assess progress.	4. Teacher notes changes in Jack's approaches to writing as he begins to work together with Bart
5. Record only factual statements.	5. Record that David leaves his desk frequently (not that he is nervous, uninterested, or unmotivated)
6. Obtain adequate samples of behavior prior to arriving at an interpretation.	6. Mrs. B. observed Simon in independent writing for 5 to 6 successive days (see description in the text)

reported that the more they use them, the easier the technique becomes (Lamme & Hysmith, 1991).

These guidelines can assist the teacher to develop information about the growth of their students and/or problems that require attention. For example, Mrs. B., a fifth-grade teacher who implemented a writing period in her class, documented students' collaborative efforts and their approaches to writing stories. Her observations of Simon over several days indicated that he used the option of working in the adjacent library to go in and out of the class from 7 to 10 times an hour. Although he carried paper and pencil, he only occasionally stopped in a location long enough to write more than a few words. He alternated between going in and out of the library, strolling among his classmates, and pausing for a minute or two at a desk or table to jot down a few words. This repeated sequence of actions over several days led to the conclusion that Simon was avoiding dealing with his poor writing skills (Gomez et al., 1991, p. 624).

One difficulty associated with anecdotal records is the logistics of documenting observations as they occur. Some teachers suggest jotting notes on computer labels or blank sticky labels and transferring them to students' portfolios. One problem with this method, however, is that the labels often can be lost.

Other teachers use some form of notebook or journal, organized by topic, such as writing workshop and math activities (Lamme & Hysmith, 1991). One teacher uses a 25-picture photo album filled with cards, one for each child. This allows her to flip quickly to a particular child's card when needed. Others divide the pages in a 3-ring binder with index tabs for quick flipping and recording (Hemme & Goyins, 1992).

Advantages and limitations. The advantage of anecdotal records is that behaviors can be captured that otherwise would not be noted. Teachers who have implemented anecdotal records in conjunction with portfolios report that they see more than they have previously noticed about the ways that children in their classrooms learn (Gomez et al., 1991; Lamme & Hysmith, 1991). Among them are a student beginning to find a voice in his writing and a first grader developing her own algorithms for understanding a problem.

One disadvantage of anecdotal records is arranging for time to observe students. Some teachers have organized their classes so that students spend some time working individually or in small groups. Students' approaches to problems, as in the observation about Jack described earlier, and other actions may be observed at these times.

Another disadvantage is the time required to record an unusual event or incident during teacher-directed instruction. One solution is to jot a few brief notes about the event and expand on them later.

Interviews

Two major uses of interviews in the elementary school years are to obtain information about students' attitudes and perceptions of their reading or other subjects and as a part of portfolio assessment. Two of the goals associated with portfolio assessment are (1) to document student growth over time and (2) to encourage students to become self-reflective learners and to have a stake in the assessment process (see Chapter 9 for a discussion of these goals). Interviews are useful to assess progress toward these goals.

Characteristics. The types of interview formats are standardized and semistructured. Standardized interviews consist of a set order of carefully worded questions accompanied by clarification and other follow-up questions (Patton, 1990). The semistructured interview, in contrast, simply identifies in advance the issues or topics to be explored.

Interviews implemented for research purposes may be from 30 to 60 minutes in length. In the classroom, however, interviews are approximately 10 to 15 minutes per child. Because interviews represent a major time investment, they typically are used to probe students' thinking processes and/or their assessments of their work. In reading, interviews can provide useful information about students' perceptions of the reading process, opinions of their reading skills, and reading performances (McLoughlin & Lewis, 1994, p. 311). Although questionnaires may be used for mature students, interviews are preferable for young students and those with poor reading skills. Examples of useful questions are: "What types of reading activities are easiest for you?" "Which are the hardest?" "If you could read a story about anything in the world, what would it be about?" "What magazines do you read or look at?" "Would you rather read true stories or stories the writer makes up?"

In portfolio assessment, in some classrooms, students examine the materials in their portfolios and are asked to reflect on the items that they enjoyed, those in which they noticed improvement, and those from which they benefitted (Lamme & Hysmith, 1991). In the interviews, the children were asked first to name a project or task they enjoyed and why. Then the interviews proceed to explore the other two topics.

In such interviews, follow-up questions should be planned to assist students who initially have difficulty in identifying changes or improvements in their work. For example, the teacher may ask the child to look through his or her stories and find places that are different from earlier drafts or where the child painted a more complete picture (Gomez et al., 1991).

Interviews to review portfolios may be conducted individually or in small groups of two or three students. When used to assess growth, interviews should be implemented at least once each marking period.

Problem-based format. A variation on the questions-only format is to give the student a problem and ask for an explanation of his or her solution processes. Then, depending on the student's responses, he or she is given an easier or more difficult problem. The teacher carefully records the problem types that are solved and the solution strategies used by the student. Preparation for this type of interview requires the selection of four to five problems that reflect the range of capabilities in the class.

One elementary school teacher uses problem-based interviews of each child three times a year. This information supplements her informal observations about the child's level of development in solving various types of addition/subtraction problems (Fennema, Franke, Carpenter, & Carey, 1993). The solution strategies used by the children ranged from representing the problem concretely (with manipulables) and counting to the use of standard algorithms and invented algorithms (p. 572).

Advantages and limitations. The two advantages of interviews in the classroom are that they can assess students' thinking strategies and can assist them in learning to evaluate their own work. The disadvantages are that they are time-consuming and may be difficult to schedule.

Summary

Observational methods are important because they can tap into learning and thinking processes in the classroom context. They also are used to assess the capabilities involved in complex performances and student products. Two open-ended methods of assessing student behavior are anecdotal records and interviews. Anecdotal records are factual descriptions of actions and events by the teacher. They are concrete, factual statements about students' actions or interactions that inform instruction or assess progress. A major advantage of anecdotal records is that they can capture behaviors that otherwise would not be noted. Although recording information can be difficult, the process becomes easier with practice. Other concerns are arranging time for observations and addressing validity criteria.

Interviews are used in the classroom to probe students' thinking processes and/or their assessments of their work. Interviews to review portfolios may be conducted individually or in small groups of 2 or 3. Problem-based interviews require that the teacher first identify four to five problems that represent the range of skills in the class. Each child in the interview receives a problem to solve and explains his or her thinking. Depending on the student's responses, the teacher selects an easier or more difficult problem. The advantage of this method is that it provides information about students' thinking. A disadvantage is the time commitment that is required.

✦ Observational Instruments

Unlike open-ended assessments, checklists and rating scales document behaviors or characteristics that have been identified prior to the observation. These instruments are useful in recording the important skills or capabilities demonstrated in a student performance or reflected in a student product. They are intended to record information that is needed on every student.

Checklists

Checklists were originally developed to record appropriate actions as a student is completing an activity. For example, an early example of a checklist on using the microscope consisted of a sequential list of behaviors, such as "wipes slide with lens paper," and "places drop or two of culture on slide" (Tyler, 1930). Since that early use, checklists also have been developed to document the mastery of identified skills, and to identify student problems in completing complex activities, such as reading.

Characteristics. A checklist is a set of specific key behaviors that represent the competency or activity of interest. The teacher or other evaluator checks "yes" if the behavior or characteristic is present and "no" if it is absent. Table 7-2 illustrates an example of a partial checklist to evaluate oral reading. As indicated by this example, the behaviors are concrete and observable. Also, they are behaviors that are reasonable to evaluate as present or absent (in contrast to behaviors that

Table 7.2 Example of a Partial Checklist to Evaluate the Oral Reading Skills of First Graders

	Yes	No
Used context clues?	________	________
Used picture clues?	________	________
Used beginning/ending sounds?	________	________
Used other phonetic clues?	________	________
Read word for word?	________	________
Guessed at meaning?	________	________

Source: Adapted from Lamme and Hysmith (1991, p. 636).

may exist to a greater or lesser degree). Ideally, the number of behaviors should be fewer than 10, and they should be arranged in a logical sequence.

Checklists should *not* mix inferential judgments with observable, specific behaviors. For example, an instrument to evaluate oral reading should not include inferences, such as "reads fluently." One problem is that "reads fluently" can be interpreted by different individuals in different ways. Another is that fluent reading is not an all-or-nothing capability. Like solving problems and other complex capabilities, it develops over time, varies from novice to expert performance, and varies from one context to another. Checklists, in contrast, address only specific, easily observed behaviors that either are or are not present.

On occasion, negative behaviors that reflect major errors in a specific procedure may be of interest. Examples in the procedure for using the microscope are "Wipes slide with finger" and "Breaks cover glass." A checklist may be constructed in either of two ways to address these behaviors. One is to rewrite them as positive behaviors using the word "avoids." The teacher then puts a checkmark in the "yes" column for "avoids wiping slide with finger" if the student did not wipe the glass inappropriately. However, this practice requires that the teacher record a nonbehavior, that is, the avoidance of an action. The other approach is to include the negative behaviors, checking "no" if they were not executed.

Checklists also may be scored. For example, in evaluating proficiency at a task, +1 is assigned to positive behaviors and −1 to negative behaviors.

Implementation. Checklists should be used when important information is identified that is to be gathered on every child in the classroom. In conjunction with portfolio assessment, teachers in several elementary classrooms used checklists to monitor student progress in sustained silent reading, book buddies, and reading-aloud times (Lamme & Hysmith, 1991).

Rating Scales

A rating scale is appropriate for classroom observations when (1) the characteristics or dimensions of a performance or product may be identified and (2) these characteristics or dimensions exist to a greater or lesser degree. Examples of performances that may be evaluated with rating scales include conducting experiments, delivering speeches, and executing dance routines. Student products include drawings, paintings, project reports, and themes.

Two types of rating scales are appropriate for student performances and products. They are the primary trait or dimensions-of-performance approach and modified primary trait or continuum scales.

The Dimensions-of-Performance Approach (Primary trait scale)

The focus of the rating scale is the key characteristics or dimensions of a complex capability or performance. For example, a speech teacher evaluating student presentations may develop a scale that includes the dimensions of capturing audience attention, establishing rapport, and coherence. In contrast, the characteristics to be evaluated for an essay may be purpose, organization, details, presentation of ideas/information, and mechanics/grammar.

Characteristics. The components of a primary trait rating scale are (1) the listing of the dimensions to be rated and (2) the scale (referred to as a Likert scale) for rating each dimension. The directions may state either that the learner is to circle or to check a number on each scale that indicates the extent of the particular characteristic.

Table 7-3 presents a partial example of a numeric rating scale. In this example, each characteristic is rated on a scale of 1 to 5. Although the scale selected for an instrument may range from 1–3 to 1–10, the recommended number is five categories. The use of more than five categories risks jeopardizing the consistency of raters' decisions.

Implementation. Of major importance in constructing a primary trait rating scale is the careful identification of the dimensions to be rated. They should represent essential characteristics of the trait or capability that is the focus of the

Table 7.3 Rating Scale of Student Prediction Skills During Reading

1. Can predict content of narrative or exposition from title.

1	2	3	4	5
Never	Occasionally	50% of the time	Most of the time	Always

2. At appropriate stopping points in a narrative, can predict the next event.

1	2	3	4	5
Never	Occasionally	50% of the time	Most of the time	Always

3. Can determine if his/her predictions were accurate on finishing the material.

1	2	3	4	5
Never	Occasionally	50% of the time	Most of the time	Always

assessment and they should be directly observable. Cronbach (1990) suggests that rating scales should be derived from recordings of the "think-aloud" strategies of experts as they work through the problem or task. In this way, important qualities of accomplished performance are less likely to be omitted.

Also important is "anchoring" each numerical rating with a verbal description that is as concrete as possible. This practice helps to ensure consistent interpretations by different raters (and contributes to the reliability of the instrument).

Rating scales also may be used for either of two roles in assessing student performance. One is to provide feedback to students during the development of a project (formative evaluation). This role is particularly important for portfolios in which the goal is to demonstrate student growth over time. For example, in the area of writing, Moss et al. (1992) suggest a rating scale for providing feedback to students on revisions of their interpretative essays on literature selections. In order to reflect growth, the ratings are combined with an analysis of the contributions of the latest draft of the essay. Each identified feature of the essay is rated on a 4-point scale (as indicated in Table 7-4). Note that the anchors for the scale points do require some interpretation, for example, "some evidence," "extended evidence," and "appropriately sustained evidence." Although permissible when used by one teacher for feedback, they should not be used for summative evaluations involving multiple raters. Instead, concrete easily interpretable anchors are needed.

The other role for ratings in assessing student performance is to determine students' level of achievement (summative evaluation). Several requirements are particularly important in determining achievement level. First, the dimensions should be those that are educationally significant and directly observable. Second, the dimensions should be defined clearly and the descriptors for each of the scale levels should be described in concrete terms.

To reduce bias during the scoring of student products, the products should be scored anonymously. (Students may place their names on the front page, which is then folded back on all products prior to scoring.) The purpose is to reduce factors extraneous to the actual performance from entering into the ratings. In addition, assess the performance of all students on one task before beginning the scoring of the second task. The rater should not rate all the tasks for one student in sequence because the student's performance on the first task may subtly influence subsequent ratings.

The ratings of the individual characteristics also may be summed in order to determine a total score for the performance or product. Because positive characteristics are selected for rating, the higher the individual score, the more proficient and complete is the performance.

Table 7.4 Example of a Partial Rating Scheme for Feedback on Interpretative Essays

Student: Barry Topic: On Lord of the Flies

Genre: Response to literature Date: 1/18/90

	Rating of Draft	Contributions of Revision
VISION		
something to say	3	1
voice	2	1
seeing beyond ordinary	2	1
conceptual framework	2	1
DEVELOPMENT		
elaboration	3	1
specificity	3	1
explanations	3	1
structuring	3	+
comprehensiveness	2	1
CRAFT: LANGUAGE FORM		
word choice	3	+
sentence structure	3	+
clarity/cohesiveness	3	+
form appropriate to genre	3	+
standard conventions	3	+
CRAFT: LITERARY STYLE		
figurative language		
concrete imagery	1	1
show-not-tell tone	1	1

Rating

1 = some evidence of feature

2 = extended evidence of feature

3 = appropriately sustained evidence of feature

4 = integrated/sophisticated evidence of feature

Revision

+ = revision increased evidence of feature

1 = revision does not change evidence of feature

— = revision reduces evidence of feature

Source: Adapted from Moss, P., Beck, J., Ebbs, C., Matson, B., Muchmore, D., Steele, D., Taylor, C., & Herter, R. (1992). Portfolios, accountability and an interpretative approach to validity. *Educational Measurement: Issues and Practice, 11*(3), 16. Copyright 1992 by the National Council on Measurement in Education. Reprinted by permission of the publisher.

The Continuum Approach (Modified primary trait scale)

Recall that Chapter 2 discussed the continuum approach to developing criterion-referenced assessments. Performances such as writing narratives, debugging computer programs, and interpreting X-rays can be organized according to level of competence from novice to expert (Glaser & Chi, 1988). The continuum approach to developing rating scales is consistent with this model.

Characteristics. The components of a rating scale on a continuum are (1) verbal descriptions of levels of proficiency of a complex capability and (2) a score associated with each level. The highest level on the continuum may either represent excellent (outstanding) performance or adequate performance. For example, one scale developed for writing consists of four levels from inadequate (level 1) to adequate/competent performance (level 4) (Herman, Gearhart, & Baker, 1993). The example in Table 7-5 uses 6 levels from "minimal evidence of achievement" to "exceptional achievement." This scoring rubric is used to score essays in which students make a judgment about an object or event and support the judgment with evidence.

The continuum scales also are referred to as *scoring rubrics* because each numerical rating is accompanied by a description of the characteristics associated with it (Neill et al., 1995). (The term described the red or "rubric" letters used in Christian prayer books to give directions on the appropriate conduct of religious services [Mitchell, 1992, p. 341].)

Some sources refer to continuum scales as an example of holistic scoring. Holistic scoring, originated for the scoring of essays, involves placing each paper in one of several piles that represent different levels of quality. In other words, the rater estimates the overall quality of the product. Then a numerical score on a range that corresponds to the number of piles (such as 1 to 5 or 1 to 7) is assigned to each group of papers. In contrast, the continuum model relies on verbal descriptions of the expected level of proficiency for each numerical rating. Moreover, these descriptions are developed in advance of the scoring. That is, the range of performance in a particular set of papers does not determine the scoring range. Further, each essay to be graded is compared to the verbal descriptions for each numerical rating.

Implementation. Of importance in developing the scale is that it should not be used for specific knowledge that is more appropriately assessed in a test format. Equally important is that the levels constitute a true hierarchy of performance from inadequate to complex. If a characteristic identified at level 5, for example, occasionally is observed in products rated as level 3, scores generated by the scale lack validity. For example, one continuum scale developed for writing in first

Table 7.5 Example of a Scoring Rubric for Evaluation Essays

	Achievement in Evaluation
Score Point	**Description of Achievement**
6 Exceptional Achievement	The student produces convincingly argued evaluation; identifies a subject, describes it appropriately, and asserts a judgment of it; gives reasons and specific evidence to support the argument; engages the reader immediately, moves along logically and coherently and provides closure; reflects awareness of reader's questions or alternative evaluations.
5 Commendable Achievement	The student produces well-argued evaluation; identifies, describes, and judges its subject; gives reasons and evidence to support the argument; is engaging, logical, attentive to reader's concerns; is more conventional or predictable than the writer of a 6.
4 Adequate Achievement	The student produces adequately argued evaluation; identifies and judges its subject; gives at least one moderately developed reason to support the argument; lacks the authority and polish of the writer of a 5 or 6; produces writing that, although focused and coherent, may be uneven; usually describes the subject more than necessary and argues a judgment less than necessary.
3 Some Evidence of Achievement	The student states a judgment and gives one or more reasons to support it; either lists reasons without providing evidence or fails to argue even one reason logically or coherently.
2 Limited Evidence of Achievement	The student states a judgment but may describe the subject without evaluating it or may list irrelevant reasons or develop a reason in a rambling, illogical way.
1 Minimal Evidence of Achievement	The student usually states a judgment but may describe the subject without stating a judgment; either gives no reasons or lists only one or two reasons without providing evidence; usually relies on weak and general personal evaluation.
No Response	
Off Topic	

Reprinted by permission of the publisher from Mitchell, R. (1992). *Testing for learning.* New York: The Free Press, p.35.

grade does not list the skill, adding to the story, until level 11. However, this activity may appear at a lower level. If so, adding to the story is not representative of advanced writing in first grade.

The continuum model is more suitable for student products rather than an ongoing performance. Observing the minute-by-minute execution of a dance routine, for example, and accurately assigning it a place on a continuum are problematic at best.

To date, the continuum model is applied most often to performance assessments and portfolios. Examples are essays that reflect responses to literature and summaries of research investigations. However, when the purpose of the portfolio is to demonstrate student growth, the selections should not be assigned a single numerical score. Because growth in different dimensions of a complex capability is likely to be uneven, a primary trait scale should be used instead.

Since the introduction of scoring rubrics in relation to student products, they also have been used as reporting systems, in lieu of grades, to parents and others. Chapter 12 includes an example.

Validity and Reliability

Critical to establishing the validity of both types of rating scales is the identification of elements in the scale. For primary trait scales, the particular dimensions that are identified should be key aspects of the capability. Equally important is that the dimensions should be directly observable.

Similarly, the descriptions of skill levels in continuum scales should not be trivial details of performance. When the fully functioning capability is not captured in the rating scale, the validity of the assessment is in question (Messick, 1984).

Also important for both validity and reliability is that descriptors should be as concrete as possible and readily interpretable. To the extent that they are not, raters will be evaluating aspects of performance other than those intended. Further, ratings by different individuals will be inconsistent.

When rating scales are used for large-scale assessments, validity also may be checked by comparing the ratings assigned to student performances or products with other information. For example, Baker et al. (1991) found that Advanced Program students scored twice as high as the slower students on overall essay scores in history and more than three times higher in the use of principles. For large-scale assessments, training sessions for raters enhance reliability. Interrater reliability also is calculated for large-scale assessments.

One factor that influences the reliability of ratings is the beliefs and attitudes of the rater that can bias the ratings in different ways. The types of bias are described in Table 7-6. The tendency to rate all products or dimensions either at

Table 7.6 Bias Errors in Ratings

Error	Definition
Generosity error	The tendency to rate all individuals at the high end of the scale
Severity error	The tendency to rate all individuals at the low end of the scale
Central tendency error	The tendency to rate all individuals near the center of the scale
Halo effect	The influence of the rater's general impression of an individual on the rating of particular skills or behaviors
Logical error	The inappropriate association of two characteristics as being similar and rating them in the same way
Response set	The tendency to rate all dimensions or characteristics on a scale in the same manner as the first few items

the high, low, or middle of the scale calls into question the rating assigned to any particular student. In addition, the ratings for a group of students may be so similar that the ratings do not differentiate student capabilities.

In contrast, halo effect and logical error involve the tendency to confuse the characteristics of individuals who are being evaluated. Halo effect is the tendency to be influenced by general impressions of an individual in the rating. Situation 3 in example (b), Table 5-6, in which the secretary's efficiency is influenced by general impressions of her neatness and willingness to work, is an example of halo effect. In the classroom, children who are obedient and quiet are often viewed favorably by teachers. However, the teacher should guard against being influenced by these impressions in evaluating ability.

Logical error refers to inappropriate associations of student characteristics. An example is expecting gifted students to have poor social adjustment and rating them lower on social skills.

Finally, response set is often the result of inattention to specific dimensions on a primary trait scale. Careful reading of each item guards against this problem.

Also of importance in scoring is that the teacher should not extend the process over several days, but should complete the scoring in as few sessions as possible. However, he or she should discontinue scoring when becoming fatigued.

Advantages and limitations

The current emphasis on open-ended assessments has increased the role of rating scales in measuring achievement. An advantage of rating scales over anecdotal statements and checklists is that they provide a structure for the assessment that can capture the fully functioning complex skills. Rating scales are also convenient to use.

A limitation of rating scales is that they are subject to personal bias errors. Careful attention to design of the scale and awareness of the potential problems are helpful in reducing these errors.

Summary

Anecdotal records and interviews are open-ended methods of recording student behavior. In contrast, checklists and rating scales provide a common structured format for recording the key characteristics of student achievement. A checklist is a set of specific discrete actions that represent a particular capability. The evaluator makes a yes-no judgment about the occurrence of the behaviors. Checklists are useful when important information is identified that is to be obtained on every student.

Rating scales are appropriate for complex capabilities that involve the integration of several skills. The two types of scales are primary trait (dimensions-of-performance) and modified primary trait or continuum scales. Primary trait scales involve the separate rating of essential dimensions or characteristics of complex performance. Important in the development of the instrument is the careful selection of both the dimensions and the verbal identifications of the scale points. Primary trait scales may be used to evaluate student performance and products for both feedback to students and to determine achievement level. When used to determine achievement, the ratings for the dimensions may be summed for a total score.

Modified primary trait or continuum scales reflect levels of proficiency of a complex skill. Referred to as a scoring rubric, each rating is accompanied by a verbal description of the characteristics of the achievement at that level. This approach to evaluating achievement is consistent with the continuum model of criterion-referenced assessment. Of major importance in the construction of the instrument is that the levels constitute a true hierarchy of performance. The continuum model has been applied most often to performance assessments and portfolios, and is more suitable for student products rather than an ongoing performance.

Essential to the validity of rating scales for performance is the identification of elements in the instrument (dimensions or levels of performance). Also important is that verbal descriptors should be as concrete as possible. Validity also may be checked by comparing the rating with other information about achievement.

Reliability is enhanced by training for raters, grading student products anonymously, and avoiding fatigue during scoring.

Chapter Questions

1. A checklist to evaluate delivering a speech includes the following items: Stands up straight; uses gestures when appropriate; maintains eye contact with audience; and finishes on time. Discuss the validity problems with this set of items.

2. In Chapter 2, you were asked to name two skills that are appropriate for the continuum model of criterion-referenced assessment. Select one of the skills and describe the rating scale you would use.

3. Mr. Johnson's sixth-grade class is working in small groups to research and develop position papers on the economic and political conditions that led to World War II. Outline a plan for Mr. Johnson to effectively use anecdotal records during these activities.

4. A rating scale for assessing silent reading includes the following items: Has proper book position; avoids vocalizing (lip movements); seems to enjoy silent reading; and avoids head movement. Identify and discuss the major problem with this set.

5. A middle school teacher believes that all student products should be stringently graded in order to prepare students for high school. What problems are likely to be associated with his ratings of student projects?

References

Alexander, P., Schallert, D., & Hare, V. (1991). Coming to terms: How researchers in learning and literacy talk about knowledge. *Review of Educational Research, 61*(3), 315–343.

Baker, E., Freeman, M., & Clayton, S. (1991). Cognitive assessment of history for large-scale testing. In M. Wittrock & E. Baker (Eds.), *Testing and cognition* (pp. 131–153). Englewood Cliffs, NJ: Prentice Hall.

Cronbach, L. J. (1990). *Essentials of psychological testing* (5th ed.). New York: Harper & Row.

Dole, J. A., Duffy, G., Roehler, L. R., & Pearson, P. D. (1991). Moving from the old to the new: Research on reading comprehension instruction. *Review of Educational Research, 61*(2), 239–264.

Fennema, E., Franke, M. L., Carpenter, T. P., & Carey, D. A. (1993). Using children's mathematical knowledge in instruction. *American Educational Research Journal, 30*(3), 555–583.

Glaser, R., & Chi, M. (1988). Overview. In M. Chi, R. Glaser, & M. Farr (Eds.), *The nature of expertise*, (pp. xv-xxxvi). Hillsdale, NJ: Erlbaum.

Gomez, M. L., Graue, M. E., & Block, M. N. (1991). Reassessing portfolio assessment: Rhetoric and reality. *Language Arts*, 68(8), 620–628.

Hemme, E., & Goyins, T. (1992). Portfolio, please! *Instructor, 101*(8), 49.

Herman, J., Gearhart, M., & Baker, E. (1993). Assessing writing portfolios: Issues in the validity and meaning of scores. *Educational Assessment, 1*(3), 201–224.

Hunt, N., & Marshall, K. (1994). *Exceptional children and youth*. Boston: Houghton Mifflin.

Lamme, L., & Hysmith, C. (1991). One school's adventure into portfolio assessment. *Language Arts*, 68(8), 629–640.

McLoughlin, J. A., & Lewis, R. (1994). *Assessing special students* (4th ed.). Columbus, OH: Merrill.

Messick, S. (1984). The psychology of educational measurement. *Journal of Educational Measurement, 21*(3), 215–237.

Mitchell, R. (1992). *Testing for learning*. New York: The Free Press.

Moran, M. R. (1996). Educating children with communication disorders. In E. L. Meyen (Ed.), *Exceptional children in today's schools* (pp. 281–314). Denver: Love Publishing.

Moss, P., Beck, J., Ebbs, C., Matson, B., Muchmore, D., Steele, D., Taylor C., & Herter R. (1992). Portfolios, accountability and an interpretative approach to validity. *Educational Measurement: Issues and Practice*, *11*(3), 16.

Neill, M., Bursh, P., Schaeffer, B., Thall, C., Yohe, M., & Zappardino, P. (1995). *Implementing performance assessments*. Cambridge, MA: FAIRTEST: The National Center for Fair and Open Testing.

Patton, M. (1990). *Qualitative evaluation and research methods*. Newberry Park, CA: Sage.

Schoenfeld, A. H. (1985). Metacognition and epistemological issues in mathematical understanding. In E. A. Silver (Ed.), *Teaching and learning mathematical problem solving: Multiple research perspectives* (pp. 361–379). Hillsdale, NJ: Erlbaum.

Stallings, J., & Mohlman, G. G. (1990). Observation systems. In H. J. Walberg & G. D. Haertel (Eds.), *The international encyclopedia of educational evaluation* (pp. 639–644). Oxford: Pergamon Press.

Tyler, R. W. (1930). A test of skill in using a microscope. *Educational Research Bulletin*, 9(11), 493–496.

Chapter 8

Performance Assessment

Major Topics

Examples of performance assessment:

Executing a dance routine

Writing a letter in a foreign language to a pen pal in another country

Writing a letter to the editor of a local newspaper on an issue of concern to the class

Conducting an experiment on the absorbency of paper towels

Overview

In the school setting, performance assessment historically referred to nonverbal psychological tests that required students to manipulate materials. An example is the Block Design Subtest of the WISC-III. In the work setting, performance assessment refers to work sample tests. A supervisor observes and scores an employee's performance while he or she executes essential job tasks (Siegal, 1986).

Currently, performance assessment in the classroom is one of the major categories of assessment referred to as "alternative" or "authentic." Performance assessments are "on-demand" assessments usually administered under standardized conditions. The other type of alternative assessment, the portfolio, is a collection of the student's work over a period of time, such as a semester.

Alternative assessment began as a part of the curriculum development efforts that focus on meaningful learning. The intent is, as much as possible, to develop assessments that reflect the actual challenges faced by writers, business people, scientists, or community leaders (Wolf, LeMahieu, & Eresh, 1992; Wiggins, 1989). Examples are writing essays, designing proposals, arguing critically, and synthesizing diverse components (Wiggins, 1989, p. 704). Thus, the major requirements for alternative assessments differ from those of multiple-choice tests.

Alternative assessments are so named because they were developed to overcome limitations of multiple-choice tests. In addition, the tasks sometimes are referred to as authentic because they are related to real-world tasks (Wiggins, 1989). However, the extent to which an assessment is authentic varies along a continuum. In writing, for example, multiple-choice tests on grammar and mechanics are at the low end of the continuum (Thomas & Oldfather, 1997). Actual samples of writing for a performance assessment are next on the continuum. Samples of writing collected from projects in which students write for real purposes and audiences are at the top end of the continuum. An example is letters to the editor about an issue of concern to the students (p. 109).

Basic Characteristics

Performance assessment may be described as "a type of testing that calls for demonstration of understanding and skill in applied, procedural, or open-ended settings" (Baker, Freeman, & Clayton, 1993). The situations at the beginning of the chapter are examples.

Performance assessments are sometimes referred to as direct measures of cognitive abilities. However, all measurements of skill and knowledge are indirect, regardless of the type of setting for tasks. They are indirect because they involve inferences about internal and mental capabilities. Further, these inferences are, in part, a product of the examiner's judgment. Thus, the term direct assessment should not be used because it promises too much (Messick, 1994, p. 21).

Major requirements. All alternative assessments should meet the four basic requirements illustrated in Table 8-1. First, unlike multiple-choice items, alternative assessments measure complex abilities. That is, they are not intended to measure the acquisition of basic knowledge. Second, and equally important, they should focus on important and teachable processes, such as developing a persuasive argument.

Table 8.1 Requirements for Alternative Assessments (Performance Assessments and Portfolios)

Requirement	Rationale
1. Measure complex abilities.	Multiple-choice items are proxies or surrogates for important capabilities.
2. Focus on teachable processes.	Tasks are not items of content nor do they depend on insight for their solution.
3. Inform teachers about students' strengths and weaknesses.	An important function of assessment is to inform instruction.
4. Require products or behaviors that are valued in their own right.	Tasks do not focus on trivial or trite performances; a hands-on task is not necessarily a performance assessment.

Sometimes efforts to design complex tasks lead to situations that appear to require complex thinking but, instead, depend on the recall of only an item of content or a flash of insight. An example is a science task in which the student is to assume that he or she is stranded on a mountainside in cold, dry, windy weather. The student is to determine which of two fabrics would keep him or her warmer. Determining the answer depends on the insight of taking two containers and filling them with warm water in order to check the insulating capacity of the fabrics. (After wrapping each container in a fabric, periodic temperature readings indicate which container loses heat faster.) In other words, if the student does not figure out this creative use of the two containers, he or she cannot solve the problem. Such a situation is a puzzle, but it is not an adequate performance assessment.

The third requirement is that the task should inform teachers about strengths and weaknesses with reference to complex mental abilities. Finally, the tasks require products or behaviors that are valued in their own right. As already indicated, not every hands-on task is a performance assessment.

Each of the examples at the beginning of this chapter meets these four requirements. Executing a dance routine involves developing a mental model of the sequence of physical actions to be performed and then executing the model with grace and precision. Similarly, in the two writing situations, students must decide on the important information to be communicated and then apply their prior knowledge and verbal skills to express these ideas. Conducting an experiment requires that the students first decide the types of information they need to address the question (towel absorbency) and ways to measure it. Then, they must draw on their prior knowledge to develop a plan of action, implement their plan, and evaluate the results.

Further, these processes are teachable, such as the execution of dance moves, communicating through writing, and strategies for addressing research questions. In addition, execution of these tasks indicates students' strengths and weaknesses that may be addressed through instruction, such as inadequate knowledge base, misconceptions, or poor learning strategies (Baker et al., 1991). Finally, each situation reflects processes and behaviors that are valued in their own right. They are not trivial tasks.

Process and product assessments. A performance assessment may require a student to either create some product or engage in some activity (Haertel, 1992). That is, some performance assessments may address particular behaviors, others may address a completed product, and some assessments may address both. Of the examples at the beginning of the chapter, executing a dance routine is a process assessment. The teacher observes the dancer and completes a checklist or rating scale while the performance is ongoing.

In contrast, the two writing tasks are product assessments. A scoring guide (rubric) appropriate for the task is developed and the teacher applies the rubric to the completed essays. Evaluating the student(s) conducting an experiment, on the other hand, involves both process (execution of the experiment) and product (the results).

The choice of whether to evaluate a performance or a product depends largely on the nature of the knowledge domain (Messick, 1994). In the performing arts, such as acting and dancing, the performance and the product are essentially the same. Therefore, the task is simply to evaluate the performance as it occurs. However, in other domains such as creative writing, several approaches to accomplishing the task are acceptable. Therefore, the product is the focus of the assessment. In some domains, such as auto mechanics, both the outcomes and procedures are important. As in the example of conducting an experiment on towel absorbency, both the execution of the task and the product are assessed.

Formats and Applications

Process skills such as demonstrating problem approach and strategy use may be demonstrated through activities such as conducting experiments, participating in research projects, team debates, and mock trials. One difficulty in group activities, however, is that of evaluating the contributions of each student.

Some capabilities, such as synthesizing; interpreting or critiquing ideas; analyzing, interpreting, and/or manipulating data may be assessed through student products. Examples are short paragraphs (elementary school students), tape recordings, essays, project reports (oral or written), and charts, diagrams, graphs, or models accompanied by verbal explanation.

One format for performance assessment that is yet to be implemented routinely in the public school setting is computer simulations. Briefly, a simulation is a situation that imitates reality in which the individual is required to make decisions and take action in response to real-world events. Historically, simulations have been widely used in the training and testing of military personnel, airplane personnel, and astronauts.

In education, simulations have been used extensively in medical and nursing schools in the form of written or computer-based exercises referred to as patient management problems. The student is first presented with a brief scenario, such as an unconscious patient, and a set of possible actions (both right and wrong). The student may typically choose more than one action and then receives feedback about the outcomes of these actions, such as the results of an x-ray requested by the student. The student then makes another decision, learns the outcome, and moves on to the next decision. The student is not informed during the simulation whether his or her choices are correct. Instead, he or she continues making decisions until the patient "recovers" or the patient "dies." In other words, there are many paths through the exercise, and the student only learns of the accuracy and/or efficiency of his or her decisionmaking in a postassessment debriefing with the instructor. At least one state uses patient management problems in the licensure examination for respiratory care therapists (Hixon, 1985, 1987). One application for public school use is the computer simulation in science in which the student must discover the preferences of sow bugs for dry or damp soil and light or dark (Shavelson, Baxter, & Pine, 1992).

Performance assessments were developed to serve as classroom assessments of learning and have been used both as informal and formal assessments in several subject areas, including history, social studies, writing, mathematics, and science. Some schools have implemented performance assessments as an integral component of student portfolios (see the following chapter).

Some statewide testing programs use performance assessments to evaluate students' writing skills. An example is the Illinois writing assessment that tests students' abilities to develop convincing points of view or ideas. Students respond to a single prompt within a 25-minute time limit. Essays are scored on focus, support for ideas, organization, mechanics, and overall effectiveness (Chapman, Fyans, & Kerins, 1984). The California Learning Assessment Scale (CLAS), used in 1994, and writing assessment programs in Milwaukee, Wisconsin, and Arizona also require students to develop some form of essay. Milwaukee ninth graders are allowed 90 minutes to write a business letter (such as a job application or consumer complaint) and an essay on a topic such as problems with their friends, neighborhood, or school (Archbald & Newmann, 1992).

One shortcoming of the use of performance assessments in large-scale testing is that some authenticity is lost. For example, essays or letters are not written within stated time limits in the real world.

Summary

Performance assessments formerly were viewed only as nonverbal psychological tests or samples of essential job tasks. Currently, performance assessment is one of the two major types of alternative (as opposed to multiple-choice tests) or authentic assessment (related to real-world tasks). Performance assessments are "on-demand" tasks that usually are administered under standardized conditions. The intent is for the student to demonstrate understanding and skill in applied, procedural, or open-ended situations.

The four major requirements for alternative assessments are (1) to measure complex abilities, (2) to focus on important and teachable processes, (3) inform teachers of students' strengths and weaknesses, and (4) consist of products or behaviors that are valued in their own right. The nature of the knowledge domain typically determines whether a performance or a product is evaluated. Domains such as acting and dancing evaluate performance; areas such as writing typically evaluate products. In some domains, such as auto mechanics, both the performance and the product are assessed.

Types of performance assessments include conducting experiments; participating in research projects; team debates; mock trials; essays; tape recordings; and student construction of charts, diagrams, and models; and simulations. Although originally designed as classroom assessments, performance assessments are found in some statewide testing programs. One shortcoming of this use, however, is that some artificiality, such as time limits, is introduced into the assessments.

✦ Guidelines for Development

"The goal of one science task was for each child to (1) observe the characteristics (size, color, and shape) of various lima beans, kidney beans, peas, and corn; and (2) classify them into two logical groups. One child wrote 'good for soup' and 'good for chili'" (Mitchell, 1992)

As indicated by the previous example, a response to the surface features of a task does not guarantee that complex thinking processes are involved (Baker, O'Neill, & Linn, 1993; Linn, Baker, & Dunbar, 1991). Major steps in developing performance assessments are the design of the performance task and the development of scoring procedures.

Task Design

Important issues in task design are approaches that are to be avoided, selecting the capability to be assessed, and factors influencing task selection.

Approaches to be avoided. At least three approaches are to be avoided in setting the framework for a performance assessment. These inappropriate

Table 8.2 Approaches to be Avoided in Developing Performance Assessments

1. Do not begin with a newspaper story, an historical event, or some other scenario and then search for a task to be assessed.
2. Do not focus on a term or concept.
3. Do not select a specific principle or rule to be demonstrated.

approaches are listed in Table 8-2. One problem that is attempting to attach a performance to a scenario or turn it into a hands-on task often results in either a trivial task or one that does not require complex thinking. Also, beginning with an event makes it difficult to then identify capabilities that the event may reflect.

Moreover, task design should not focus on a term or concept or a specific role or principle to be demonstrated. The purpose of performance assessment is not to demonstrate content mastery or execution of a simple cognitive skill. Test items, such as the examples in Chapter 5, are appropriate for these skills.

Also, one is likely to end up with an elaborated word problem (instead of a performance assessment). An example is the mathematics item in Figure 8-1. It is an elaborated word problem and not an adequate performance assessment. The primary performance being assessed is drawing two geometric figures in which a major dimension is twice the length of a dimension shown in a dotted line on

"Double the dotted line segment"
Part 1
For each of the figures shown, draw a new enlarged figure that has the same shape. The dotted line segment in each new figure should double the length of the dotted line segment in the original figure.

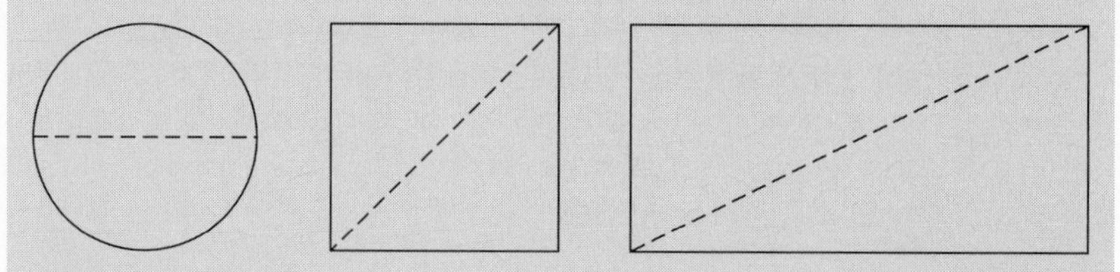

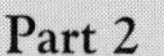

Part 2
Describe mathematically how the pairs of old and new figures are the same and how they are different.

FIGURE 8-1
Example of a mathematics performance assessment item with a substantial verbal component.

From "How Three Different Grade Groups Took the 4-Section CLAS Exam" by D. DeVise, March 10, 1994, *Press-Telegram*, Los Angeles, CA.

another figure. (This task also presents a measurement problem in that verbal ability and reading skills are part of the task.)

Identifying capabilities and possible formats. The first steps in developing a performance assessment are (1) identify a complex capability that is teachable and (2) identify possible formats for the assessment. The basis for identifying the capability is the teacher's goals and objectives that represent complex capabilities. Examples are developing a persuasive argument, interpreting positions on major social or economic issues, and evaluating stories one has read.

Possible formats for some objectives are illustrated in Table 8-3. The objective of interpreting positions on social or economic issues, for example, involves the analysis and synthesis of ideas. Potential formats include paragraphs and tape recordings (elementary school children), essays, reports, mock trials, team debates, and simulations. In contrast, the objective of interpreting data on crop

Table 8.3 Examples of Objectives and Performance Assessments

Sample objectives	Appropriate formats	Sample assessments
1. Interpret major positions on key social or economic issues.	Essays, project reports (oral or written), mock trials, team debates, simulations	Choose a period of economic and/or technological change in American history, select a negative side effect of the change, and recommend a solution.
2. Evaluate the stories and books read during free reading time.	Tape recordings or short paragraphs (elementary school students)	Twice monthly third graders take turns tape recording their comments on books/stories they have read.
3. Interpret data on crop productivity, weather conditions, and farming methods.	Essays or project reports (oral or written), supported by charts or graphs; simulations	Students construct charts, graphs, or diagrams to support their conclusions accompanied by explanations.
4. Determine the effects of one variable on another.	Conducting experiments in physical settings; computer simulations	Conduct an experiment to determine the absorbency of paper towels (Shavelson et al., 1992)
5. Solve problems in which two variables interact with each other.	Conducting experiments in physical settings; computer simulations	Conduct a computer simulation experiment on the preferences of sow bugs for light or dark and damp or dry soil (Shavelson et al., 1992)

productivity, weather conditions, and farming methods involves analyzing and interpreting data. This objective may be assessed through the student's construction of charts, graphs, and/or diagrams accompanied by verbal or oral explanation.

Factors influencing task selection. Identifying the capabilities to be assessed and appropriate formats are first steps in designing performance assessments. Completing the next step, developing the particular task itself, is influenced by at least three factors. They are the developmental level of the student, required prerequisite knowledge and skills, and time, space, and equipment requirements.

In general, tasks with a great deal of information and several variables or factors to consider are too difficult for young children. However, elementary school children can be successful on tasks that involve interpretation, evaluation, and experimentation when the tasks are properly designed. For example, in third-grade language arts classes at one school, children evaluate the books they read. They take turns twice monthly at the resource table tape recording their comments. The teacher later notes the level of the child's comments on a scale that ranges from simply liking the book to relating the book to his/her experiences or other books, to analyzing something about the book (plot, setting, characters) (Lamme & Hysmith, 1991, p. 633).

Young children also can learn to manipulate and experiment with data. Younger students can address the situations in which they investigate a particular variable, such as the absorbency of paper towels. Middle school children, in general, also can handle situations in which the relationships of two variables are involved. However, situations in which more than two variables interact with each other to influence other variables should not be introduced until students are able to construct mental models of all the possible combinations. An example of a multivariable task is a computer simulation of a water pollution problem. The task is to determine which combinations of five variables (temperature, waste type, dumping rate, type of treatment, and type of body of water) most affected oxygen and waste concentration of the water (Lavoie & Good, 1988). The researchers tested the students' subject-matter knowledge and level of Piagetian reasoning prior to the simulation. They found that both were key factors in successful resolution of the problem. Specifically, concrete operational thinkers as identified by Piaget are unable to systematically address problems in which more than two variables interact to produce effects.

The breadth and scope of subject-matter knowledge is a component of tasks that focus on interpretation, writing, and problem-solving tasks in specific domains. Research indicates, for example, that knowledge of a topic contributes to writing performance (Breland, Camp, Jones, Morris, & Rock, 1987; Quellmaz, 1984). Cognitive research indicates that successful problem-solving performance depends on (1) the availability of relevant domain knowledge and (2) the student's capability of accessing that knowledge (see, e.g., Chi, Glaser, & Farr, 1988).

Objective 1 in Table 8-3 is an example in which prerequisite knowledge is essential to successful completion of the task. Prior to the end-of-semester performance assessment, student knowledge of the content can be assessed on unit tests.

Time and space requirements also are considerations in designing performance assessments. Conducting experiments, for example, requires time, space, and special equipment. The time may be reduced by asking students to keep notebooks describing their procedures and outcomes, instead of actual observation by the teacher (Shavelson, Baxter, & Pine, 1992). However, this substitution should be restricted to assessments that are not major components in the student's final grade.

Scoring Methods

As indicated in Chapter 7, two types of instruments may be used to score performance assessments. They are checklists and rating scales. In most cases, however, rating scales are used because the complex performance consists of qualities or components in greater or lesser degree.

Developing a scoring mechanism for a complex task begins with the capability that is the focus of the task. That is, is the student expected to (1) apply scientific investigation methods to a problem he or she has not encountered before, (2) evaluate readings he or she has completed, or (3) combine particular separate skills in the execution of a dance routine? The next step is to determine if the purpose of the rating is to document (1) the characteristics or traits that are components of accomplished performance or (2) the levels of proficiency that reflect a progression from novice to accomplished performance. The first requires a primary trait scale and the second is reflected in a continuum scale. Table 7-4 in Chapter 7 is an example of a primary trait scale to provide feedback to students in interpretative essays, and Table 7-5 is an example of a continuum model. For objective 2, Table 8-3, third-grade teachers developed a continuum of children's responses to literature that indicates increasing depth and understanding. Level 2 in the continuum involves a general positive or negative statement, such as "It was good"; level 3 includes a general explanation, such as "I like it because it's funny." Level 4 involves relating the book to his or her own experiences or other books, and level 5 involves analyzing something about the book (Lamme & Hysmith, 1991, p. 633). The teacher places each child's comments at a level on the scale. During independent reading or small-group sessions, the teacher encourages children at the lower ends of the scale to think about other aspects of the books they have read.

Summary

The two major steps in developing performance assessments are the design of the particular tasks and the development of scoring procedures. Approaches to avoid in designing the task are beginning with a story or event, beginning with a term or concept, and selecting a single principle to be demonstrated. Instead, the teacher should review curriculum goals and objectives to identify the complex capabilities appropriate for performance assessment. Examples include interpreting, analyzing or synthesizing ideas, and interpreting or manipulating data. Identifying the broad capability also indicates several types of possible formats, such as essays, conducting experiments, and simulations. Developmental factors, extent of prerequisite knowledge required, and time and space requirements also influence the design of the particular task.

Developing scoring criteria begins with the identification of the essential characteristics of the capability to be assessed. If the task is to demonstrate the operation of a piece of equipment, then a checklist of the essential steps is developed. The purpose is to identify the presence or absence of particular behaviors. Performance assessments for complex cognitive skills may be scored using rating scales that either address separate dimensions of the skill or place the student on a continuum of levels of proficiency.

✦ Issues in Designing and Using Performance Assessments

Lucy, in a well-known Peanuts cartoon, loudly questions the "C" grade on her coat-hanger sculpture: "How could a coat-hanger sculpture get a C? Was I judged on just the sculpture? But only time can judge works of art. Was I judged on talent? How can I be judged on something that I do not control? Was I judged on effort? Then the grade is unfair, because I worked as hard as I could. Was I judged on what I learned? Then isn't my teacher also being judged on her skills in transmitting her knowledge to me? Shouldn't she share my C?"

Lucy's comments reflect one of the validity issues faced by performance assessments—that of the focus of the scoring guide. In addition to other validity concerns, reliability, fairness, and implications for classroom practice also are important.

Validity

The danger in developing performance assessments is ending up with complicated, unwieldy tasks unrelated to the original purpose for the assessment. Further, the open-ended nature of the assessments leads to particular questions about validity that are not found in the development of multiple-choice tests. The specific validity questions to be asked about performance assessments are (1) Is the task assessing complex capabilities? (2) Are the processes that are assessed teachable? (3) Can the complex capabilities be disentangled from component skills or knowledge? and (4) Does the scoring mechanism capture the essential characteristics of the capability? In addition, for large-scale performance assessments, representation of the subject domain is also important.

A review of the performance task should indicate the basis for successful performance. Tasks that require the recall of specific items of content are not assessing complex capabilities. Assessments that require a flash of insight are complex, but the process of insight is not teachable.

When the task requires complex cognitive skills, such as the interpretation of ideas, the next issue is the nature of the essential prerequisite knowledge. For example, Linn (1994) notes that the reading and writing skills required in many performance-based assessments, even in areas such as mathematics, frequently are substantial (p. 12). An example is the elaborated word problem in Figure 8-1. As indicated in Chapter 2, the student may understand the relationship that is sought in the problem, but fail the task because of poor reading or writing skills. One solution to this validity problem is to rewrite a task in some way, such as using simpler terms or making use of charts or diagrams. Also important, however, is to separately assess prerequisite knowledge of a topic when that knowledge can influence the student's performance on complex tasks.

The nature of the scoring guide also is a validity issue. On occasion, the scoring addresses aspects of performance quality rather than different components of the complex skills (Messick, 1984, p. 20). However, Messick (1984) maintains that aspects of performance quality, such as voice, should not be included because (1) it is not teachable and (2) is not a subskill (component) of writing. Instead, he suggests that writing components include skills such as presence of overall plan or controlling ideas, and clear presentation of information/ideas. These components of writing are skills that are teachable.

In addition to these validity issues, developers of performance assessments for statewide testing programs face another issue. That issue is domain representation—the extent to which selected assessments reflect important learning in the discipline. Some states exploring performance assessment and the committees involved in National Assessment of Educational Progress (NAEP) have developed curriculum frameworks for different subjects. An example is the 1990 NAEP conceptualization of scientific literacy. The framework consists of a two-way matrix that crosses three fields of science (earth, physical, and life science) with the three general skill areas of conceptual understanding, scientific investigation, and practical reasoning. Such frameworks are broad in scope and must be further interpreted by test developers and teachers. Nevertheless, they provide an orientation for the development of curriculum objectives and assessments.

Fairness

One of the potential roles suggested for performance assessments is the certification of students for grade promotion (Baker et al., 1993). In any high-stakes decisions about students, fairness of the assessment is an important consideration. One issue in determining fairness is the comparability of different assessment tasks. If assessments provide a range of topic options or assignments, validity evidence as to their comparability should be documented (Baker et al., 1993, p. 1215).

Another issue in determining fairness is the availability of needed equipment that can impact the assessment in two ways. One is the lack of essential equipment when the test is administered. An example is the substitution of rulers for missing yardsticks to calculate the area of the classroom (Phillips, 1994). The other issue is student access to equipment during learning. Linn et al. (1991) note that a nonthreatening assessment such as NAEP may include calculator-dependent problems, although student access to calculators may be inequitable (p. 17). However, tests intended to profile a particular student's capabilities should address this issue.

One expectation for performance assessment is that the tasks will be meaningful to students because they reflect actual challenges undertaken by individuals in their daily lives. However, a richly contextualized assessment is not necessarily uniformly good for all students (Messick, 1994). Contextual features that motivate some students may alienate and confuse others, thus distorting their performance (p. 19). For example, certain types of content or subject matter in reading passages lead to different performance consequences as a function of gender and ethnicity. Also, some data from NAEP analyses indicate that students differ by ethnicity in their rates of attempting more open-ended items (Baker et al., 1993, p. 1214). The implications are that resources must be allocated to instruction to prepare student for complex open-ended assessments (Linn et al., 1991).

Reliability

The focus of validity is the constructs and capabilities measured by an assessment and the resulting decisions that are made about students. The key question with respect to reliability is, "To what extent is the student's score a reflection of his or her true ability (and not the result of measurement error)?" Well-known sources of measurement error are unplanned cues that give away the answer, confusing or poorly written directions, use of unfamiliar terms that were not in the instruction, insufficient number of items or tasks, and inaccurate scoring. A particular problem in using performance assessments is a sufficient number of tasks. Although time-consuming, more than one task should be used to measure complex capabilities.

Another source of measurement error in open-ended assessments is the inconsistent application of scoring criteria. The classroom teacher can guard against this problem by avoiding grading when fatigued, grading only a few products at one time, and spot-checking a few products after the grading is completed.

Consistency of grading also is an issue in large-scale assessments. Studies have indicated that the error resulting from different raters can be minimized when well-defined scoring criteria are used and raters are carefully trained (Linn, 1994, p. 25).

Other sources of unreliability in scores are student unfamiliarity with the mechanical apparatus in a manipulative task and variations in the accuracy of observers who are rating the completion of manipulative tasks. Variations in the accuracy of observers can be addressed through training and through criteria that can be applied easily during the observation.

Summary

Three key issues in designing and using performance assessments are validity, reliability, and fairness. The specific validity concerns are the capabilities assessed by the task, disentangling the complex capability from prerequisite skills or content, and the characteristics that are tapped by the scoring rubric.

Performance assessments that rely on the recall of an item of content or a flash of insight are not assessing complex capabilities. Also, if the assessment depends on extensive reading and writing skills, the task should be rewritten or the student's reading and writing competence should be documented. Prerequisite knowledge required for the task should be assessed prior to administration of the performance assessment. In addition to these concerns, large-scale assessments must address the issue of domain representation of the selected assessments.

When important decisions are being made about students, issues of fairness refer to the comparability of tasks, the availability of essential equipment for the assessment, and the student's access to equipment during learning. Reliability issues germane to performance assessments include inconsistent application of scoring criteria, student unfamiliarity with the mechanical apparatus in a manipulative task, and the reactions of some ethnic groups to open-ended items and other types of questions. The implications are that resources should be allocated to instruction to prepare students for open-ended assessments.

Chapter Questions

1. One of the standards for language arts in Table 4-1 is to communicate effectively in various ways. Select a grade level and identify one to three capabilities for this standard and describe a performance task for each.

2. A proposed performance assessment first asks students to read a newspaper article on the 1940s pouring of transformer oil in area lakes to kill mosquitos and the resulting PCB contamination of fish. Students are asked to write an essay describing PCB contamination. Discuss the problems with this task as a performance assessment.

3. One elementary school is exploring a proposal to use the computers in the computer lab for children's performance assessments in writing. Discuss the validity and reliability issues.

4. This chapter stated that students can be required to keep notebooks of their procedures and outcomes while conducting experiments that are not major components of the student's final grade. Discuss the problems with using this procedure for experiments that are part of a six-weeks test.

5. Implementing performance assessments such as conducting experiments, designing zoo habitats for different species of animals, and designing a marketing plan for Zinger cola assess different capabilities than structured-response items. Discuss the implications of such assessments for instruction.

References

Archbald, D., & Newman, T. (1992). Approaches to assessing academic achievement. In H. Berlak, F. M. Newman, E. Adams, D. Archbald, T. Burgess, J. Raven, & T. A. Ramberg. *Toward a new science of educational testing and achievement* (pp. 139–180). Albany: State University of New York Press.

Baker, E., Freeman, M., & Clayton, S. (1991). Cognitive assessment of history for large-scale testing. In M. Wittrock & E. Baker (Eds.), *Testing and cognition* (pp. 131–153). Englewood Cliffs, NJ: Prentice Hall.

Baker, E., O'Neill, H., & Linn, R. (1993). Policy and validity prospects for performance-based assessment. *American Psychologist, 48*(12), 1210–1218.

Breland, H., Camp, R., Jones, R., Morris, M., & Rock, D. (1987). *Assessing writing skill. Research monograph no. 11*. New York: College Entrance Examination Board.

Chapman, C., Fyans, L., & Kerins, C. (1984). Writing assessment in Illinois. *Educational Measurement: Issues and Practice, 3*(1), 24–26.

Chi, M., Glaser, R., & Farr, M. (Eds.). (1988). *The nature of expertise*. Hillsdale, NJ: Erlbaum.

Haertel, E. (1992). Performance assessment. In M. C. Alkin (Ed.), *Encyclopedia of educational research* (pp. 984–989). New York: Macmillan.

Hixon, S. J. (1985). An investigation of the psychometric properties of a written clinical simulation exercise for respiratory care practitioners. Unpublished doctoral dissertation, Ohio State University, Columbus.

Hixon, S. J. (1987). The relationship of quantified measures of work experience to clinical problem-solving ability. Paper presented at the annual meeting of the American Educational Research Association, Washington, DC.

Lamme, L., & Hysmith, C. (1991). One school's adventure into portfolio assessment. *Language Arts, 68*(8), 629–640.

Lavoie, D., & Good, R. (1988). The nature and use of prediction skills in a biological computer simulation. *Journal of Research in Science Teaching, 25*(5), 335–360.

Linn, R. (1994, April). Performance assessment: Policy promises and technical measurement standards. Invited address, Division D, annual meeting of the American Educational Research Association, New Orleans.

Linn, R., Baker, E., & Dunbar, S. (1991). Complex performance-based assessment. Expectations and validation criteria. *Educational Researcher, 20*(5), 15–21.

Messick, S. (1984). The psychology of educational measurement. *Journal of Educational Measurement, 21*(3), 215–217.

Messick, S. (1994). The interplay of evidence and consequences in the validation of performance assessments. *Educational Researcher, 23*(2), 13–22.

Mitchell, R. (1992). *Testing for learning*. New York: The Free Press.

Phillips, S. (1994). Opportunity for success. *National Council on Measurement in Education Quarterly Newsletter, 3*(1), 2.

Quellmaz, E. (1984). Toward successful large-scale writing assessment: Where are we now? Where do we go from here? *Educational Measurement: Issues and Practice, 3*(1) 29–33.

Shavelson, R., Baxter, G., & Pine, J. (1992). Performance assessments: Political rhetoric and measurement reality. *Educational Researcher, 21*(4), 22–27.

Thomas, S., & Oldfather, P. (1997). Intrinsic motivations, literacy, and assessment practices: "That's my grade. That's me." *Educational Psychologist, 32*(2), 107–123.

Siegel, A. (1986). Performance tests. In R. Berk (Ed.), *Performance assessment: Methods and applications* (pp. 121–142). Baltimore: The Johns Hopkins University Press.

Wiggins, G. (1989). A true test: Toward more authentic and equitable assessment. *Phi Delta Kappa, 70*(9), 703–713.

Wolf, D., Mahieu, P., & Eresh, J. (1992). Good measure: Assessment as a tool of reform. *Educational Leadership*, 8-13.

Chapter 9

Portfolio Assessment

Hundreds of art portfolios are spread out in the gymnasium. Each includes creative products and slides for each of three sections (original work, concentration, and breadth) in general and/or drawing. Also included are student explanations of their work that describe their sources of ideas, influences, and assistance.

—Mitchell, 1992

Major Topics

The preceding portfolio assessment is the Advanced Placement examination for high school students seeking college credit in studio art. Teams of teachers evaluate each part of the portfolio and these evaluations are combined in an overall score.

Although not a new development in the Advanced Placement examination, portfolio assessment is relatively new to the classroom. Like performance assessment, portfolios were initiated in the classroom in the late 1980s as an alternative to paper-and-pencil tests. Also like performance assessment, the intent is to measure intellectual capabilities, to focus on teachable cognitive processes, and to inform teachers about students' strength and weaknesses (Baker, Freedman, & Clayton, 1991, p. 135).

In addition to this initial use of portfolios, they also have been advocated as mechanisms for showcasing students' best work, either at the classroom or school level. Portfolios also have been implemented in some statewide assessments. However, the formats and extent of student involvement differ for these different uses.

Types of Portfolios

Since the inception of portfolios for classroom assessment in the early 1980s, they have been implemented in different ways. Discussed in this section are the basic characteristics of portfolios, the "ideal" format, and variations on that format.

Basic Characteristics

Artists and, later, photographers have long used portfolios as portable collections of work samples to show prospective clients. Although the portfolio in the classroom also is a collection of student work, it differs from other collections in three major ways. First, a student's portfolio illustrates longitudinal growth that is evidenced by changes over time in his or her work. For example, changes may include greater depth in writing or the ability to pursue and solve more complex problems.

Second, the student's portfolio also can illustrate breadth in the subject area through the samples of different kinds of work that are included. In language arts, for example, a portfolio may contain journal entries, essays, poems, narratives, and tape recordings of class presentations.

Third, the portfolio should involve the student in the assessment process. Ideally, the portfolio would include student reflections on his or her work and provide evidence that the student is able to pursue work over time and also develop standards of excellence (Wolf, 1987/1988, p. 29).

Portfolios differ from performance assessments in four major ways (Herman, Gearhart, & Baker, 1993, p. 203). First, samples of class work, rather than responses to a stimulus under standardized conditions, are included. Second, the range of examples represents multiple opportunities to demonstrate competencies in several contexts. Third, examples of student work represent a variety of tasks. Fourth, some of the examples are various stages in the completion of work, such as early drafts of a story, revised drafts, and the final version.

In the classroom, the portfolio is not an "add-on" to existing forms of assessment; instead, it is the sole assessment system. Implementation of portfolio assessment in the classroom reflects five basic beliefs about the assessment of student learning (see Table 9-1). The focus is to demonstrate student strengths, not to document shortcomings. Therefore, examples of student work in the portfolio

Table 9.1 Five Basic Beliefs about the Sssessment of Student Learning Represented in Portfolios

1. The focus is on student strengths and potential, not simply on needs and deficits (Thomas & Oldfather, 1997).
2. Selected examples of student achievement should reflect growth over time.
3. Assessment should provide opportunities for students to do more than use "algorithms to solve tidy problems" (Darling-Hammond, Ancess, & Falk, 1995, p. 5).
4. Assessment should provide detailed information on the day-by-day progress of students.
5. Assessment should assist less traditionally skilled students to develop their capabilities (Wolf, Bixby, Glenn, & Gardner, 1991).

should document growth in complex capabilities, such as interpreting and analyzing literature, developing a short story, or conducting research on the Civil War. Items in the student's portfolio are examples of his or her work produced in the classroom.

Unlike other forms of assessment, the portfolio is closely linked to day-by-day instruction. Thus, it is an example of the integrated teaching-assessment model described in Chapter 4.

The "Ideal" Format

The "ideal" format, developed in the arts and humanities, is so named because it is designed to fulfill two major aims. One is to model individual and personal responsibility in questioning and reflecting on one's own work. The second aim is to portray student growth in order to assist learners to become thoughtful and informed evaluators of their own histories as learners (Wolf, 1989, p. 36). The portfolio, in other words, is a working document in which entries change throughout the year as the student develops maturity and insight about the subject and his or her own learning. Student growth is documented by a qualitative analysis of early versus later works.

The "ideal" portfolio consists of three major components (see Table 9-2). Documentation of the development of a major project is referred to as a biography of the work (Wolf, 1989). A portfolio in art, for example, may contain a series of sketches from the student's sketchbook, with accompanying notes. A writing portfolio may contain notes, diagrams, drafts, and the final version of a narrative.

In addition to depth, the portfolio also should demonstrate breadth of development. A portfolio in social studies, for example, may include several drafts of a

Table 9.2 Components of the "Ideal" Portfolio

Component	Example
1. Documentation of the development of major works	Notes, diagrams, drafts, and the final version of a narrative (writing portfolio)
2. Evidence of the range or variety of student work	Student journal that provides evidence of the depth and breadth of the student's reading interests, personal responses to literature, and analytic papers of the student's interpretations of literature (reading portfolio) (Thomas & Oldfather, 1997)
3. Student reflections	Student description of the basic features of his or her work, the changes over time, and progress yet to be achieved (Wolf, 1989, p. 37)

report on the lives of soldiers during the Civil War with photos and excerpts from letters and journals, an analysis of the issue of state sovereignty and slavery expressed in the Lincoln-Douglas debates, and interviews with descendants of Civil War soldiers (Thomas & Oldfather, 1997, p. 109).

Of particular importance is that students become proficient in reflecting on and analyzing their work. Therefore, at different times during the semester, the classroom teacher asks students to review their portfolios from the viewpoint of an informed critic. Each student notes strengths and weaknesses, identifies progress since the prior review, and describes the goals he or she has yet to achieve (Wolf, 1989, p. 37). Students also may return to earlier works to make comparisons with later works.

In the classroom, teachers and students discuss the processes involved in developing worthwhile work, the elements of a helpful critique, and ways to incorporate comments into ongoing work (Wolf et al., 1991, p. 58). In this way, the portfolio becomes a context in which students can learn to view assessment as an occasion for learning (Wolf et al., 1991). At the end of the year, a final selection of portfolio entries is made that then goes forward with the student the next year.

Particular strengths of portfolio assessment are identified by Wolf (1989). They are the development of student responsibility for learning, the renewed emphasis on process, and a focus on a developmental view of learning (Wolf, 1989).

Variations on the "Ideal" Format

Since the introduction of portfolio assessment in the 1980s, variations of the early format have been implemented in classroom settings. In one elementary school, for example, each fifth-grade class makes use of a Macintosh computer with a microphone and a printer for students' oral reading. Student and teacher evaluations of reading throughout the year are recorded as well as the student's oral performance. These recordings are key components in the students' reading portfolios.

In one prekindergarten-to-grade-3 school, the teachers met by grade level and developed a scale of writing development, a scale of emergent reading, and a response to literature scale. After a 1-year tryout, the grade-level scales were consolidated into three schoolwide scales. The three consolidated scales became part of the school portfolio that documents children's progress and goes with the child from grade to grade (Lamme & Hysmith, 1991, p. 630).

Included in the portfolio, referred to as a working portfolio, are a variety of artifacts. Among them are writing folders, reading-response journals, day books, projects, and writing notebooks. Children also keep reading logs in which they record the title and author of books they read, along with ratings on a five-star scale (Lamme & Hysmith, 1991). At least once each marking period, a teacher-student interview focuses the child's thoughts about his or her reading and writing and what he or she is learning (Lamme & Hysmith, 1991).

Other Portfolio Formats and Uses

The use of portfolios as a classroom assessment mechanism was designed to serve as a learning tool for students and a basis for planning by the classroom teacher. The primary purposes were to document growth, identify strengths and weaknesses, identify diversity in student work, and provide some ownership of the assessment process by students. Since that beginning, others have implemented portfolios for different purposes, resulting in some alterations in format as well as some tensions with the original goals. At present, four different types of portfolios may be identified. They are the showcase, the documentation, the class, and the evaluation portfolio.

The documentation portfolio. This format is similar to the "ideal" portfolio in that it provides an ongoing record of student progress. However, the emphasis is in the direction of documenting the student's efforts, progress, and achievements (Paulson, Paulson, & Meyer, 1991) than in developing autonomous learners. The essential portfolio elements, according to Meyer, Shumann, and Angelo (1990), include criteria for selection of portfolio contents and criteria for judging merit.

The documentation portfolio, unlike the "ideal" format, also includes teacher-completed checklists, records of teacher observations of students during class, and performance tests. In other words, the documentation portfolio is not restricted to evaluations of student products that appear in the file. However, one difficulty with the documentation portfolio is the amount of information that it may contain and the difficulty in evaluating a widely heterogeneous collection.

The showcase portfolio. A showcase portfolio is a collection of the student's best or favorite work selected primarily by the student. Sometimes the showcase portfolio is developed from the student's ongoing working portfolio that is maintained throughout the year. Some teachers in one elementary school, for example, used expandable folders for the showcase portfolio that the students then decorated. Other teachers used classroom collection books (Lamme & Hysmith, 1991).

Of major importance is that the student should make the selections of his or her work for the showcase portfolio. That is, the selections should represent what the student believes is best about his or her work. However, teachers should be aware of the fact that students often do not select the strong pieces for their portfolio (Moss et al., 1992; Simmons, 1990). One student, for example, included two pieces of expository responses to literature. The second selection was not as well organized as the first. However, the student selected it because it was a richer interpretation and, therefore, an example of growth (Moss et al., 1992).

The class portfolio. The focus of the showcase and documentation portfolios is to illustrate the achievements of the individual student. In contrast, the class portfolio is a summary document. It is useful for reporting to parents and administrators. However, the class portfolio does not include student reflections.

One class portfolio used a three-section binder that consisted of (1) summary sheets for all students, describing performance in terms of curriculum goals; (2) the teacher's notes on each student; and (3) the teacher's curriculum and instructional plans for the year (Valencia & Calfee, 1991). In addition to qualitative judgments, the teacher's notes also should refer to student works, test data, and conference notes for each student. One problem associated with the class portfolio, however, is the extensive time required for compilation.

The evaluation portfolio. The purpose of the evaluation portfolio is to report to the general public or government agencies. One inner-city high school participating in a reform effort retains senior exit portfolios in students' official files with several items for each subject discipline included. In mathematics, for example, the entries consist of a mathematics position paper, a math model, and representation or argument about a mathematical idea (Jervis, 1995).

As indicated in the prior example, the contents and criteria are specified in advance. One problem with this procedure, however, is that the assessment may more closely resemble multiple measures in a domain than portfolios (Purves, 1993). For example, the specification by a school district of a brief narrative, a business letter, and a persuasive essay is, in reality, a set of multiple assessments.

Another use of portfolios is to report to the public. An example is the analysis of student writing in the Pittsburgh school district. Of importance is that the scoring criteria grew out of teachers' extensive participation in both state and district curriculum projects in writing. The focus of these efforts was on goals for writing and ways to consider student writing (LeMahieu, Gitomer, & Eresh, 1995, p. 25). The scoring criteria were derived by many teachers and administrators reviewing a large volume of student work and developing a shared vocabulary applicable to all potential entries in a portfolio. Supervisors also worked with teachers in analyzing samples of student portfolios as classroom assessments.

The purpose of the portfolio was to present as complete a picture as possible of the student's writing. Students chose the four selections for their portfolios. They were (a) an important piece, according to the student's criteria, refined in class discussions; (2) a satisfying piece; (3) an unsatisfying piece; and (4) a free choice. Each was accompanied by early drafts and student reflections (LeMahieu et al., 1995, p. 12).

Portfolios selected for district analysis were identified 1 week before scoring through stratified random sampling. Demographic variables, grade level, and school were used to stratify the sample that was 8 percent of the students in grades 6 to 12. Then 25 raters (19 classroom teachers and 3 administrators with writing responsibilities) each scored two portfolios. Interrater reliabilities across grade levels were 0.84 (accomplishment as a writer), 0.80 (use of processes and resources), and 0.80 (growth and engagement as a writer) (p. 15).

Summary

Like performance assessments, portfolios were initiated as alternatives to paper-and-pencil tests. In the classroom, portfolios are intended to provide new opportunities for teachers and students and to illustrate student growth. Portfolios differ from performance assessments in four ways: (1) they are samples of student work rather than responses to a stimulus under standardized conditions, (2) the examples are multiple opportunities to demonstrate competence, (3) the samples represent a variety of tasks, and (4) some of the examples reflect various stages in the completion of a work.

The original use of portfolios, referred to as the "ideal" format, is designed to fulfill two major aims. They are to model personal responsibility in questioning and reflecting on one's own work and to illustrate student growth. The portfolio is a working document that includes (1) biographies of works from early ideas or drafts to the final version, (2) a range and variety of student works, and (3) student reflections. Variations of this format influence the use of several types of teacher evaluation in the portfolio and the use of established benchmarks to evaluate progress.

Other types of portfolios are the documentation, the showcase, the class, and the evaluation portfolio. The documentation portfolio typically does not emphasize student reflections and includes records of observations of students during class and performance tests in addition to evaluations of student products.

The showcase portfolio is a collection of the student's best or favorite work selected primarily by the student, whereas the class portfolio is a summary document. The purpose of the evaluation portfolio is to report to the general public and governmental agencies. When the contents and criteria are specified in advance, the assessment may more closely resemble multiple measures in a domain than do portfolios. Although one statewide assessment reported difficulties with scoring, one district assessment obtained acceptable reliability indices. Important in the district implementation was the involvement of large numbers of teachers in the development of the scoring system, the integration of portfolios into the classroom assessment of writing goals, and the use of a small team of raters.

Issues in Development and Implementation

> *"Considerable professional development is required to effectively implement portfolio systems. Given that the intent is to alter the focus of classroom instruction, the costs of generating the data for public accounting should be viewed as separate from the costs associated with portfolios as instructional systems." (LeMahieu, et al., 1995, p. 27)*

Assessing the costs of professional development and generating summary data are two issues in developing and implementing portfolio assessment. Others are implications for teachers, students, and the curriculum, addressing potential tensions between classroom and large-scale assessments, scoring, and validity and reliability.

Costs

Portfolio assessment, like performance assessment, is labor-intensive. Implementation within the classroom requires released time for teacher planning individually and in groups. One mechanism for reducing teacher time is to implement evaluations of student work as an everyday instructional activity. In this way, the contents of the portfolio are not an "add-on," but grow out of student work throughout the year.

The costs for large-scale assessment can be considerable, depending on the ways that the portfolios are selected and scored. Included are honoraria, released time, and per-diem expenditures for large numbers of teachers to score portfolios in regional or state meetings. For example, costs for the 1993 Vermont portfolio assessment amounted to approximately $13.00 per portfolio.

Sampling portfolios from the total set can provide information about student capabilities and also reduce costs. Using a small team of raters also can reduce costs. Expenditures for the Pittsburgh school district were $18,750 for the 25-member team for 1 week to evaluate 1,250 writing portfolios and $10,000 for technical analyses of possible scoring bias, validity, and reliability (LeMahieu et al., 1995). This outlay compares very favorably to the district's expenditures for a standardized writing assessment.

Implications for Teachers, Students, and the Curriculum

One advantage of portfolio assessment is that it assists teachers to uncover a wide range of student strengths and weaknesses (Jervis, 1995). Another is that it enables teachers to see students as individuals (Gomez, Graue, & Block, 1991; Jervis, 1995; Lamme & Hysmith, 1991). However, portfolio assessment, whether implemented within classrooms only or as district or statewide assessment, requires a number of initial decisions, changes in both teacher and student roles, and a restructuring of classroom activities.

Initial decisions in implementing portfolio assessment. As indicated in Table 9-2, the use of portfolios in the classroom reflects particular beliefs about the assessment of student learning. These beliefs, as discussed in the following section, alter teacher and student roles in the classroom. As a result, the teachers in a subject area or the school make the commitment to implement portfolio assessment, rather than individual teachers.

The commitment to portfolio assessment leads to three essential group decisions prior to implementation (Johnson, Willeke, Bergman, & Steiner, 1997). First, establish a focus for the portfolio by identifying the goals it should reflect. This decision involves discussions of teachers' views of the contribution of the subject area to the development of student potential. Thus, portfolio assessment means less reliance on content coverage and textbook-sequenced instruction. Instead, the focus is directed toward developing complex cognitive abilities, such as critiquing and evaluating ideas and learning to communicate effectively. One perspective on the role of the subject area is that students should be able to "frame problems, find information, evaluate alternatives, create ideas and products and invent new answers to messy dilemmas" (Darling-Hammond et al., 1995, p. 5).

Second, the teachers should develop selection criteria for the inclusion of items in the portfolio. Also, should complete freedom in creating the portfolios be allowed, or should the portfolios include both common and personally selected items? This discussion assists in addressing the problem expressed by some teachers in determining the information that is important to collect, the best method of recording information, and monitoring the system (Lamme & Hysmith, 1991).

Third, the group should develop a mechanism for evaluating the portfolios. Proponents of the "ideal" format recommend that each teacher should evaluate each portfolio at the end of the year with a written summary. However, others suggest the use of rating scales (see the section on scoring).

When these decisions have been made, the school should communicate the change in assessment to parents. Particularly important is to explain the expectations for students and the kinds of information to be developed about student learning.

Changes in teacher and student roles. In the classroom, the focus becomes that of developing the complex capabilities identified as the focus of the curriculum. The teacher's role is that of coach, facilitator, and guide. Depending on the subject area, the teacher may be providing feedback and suggestions on students' developing research on U.S. history topics, children's writing skills, or student drawings. For students, portfolios, in and of themselves will not lead to student self-understanding (Gomez et al., 1991, p. 627). Instead, teachers must involve students in the activities.

First, the teacher should discuss portfolio assessment with the students and incorporate student suggestions for implementation. For example, a practical consideration is the type of container for student work. Paper briefcases or file folders with flaps and attached strings are useful, but are somewhat expensive. Other possibilities are cardboard boxes and double grocery bags (for strength) with the top edges folded down. Also to be decided is the classroom location for the containers, which must be easily accessible to students. After a few weeks, discuss with the class how the process is working and suggestions to improve it.

As the semester progresses, the teacher should help the students see what each product shows about them and what their portfolio indicates about their learning. In other words, portfolio assessment requires a more collaborative role for students and teachers.

A key factor in the implementation of portfolio assessment is the teacher's belief system. For example, language arts teachers with high levels of implementation reported a match between their teaching philosophy and portfolio assessment as well as few implementation problems (Lamme & Hysmith, 1991). In contrast, teachers with low levels of implementation viewed portfolios as an "add-on" rather than as a transition to a different form of assessment.

Restructuring classroom activities. The changed role for teachers means less reliance on content coverage and textbook-sequenced instruction, skill worksheets, and chapter questions. Thus, teachers face decisions about the types of hands-on activities and problem-based activities to use in the classroom and ways to incorporate performance activities and observations into the curriculum. For example, learning to communicate effectively may involve tape-recorded evaluations by students of books they have read, brief essays on topics of interest selected by the students themselves, tape recordings of oral reports, and drafts of a longer report on a topic of interest or a story that the student is continuing to work on.

Implementation also requires a restructuring of class time so that teachers may work with and observe individual students. Most teachers set up times for independent reading and writing or group work in mathematics and observe or confer with individual students during those times.

Potential Tensions Between Classroom and Large-Scale Assessment

Portfolio assessment is typically implemented in the classroom to assist students in developing complex intellectual capabilities. The purpose of portfolio assessment in large-scale testing is to provide quality data about student achievement that can be compared across grade levels, schools, and districts. Potential tensions between these two levels of assessment can be lessened through several actions. First, achievement goals at the external assessment level (district or state) should be compatible with school and district goals. Second, practices must be consistent with the goals. For example, if the goal of large-scale assessment is to understand the performance of the educational system, efforts to get a score for every student are likely to have a negative impact on opportunities to learn (LeMahieu et al., 1995, p. 28). Third, steps should be taken to ensure the involvement of school personnel and development of scoring criteria and to assist teachers with implementing portfolio assessment.

Scoring Methods

Implementation of methods for scoring depend in part on the purpose established for the portfolio. The two major purposes are (1) facilitating learner growth and development, and (2) documenting student achievements (the evaluation portfolio).

Facilitating learner growth. In the ideal portfolio format, entries change throughout the year as the student develops maturity and insight into the subject. Also, early entries serve as focal points for teacher-student conferences about possible directions for the student to pursue (Wolf, 1987/1988).

The purpose of scoring guidelines for this role of portfolios is for the teacher to be able to quickly identify student strengths and weaknesses on revisiting the portfolio. Rating scales that list the essential dimensions of the capability may be used to provide feedback to students on the drafts of their work. Table 7-4 is an example of a rating scale to provide feedback to students on the features of drafts of their interpretative essays.

An example of a mechanism to record growth in children's writing was developed by K–2 teachers. The scale begins with simple activities, such as "attempts to write in scribbles or draw patterns" and moves to more complex items, such as "child writes the start of a story" (Lamme & Hysmith, 1991, p. 531).

Documenting student achievements. The scoring methods described in Chapter 7 for performance assessments are also appropriate for entries in the documentation and evaluation portfolios. Of major importance is that the characteristics and benchmarks that are evaluated should be public and students should understand their meaning.

Two criteria are of major importance when decisions about students or programs are based on portfolios. One is that the scoring system must be unambiguous and clearly interpretable. The other is that the inferences about student proficiency must be compatible with the capabilities that can be demonstrated in portfolio selections. For example, one Chapter 1 evaluation used portfolios as evidence that students had mastered elements on a checklist of 11 to 16 skills. Further, teachers were to score the portfolio on a 3-point mastery scale with the levels of some of the time, most of the time, and not yet (Benoit & Yang, 1996). Difficulties in scoring the portfolios and other problems were likely associated with a poor match between the basic skills checklist and the capabilities that can be illustrated in portfolio entries and the wide interpretations that can be made of the 3-point scale.

Fairness

Like performance assessments, portfolios are expected to provide opportunities for less traditionally skilled students to develop their abilities (Wolf et al., 1991). One study indicated, for example, that the poor writers in a sample of fifth graders improved to the level of average writers when writing portfolios were instituted. This method allowed the students ample time to develop their work. The lowest group worked the longest (16 days) on papers nearly as lengthy as those developed by the highest group (Simmons, 1990).

However, as indicated in Chapter 8, some students may have difficulty with open-ended tasks. Also, implementing portfolio assessment will not necessarily introduce fairness in learning opportunities or evaluations. For example, Ball (1993) found that teachers assigned lower formative ratings to students who used orally based patterns than those who used linear, explicit, and impersonal writing (p. 264). For portfolio assessment to address equity concerns, bridges between informal forms of communication and academic discourse may be needed.

Validity and Reliability

Two issues of particular concern in the documentation and implementation portfolios are validity and reliability of the assessments.

Validity. Of importance in establishing validity are (1) the capabilities or constructs that are represented by the portfolio entries, (2) the fit between the scoring rubric and the pieces in the portfolio, and (3) representation of the subject domain by the pieces in the collection.

Like performance assessments, the complex capabilities that can be reflected in a portfolio should be identified prior to implementation as an assessment tool. Unfortunately, a typical practice in statewide assessments is to specify which types of pieces are to be included and to assume that they will represent complex intellectual capabilities. This practice, however, can contribute to problems in scoring. For example, teachers in the Vermont portfolio assessment sometimes disagreed about the applicability of some scoring dimensions to specific attributes of a particular piece (Koretz et al., 1994, p. 12). Also, raters had to stretch general-purpose criteria to the scoring of a wide variety of tasks (p. 12). These difficulties contribute to lack of validity of the scores.

Domain representativeness is a validity concern for district and statewide portfolio assessments. Clear definitions of the domains that assessments are intended to tap and adequate measures of related constructs are needed to establish validity (Koretz et al., 1994).

Reliability. The term *reliability* has several meanings. In relation to portfolio assessments, reliability is typically interpreted as interrater agreement. Specifically, reliability is viewed as the consistency with which raters assign scores to particular pieces of work.

Several factors can contribute to lack of consistency in scoring. They are (1) unclear or inconsistent terms in the scoring criteria, (2) complexity of the scoring system, (3) insufficient training of raters, and (4) wide variations in the types of pieces in the collection and in the conditions of development of student work. For example, some students or classes may have access to more parental or teacher assistance than others. Also, if some classes are permitted several rewrites of their work and others are not, comparisons across classes will not be reliable.

Summary

Implementation of portfolio assessment involves the costs of released time for training and scoring sessions as well as time for classroom planning. Portfolio assessment also requires significant amounts of both in-class and after-school time. Costs of large scale assessments can be reduced by using stratified random sampling to select a portion of the total number of portfolios for scoring and by using a relatively small team of scorers.

Among the changes associated with portfolio assessment are new roles for students and teachers, a classroom focus on problem-based activities, and time allocated to independent work sessions. Advantages of portfolio assessment are the identification of a wide range of student strengths and weaknesses and enabling teachers to see students as individuals. Potential tensions between classroom and large-scale portfolios can be reduced by consistent goals, a shared interpretative framework by those using the portfolio assessment, and heavy involvement in the development of the system.

Coding systems for portfolios implemented to facilitate learner growth should address strengths and weaknesses, reflect major growth changes, and be easily interpreted. Scoring guides for documentation and evaluation portfolios should address complex capabilities, be unambiguous, and fit the types of portfolio entries that are evaluated. Like performance assessments, portfolios are expected to provide opportunities for less traditionally skilled students. However, some students may have difficulty with open-ended tasks, and implementing portfolio assessment will not automatically introduce fairness in learning opportunities or evaluations.

When portfolios are used in district and statewide assessments, validity and reliability also are key issues. Establishing validity involves identifying the capabilities or constructs to be represented in the portfolio entries, ensuring the fit between the scoring criteria and portfolio pieces, and between the portfolio entries and the subject domain.

Reliability in relation to portfolio assessments is typically viewed as consistency among raters. Factors that contribute to unreliability of scores are unclear or inconsistent terminology, complex scoring systems, inadequate rater training, and wide variations in the preparation of portfolio entries.

Chapter Questions

1. A study noted in this chapter found that some teachers assigned lower formative ratings to students who used orally based patterns than those who used linear, explicit, and impersonal writing (Ball, 1993). Discuss the implications for both teaching and the methods for rating student writing.

2. A middle school science textbook with 15 chapters that each introduces new terms, concepts, and principles identifies end-of-chapter exercises as entries for student portfolios. Discuss the philosophical conflicts between this directive and the recommended use of portfolios.

3. Discuss the philosophical validity and reliability issues involved in assessing the entire contents of portfolios, in which the entries may vary for different students, on a 4-point continuum scale from unsatisfactory to above average.

4. Why is it important for students to make the choices of entries to be placed in showcase portfolios?

5. Discuss potential advantages and disadvantages of portfolio assessment for poor readers.

References

Baker, E., Freeman, M., & Clayton, S. (1991). Cognitive assessment of history for large-scale testing. In M. Wittrock & E. Baker (Eds.), *Testing and Cognition* (pp. 131–153). Englewood Cliffs, NJ: Prentice Hall.

Ball, A. (1993). Incorporating ethnographic-based techniques to enhance assessments of culturally diverse students' written exposition. *Educational Assessment, 1*(3), 255–281.

Benoit, J., & Yang, H. (1996). A redefinition of portfolio assessment based upon purpose: Findings and implications from a large-scale program. *Journal of Research and Development in Education, 29*(3), 181–193.

Darling-Hammond, L., Ancess, J., & Falk, B. (1995). *Authentic assessment in action: Studies of schools and students at work*. New York: Teachers College Press.

Gearhart, M., Herman, J., Baker, E., & Whittaker, A. (1992). Writing portfolios: Potential for large-scale assessment. Los Angeles: University of California, Center for the Study of Evaluation.

Gomez, M., Graue, M., & Block, M. (1991). Reassessing portfolio assessment: Rhetoric and reality. *Language Arts, 68*(8), 620–628.

Herman, J., Gearhart, M., & Baker, E. (1993). Assessing writing portfolio issues in the validity and meaning of scores. *Educational Assessment, 1*(3), 201–224.

Jervis, K. (1995, April). Moral tug of war in an urban high school: A portfolio story. Paper presented at the annual meeting of the American Educational Research Association, San Francisco.

Johnson, R. L., Willeke, M. J., Bergman, T., & Steiner, D. J. (1997). Family literacy portfolios: Development and implementation. *Window on the World of Family Literacy, 2*(2), 10–17.

Koretz, D., Stecher, S., Klein, S., & McCaffrey, D. (1994). The Vermont Portfolio Assessment Program: Findings and implications. *Educational Measurement: Issues and Practice, 13*(3), 5–16.

Lamme, L., & Hysmith, C. (1991). One school's adventure into portfolio assessment. *Language Arts, 68*(8), 629–640.

LeMahieu, P., Gitomer, D., & Eresh, J. (1995). Portfolios in large-scale assessment: Difficult but not impossible. *Educational Measurement: Issues and Practice, 14*(3), 11–28.

Meyer, C., Shumann, S., & Angelo, N. (1990) *NWEA white paper on aggregating portfolio data*. Lake Oswego, OR: Northwest Evaluation Association.

Mitchell, R. (1992). *Testing for learning*. New York: The Free Press.

Moss, P., Beck, J. Ebbs, C., Matson, B., Muchmore, J., Steele, D., Taylor, C., & Herter, R. (1992). Portfolios, accountability and an interpretative approach to validity. *Educational Measurement: Issues and Practice*, *11*(3), 12–21.

Paulson, R., Paulson, P., & Meyer, C. (1991). What makes a portfolio a portfolio? *Educational Leadership*, *48*(5), 60–63.

Purves, A. (1993). Setting standards in the language arts and literature classroom and the implications for portfolio assessment. *Educational Assessment*, *1*(3), 175–200.

Simmons, J. (1990). Portfolios as large-scale assessment. *Language Arts*, *67*(3), 262–268.

Thomas, S., & Oldfather, P. (1997). Intrinsic motivations, literacy, and assessment practices: "That's my grade. That's me." *Educational Psychologist*, *32*(2), 107–123.

Valencia, S., & Calfee, R. (1991). The development and use of literacy portfolios for students. *Applied Measurement in Education*, *4*(3), 333–346.

Wiggins, G. (1990). Put portfolios to the test. *Instructor*, August, 48–53.

Wolf, D. (1987/1988, January). Opening up assessment. *Educational Leadership*, *45*(4), 24–29.

Wolf, D. (1989). Portfolio assessment: Sampling student work. *Educational Leadership*, *46*(7), 35–39.

Wolf, D., Bixby, J., Glenn, J., & Gardner, H. (1991). To use their minds well: Investigating new forms of student assessment. In G. Grant (Ed.), *Review of Research in Education*, Vol. 17 (pp. 32–73). Washington, DC: American Educational Research Association.

Part Three

Related Assessment Issues

Chapter 10

Measuring Affective Characteristics

Chapter 11

Assessing Special Needs

Chapter 12

Developing a Grading System

Chapter 13

Interpreting Norm-Referenced Tests

Chapter 14

Ethical and Legal Issues in Assessment

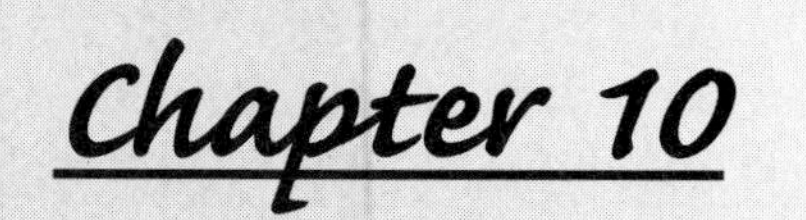

Chapter 10

Measuring

Affective Characteristics

Churchill (1940) recalls writing his name at the top of the page, then not being able to think of anything relevant. A blot and several ink smudges appeared from nowhere and for two entire hours he stared at the page. His pain was relieved only when the ushers collected the examination papers.

This incident describes perhaps the most famous anxiety attack on record (Covington, 1992). Winston Churchill, the courageous prime minister who led Great Britain through World War II, was not dyslexic, as some assumed. Instead, he suffered severe anxiety when faced with test-taking situations.

Anxiety is one of several affective characteristics found in the classroom. Others are attitudes, interests, and values. They are important in education because they are fairly stable characteristics and they influence students' reactions to school tasks and schooling in general, as well as interactions with others.

Major Topics

Overview

Affective characteristics consist of appreciations, attitudes, adjustments, interests, values, and attitudes about oneself, such as self-concept, self-esteem, and self-efficacy. Affective characteristics are unobservable internal characteristics and they may only be inferred from individuals' actions in situations or their responses to carefully designed structured or open-ended questions. Self-efficacy, for example, involves attitudes about one's capabilities to master particular situations (Bandura, 1986). Students with high self-efficacy typically set attainable goals for themselves, focus on task requirements, and persist in the face of difficulties. In contrast, students with low self-efficacy often set unrealistic goals, are easily distracted by concerns about immediate performance and other factors, and may give up entirely when faced with difficulties (Bandura, 1986).

Categories

Affective characteristics or qualities are constructs. That is, they are hypothesized characteristics that are indirectly related to observable behavior. For example, a student with a major interest in stamp collecting is more likely to attend a stamp auction than a student with an interest in baseball cards.

The domain of affective characteristics may be analyzed in several ways. Table 10-1 illustrates six categories of affective characteristics that are important in the classroom. Appreciations refer to the personal satisfaction following involvement in aesthetic activities, such as visiting an art museum, listening to great works of music, and so on. Appreciations have sometimes been stated as desirable outcomes of instruction, as indicated by courses such as art appreciation and music appreciation.

Adjustments. This category of affective characteristics refers to adaptive behavior and social-emotional development as reflected in students' responses to school rules, interpersonal relationships with peers and teachers, and personal responsibility. The present trend toward mainstreaming students with poor intellectual functioning into the regular classroom has increased the importance of obtaining information about adjustment problems. Specifically, students with learning disabilities or low intellectual functioning also may have poor work habits and/or have difficulties interacting in social situations. For example, a student may be impulsive and have difficulty in controlling his or her verbal outbursts in class (Hunt & Marshall, 1994).

Attitudes. Appreciations are particular reactions to aesthetic events or objects. In contrast, attitudes are relatively stable tendencies to approach or to avoid cer-

Table 10.1 Summary of Affective Characteristics

Affective category	Definitions	Example
Adjustments	The individual's social interactions and relationships to peers; also includes reactions to authority, criticism, and praise	Child does not initiate conversations with classmates; is either a spectator or on the periphery of playground activities.
Appreciations	Feelings of satisfaction and enjoyment in response to art, literature, music, and nature	Student expresses pleasure at the expression of motion and light in an exhibit of paintings by Degas; student purchases three prints at museum gift shop.
Attitudes	Dispositions that lead to actions toward or away from some class of objects, events, or persons (Gagné, 1985)	Student enrolls in elective science courses, collects and studies insects, and believes that some aspect of science would be an interesting career (positive attitude toward science).
Interests	Preferences for engaging in particular activities	Student, when given a choice, consistently goes camping instead of playing soccer and other sports.
Values	Personal standards in any of six areas: aesthetic, economic, political, religious, social, and theoretical (Rokeach, 1973)	Government has a responsibility to assist its weakest and most vulnerable citizens (social).
Self-attitudes	Feelings that address some aspect of the individual's self-worth (includes self-esteem, self-concept, and self-efficacy); may be positive or negative	Student attributes a low score on a test to lack of ability (low self-efficacy).

tain social objects, situations, and institutions. Examples are schooling, school subjects, and ethnic groups. Attitudes, however, are not simply preferences. Instead, they involve beliefs about the object or institution and perceptions as well as feelings.

The term "attitudes," however, is sometimes misapplied. For example, attitudes toward a subject area should not be confused with course satisfaction. Attitudes are "meanings or beliefs, not mere expressions of approval or disapproval" (Cronbach, 1963, p. 678). For example, a student's attitude for science includes his or her beliefs about the benefits that can be realized from various scientific endeavors, such as interplanetary exploration and genetic studies.

Another key aspect of attitudes toward a subject is the fit between the student's self-concept and his or her concept of the discipline. An example is the question, "What roles does science offer someone like me?" (Cronbach, 1963). Instruments developed to assess attitudes toward a subject also should address the potential match between the student's self-image and his or her view of the subject area.

Values. Rokeach (1973) defines a value as a standard that determines presentations of the self to others, judgments, and comparisons of the self with others. Values also guide actions and attitudes. As indicated in Table 10-1, the six types of values are aesthetic, economic, political, religious, social, and theoretical.

In the classroom, the social values of other cultures have become increasingly important as the diversity of students increases. As mentioned in Chapter 2, Erickson and Mohatt (1982) studied classroom interactions between Native American children and Caucasian teachers. The researchers noted that the classroom participation structures in which an adult (the teacher) functions as a "switchboard operator" to whom most talk is addressed and who allocates speaking turns is not present in the Native American culture. In the classroom situation, the Native American students engaged in much more situationally inappropriate behavior (silence, nervous giggling, and failure to answer questions) than other students (p. 140). Seating children at tables in groups, addressing the group rather than the individual child, reducing the time spent in whole-class lessons, and increasing the time spent with children in small groups are classroom practices that are congruent with the cultural etiquette (Erickson and Mohatt, 1982).

In another situation, Hawaiian teachers found that the reading comprehension scores of first-grade children increased significantly when they implemented the "talk-story" aspect of the native culture. Specifically, it is a participatory method of story telling in which more than one person, as well as members of the audience, contribute in overlapping turns (Au & Jordan, 1981).

These examples represent cultural values in which both adults and children share participatory roles in important communicative events. Classroom adjustments that are sensitive to such cultural values are referred to as "culturally congruent" or "culturally responsive" (Cazden & Leggett, 1981; Erickson & Mohatt, 1982; Ladson-Billings, 1995).

Interests. Preferences for engaging in particular activities are referred to as interests. They differ from attitudes in that the target of an attitude is a social object or an institution. The target of an interest, in contrast, is some activity.

Knowledge of student interests assists the teacher in two ways. One is in the selection of materials that are appealing to students. The other is in developing or selecting activities that may be used to reinforce positive changes in student behavior.

Self-attitudes. Beliefs and feelings about oneself are important in classroom learning. Included are self-concept, self-esteem, and self-efficacy. Briefly, self-concept is the general image that one has about her or himself, and self-esteem is the extent of confidence and satisfaction in oneself. Self-esteem and self-concept begin to develop in early childhood, are formed over several years, are highly stable, and influence students' achievement-related actions (Bandura, 1986).

Self-efficacy for school subjects, however, is a somewhat different matter. Research indicates that most kindergarten and first-grade children hold high perceptions of their ability and high expectancies of success (Dweck, 1989; Stipek, 1981; Wigfield, 1988). By the second or third grade, however, the view that success can come with effort begins to decline, and both confidence and expectancies for success are also likely to decline under failure (Dweck, 1989; Nicholls, 1978; Ruble & Rhales, 1981).

Self-concept, self-esteem, and self-efficacy are important in the classroom because they influence the student's willingness to undertake academic tasks. They also influence the student's willingness to take risks in academic and social situations. Low self-concept, also referred to as "failure syndrome," is observed in half-hearted attempts at school tasks and giving up at the first sign of difficulty (Brophy, 1996).

Common features. The six categories of affective characteristics listed in Table 10-1 share several major features. First, like knowledge and cognitive skills, they are learned. That is, they are the products of one's experiences with objects and events and interactions with others. For example, a child whose parents enjoy music and art, and who has had positive experiences in relation to them, is likely to develop an appreciation for contributions in these areas. In contrast, the child who is forced to take piano lessons and to practice daily may learn to play and also learn to dislike music.

Second, also like cognitive knowledge, affective characteristics are influenced by beliefs and perceptions. For example, a student is unlikely to have a positive attitude toward mathematics if he or she believes only "nerds" do mathematics.

In addition, affective characteristics include an emotional component, are fairly stable over time, and are oriented toward a positive or negative direction. For example, test anxiety includes feelings of discouragement and an unfavorable (negative) view of tests.

✦ Measurement in the School Setting

Affective instruments include (1) rating scales and inventories of student interests and (2) rating scales that address constructs such as appreciations, self-concept, and self-efficacy. As discussed in this chapter, teachers may construct instruments to assess student interests in potential activities or topics in the curriculum.

However, valid and reliable measures of personal and social characteristics are difficult to construct and this task should not be attempted by novices. Moreover, measures of social adjustments and other personal characteristics or feelings of students should only be initiated by a qualified licensed professional after the parent provides written informed consent. As discussed in this chapter, however, the teacher may be asked by the school psychologist on occasion to complete a behavior rating scale on a student.

A Comparison of Observational and Affective Scales

Chapter 7 describes primary trait scales that measure the essential characteristics of student performances and products. The teacher or other rater records the extent to which a feature is present while observing the students' performance or reviewing the essay, report, or other product.

Scales to measure attitudes, adjustments, appreciations, or self-attitudes typically use the same format. That is, a set of descriptors on a continuum (Likert format) accompanies each statement that represents the particular characteristic or behavior.

The measurement of affective characteristics differs from observational ratings in five ways. First, affective ratings include feelings. Second, when the respondent is completing the instrument about her- or himself, the ratings often include the perceptions or beliefs of the respondent (see Table 10-2). In contrast, observational ratings do not address feelings and they should be constructed, as much as possible, to avoid the influence of the observer's beliefs, attitudes, or global perceptions.

Third, the extent of agreement with a statement or the importance of a characteristic is often the focus of an affective scale. For example, an instrument on teacher beliefs may include an item on the importance of homework. Observational scales, however, focus on documenting the occurrence of a particular observable feature, such as uses context clues to decipher word meaning or the proficiency level of an observed capability.

Fourth, ratings of student performances and products are completed by teachers or others. Affective measures, in contrast, may be completed about oneself. Self-attitudes or beliefs in oneself are examples. When an instrument is developed

Table 10.2 Characteristics of Affective Ratings

Characteristics	Example
1. Components may include feelings.	1. When art class is canceled, I feel (a) very sad, (b) sad, (c) happy, (d) very happy.
2. Evaluations often include perceptions or beliefs.	2. Work in English class helps students in other classes.
3. Options often address extent of agreement or importance of the characteristic.	3. Options typically range from "strongly agree" to "strongly disagree" or "very important" to "very unimportant."
4. Respondent may be either oneself or someone else.	4. Students are asked to rate how well they can complete activities that are important in successful learning such as "finish assignments by deadlines."
5. Validity and reliability are often difficult to establish.	5. On self-report scales, individuals may respond in ways they believe are socially desirable.

as a self-report measure, the individual serves as both the observer and the object of the observation (Newfield, 1990, p. 146). Table 10-3 illustrates sample items from a 24-item scale to measure students' beliefs about how well they organize and manage their own learning.

Finally, the validity and reliability of affective scales are often difficult to establish. For example, one problem with self-report scales is that individuals may provide answers they believe the researcher or other evaluator is seeking or they may respond in ways that appear to them to be socially desirable or important. Social desirability tends to increase when the instrument includes very personal questions and when the information is to be used for selection of individuals for a job, a promotion, or entry into a school program (Anderson, 1981). Validity also is jeopardized by vague descriptors that require interpretation by the respondents, complex sentences that are difficult to understand, and a lack of relationship between the items on the instrument and the affective characteristics being measured.

Validity evidence provided by commercial publishers should include data on the constructs measured by a particular instrument. Researchers implement scale items with large samples and apply statistical methods to determine the particular constructs measured by the items. For example, preliminary data on the 24-item scale illustrated in Table 10-3 indicate that it assesses general organizational

Table 10-3 Examples of items from a scale to assess students' perceptions of their self-regulatory activities during learning

1. I turn off the TV/radio so I can concentrate on what I am doing.

1	2	3	4	5
Not at all		Some of the time		Very often

2. I paraphrase written information when I am studying.

1	2	3	4	5
Not at all		Some of the time		Very often

3. Before beginning a project, I get as much information as possible.

1	2	3	4	5
Not at all		Some of the time		Very often

4. If I have problems with assignments, I ask a teacher to help.

1	2	3	4	5
Not at all		Some of the time		Very often

Source: Adapted from Gredler and Schwartz (1997) based on categories of strategies identified by Zimmerman and Martinez-Pons (1986).

and planning strategies, task preparation strategies, and environmental restructuring (steps to ensure a quiet study environment) (Gredler & Schwartz, 1997). Reliability typically is determined by a statistical formula that addresses internal consistency.

The Role of Behavior Rating Scales

On occasion, a child may be having difficulties in the classroom that seem to stem from cognitive or emotional problems. The teacher or parent who notices the child's difficulties typically contacts the school counselor or school psychologist who gathers various types of information to diagnose the problem.

The information that is collected includes some type of behavior rating scale or social adjustment scale that is completed by the teacher. Some scales, such as those that address depression, also have a form that is completed by the parent.

Adjustment scales document student behaviors in several categories, such as coping with school work, games and play, relationships with other students, and other behaviors. Such instruments also are developed from a conceptual framework and undergo extensive tryout and analysis to verify the constructs that are measured.

When the scale is completed, the school psychologist plots the student's profile from the responses. This information is combined with information from the student's cumulative record and other sources. Included are descriptions of the general environments where problems occur and where they are absent and expectations in problem and nonproblem environments (Edwards & Simpson, 1996, p. 263). Data from these varied sources contribute to a diagnosis of the student's problem by a qualified professional.

The items in Table 10-3 also illustrate the inferential nature of affective scales. That is, although based on observations, affective scales involve judgments. Hunt & Marshall (1994) note that different teacher expectations of acceptable classroom behavior and the teacher's level of experience with the child can influence ratings on behavioral scales. For example, the teacher who expects every child to sit quietly in his or her seat is likely to consider walking around the classroom to be abnormal. In a class characterized by several groups using a variety of materials and resources around the room, such behavior would be considered acceptable.

The Executive Committee of the Council for Children with Disabilities (1989) suggests several practices to reduce personal bias and the influence of situational factors in the use of behavioral rating scales. Included are observations in several different settings, completion of the scale by several different individuals, collection of the information over a period of time, and consideration of predisposing factors, such as cultural differences.

Assessment of Student Interests

Teachers can construct instruments that assess student interest in various activities in a course or subject area. The purpose of such an assessment is (1) to identify individual children's preferences that may be used to reinforce appropriate behaviors in the classroom and (2) to plan subsequent classroom activities. Of importance in administering the instrument is stressing to the pupils the importance of the information to the teacher for planning. Equally important is for the teacher to use the information in planning classroom activities.

Either of two types of instruments may be constructed. One is an interest scale on which students indicate the degree of preference for each in-use or planned activity. Table 10-4 is an example of a partial scale appropriate for elementary school students.

The other type is an inventory that is a forced-choice instrument. That is, the student is required to assign listed activities to particular categories, such as most

Table 10.4 A Partial Classroom Interest Scale for Activities

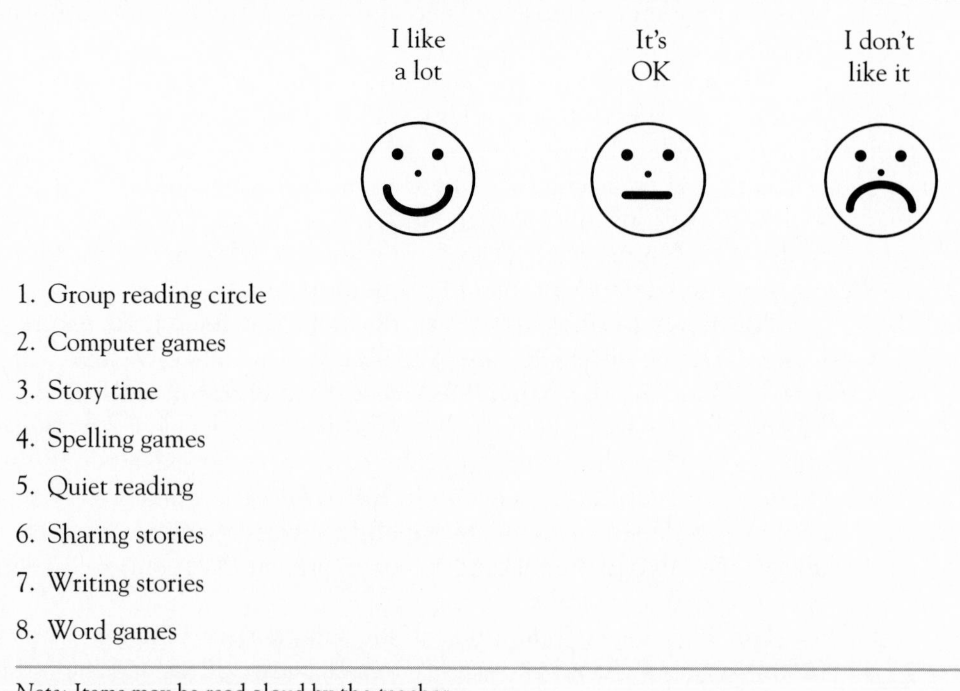

	I like a lot	It's OK	I don't like it
1. Group reading circle			
2. Computer games			
3. Story time			
4. Spelling games			
5. Quiet reading			
6. Sharing stories			
7. Writing stories			
8. Word games			

Note: Items may be read aloud by the teacher.

or least preferred or like or dislike. A disadvantage of an inventory is that a student may have no strong feelings about an activity or set of activities, but is required to choose a category.

A well-known published inventory for grades 6 to 12 is the Kuder General Interest Inventory. The instrument groups activities in sets of 3. The student must choose which of the 3 is his or her most liked activity and which is the least liked activity. This format is referred to as forced choice; if all three activities are enjoyable for the student, he or she must choose a most and least preferred.

Two published inventories that address occupational interests are the Kuder Occupational Interest Survey and the Strong-Campbell Interest Inventory. They are designed for the high school years and beyond. Of importance in administering such instruments in the school setting, however, is that interest should not be confused with ability. Also, the instability of student interests through high school indicates that interest inventories should be implemented with caution.

In the classroom, the teacher can easily construct an interest inventory for possible topics or activities considered for implementation. A listing of the items is

Table 10.5 Partial Interest Inventory for Science Topics

Directions: For each topic, circle L for *like* and D for *dislike*.

Topic		
1. Sharks	L	D
2. Coral reefs	L	D
3. Butterflies	L	D
4. Space flight	L	D
5. Dinosaurs	L	D
6. Diamonds and rubies	L	D
7. Whales	L	D
8. Jet airplanes	L	D
9. Songbirds	L	D
10. Rockets	L	D

prepared, accompanied by the two response options L (like) and D (dislike). Table 10-5 is an example.

Classroom Assessment Methods to Avoid

Some texts suggest that teachers can obtain useful information about student characteristics such as concern for others and leadership ability from methods referred to as peer appraisals. Two such methods, which are referred to as nomination methods, are the Guess-Who technique and the sociometric approach. In the Guess-Who technique, students are provided with a set of statements, such as "someone who enjoys playing and working with others" and "someone who is willing to share materials with others." Students may nominate as few or as many students as they wish.

At least four problems are associated with this method. First, it assumes that students will make valid and reliable judgments; however, their selections will be strongly influenced by their friendships. Second, some students who have the identified characteristics will not be nominated because they are quiet or shy and/or are not known well. Therefore, the information obtained from the questionnaire is incomplete. Third, a very serious problem is that students, despite admonitions to the contrary, will discuss their choices with others. A few students are likely to tease others about why they did not name them, and hurt feelings are the result. Fourth, assessments, particularly affective assessments, must have a clear and necessary purpose. A rationale for the teacher's need to obtain such information in this way is difficult, at best, to establish.

The sociometric approach first asks each student to name up to four students with whom they would like to work on a planned small-group activity. Essential requirements of this approach are for the teacher to follow through by scheduling such an activity and to honor some of the student's choices of work partners. The data provided by the students are then tabulated by recording the number of nominations received by each student. A diagram referred to as a sociogram may also be constructed with arrows from each student making selections to each of his or her nominees. The students who receive the most nominations are the most popular, and the diagram theoretically indicates the social structure of the class at a particular point in time.

The problems identified for the Guess-Who technique are also the same for the sociometric approach. In addition, the possibilities for hurt feelings by not being nominated by someone whom a student believes was a friend are greater with this approach because the selections are those a student wants to be with.

Summary

Affective characteristics are hypothesized constructs that are indirectly related to behavior. Affective characteristics are both internal and unobservable. Thus, they must be inferred from individuals' reactions in situations or their responses to carefully constructed questions.

Six types of affective characteristics are appreciations, attitudes, adjustments, interests, values, and attitudes about oneself, such as self-concept and self-esteem. Adjustments involve social relationships and social interactions; appreciations consist of feelings of enjoyment or satisfaction in response to aesthetic activities. Attitudes, in contrast, are dispositions to approach or to avoid some class of objects, events, or persons. Related to attitudes are interests, which are preferences for certain activities. Values are one's personal standards, whereas self-attitudes consist of feelings about some aspect of oneself. The common features of affective characteristics are that they are learned, are influenced by beliefs and perceptions, include an emotional component, and are oriented in a positive or negative direction.

Teachers may be involved in the implementation of affective instruments in two ways. One is the completion of behavioral rating scales at the request of the school psychologist for any students referred for cognitive or emotional difficulties. Methods to reduce the influence of extraneous factors on the ratings include observations in different settings by different individuals, collection of data over time, and consideration of predisposing factors.

Second, teachers can construct scales or inventories to assess student interest in course activities. In contrast to an interest scale in which respondents indicate the extent of interest in each activity, inventories are forced-choice instruments. The respondent assigns each activity to a particular category.

Some texts suggest peer appraisals as devices for teachers to obtain information about student characteristics, such as concern for others. However, they should not be used because of at least four problems: (1) the data are of questionable validity and reliability, (2) the nominations are likely to omit qualified students, (3) use is likely to generate some hard feelings, and (4) need for the information is difficult to establish.

Chapter Questions

1. Assume that you are a member of a research team to develop a scale to assess math anxiety. What are some of the statements that might be used to represent math anxiety on the instrument? What are some of the problems with these statements?

2. This chapter discusses problems with the Guess-Who technique in identifying children with certain qualities, such as sharing and leadership. Reflecting on prior chapters in this text, what are some other ways to obtain this type of information?

3. A national fast-food chain uses a self-report scale on personal characteristics as part of the screening process for potential hires. Discuss the problems with this procedure.

4. What are the differences between interests and appreciations? How are they similar?

5. An affective scale on self-concept asks students to express agreement or disagreement with statements such as "I feel uncomfortable in complex situations." What are some of the problems with this statement?

References

Anderson, L. W. (1981). *Assessing affective characteristics in the schools*. Boston: Allyn & Bacon.

Au, K., & Jordan, C. (1981). Teaching reading to Hawaiian children: Finding a culturally appropriate solution. In H. Trueba, G. Guthrie, & K. Au (Eds.), *Culture and the bilingual classroom: Studies in classroom ethnography* (pp. 139–152). Rowley, MA: Newbury.

Bandura, A. (1986). *Social foundations of thought and action: A social-cognitive theory*. Englewood Cliffs, NJ: Prentice Hall.

Brophy, J. (1996). *Teaching problem students*. New York: Guilford Press.

Cazden, C., & Leggett, E. (1981). Culturally responsive education: Recommendations for achieving low remedies II. In H. Trueba, G. Guthrie, & K. Au (Eds.), *Culture and the bilingual classroom: Studies in classroom ethnography* (pp. 69–86). Rowley, MA: Newbury.

Churchill, W. S. (1940, June 18). *Hansard Parliamentary Debates* (Commons), Vol. 362, cols. 51–61.

Covington, M. V. (1992). *Making the grade: A self-worth perspective on motivation and school reform*. New York: Cambridge University Press.

Cronbach, L. J. (1963). Course improvement through evaluation. *Teachers College Record* 64(8), 672–683.

Dweck, C. (1989). Motivation. In R. Glasser & A. Lesgold (Eds.), *The handbook of psychology and education. Vol. 1* (pp. 187–229). Hillsdale, NJ: Erlbaum.

Edwards, L., & Simpson, J. (1996). Children with behavior disorders. In E. L. Meyen (Ed.), *Exceptional children in today's schools* (3rd ed.; pp. 251–279). Denver: Love Publishing.

Erickson, F., & Mohatt, G. (1982). Cultural organization of participation structures in two classrooms of Indian students. In G. Spindler (Ed.), *Doing the ethnography of schooling* (pp. 132–175). New York: Holt, Rinehart, & Winston.

Executive Committee of the Council for Children with Behavioral Disorders (1989). White paper on best assessment practices for students with behavioral disorders: Accommodation to cultural diversity and in individual differences. *Behavioral Disorders, 14*, 263–278.

Gagné, R. (1985). *The conditions of learning* (4th ed.). New York: Holt, Rinehart, & Winston.

Gredler, M., & Schwartz, L. (1997). Factor analysis of a self-efficacy for self-regulation scale. *Psychological Reports, 81*, 51–57.

Hunt, N., & Marshall, K. (1994). *Exceptional children and youth*. Boston: Houghton Mifflin.

Ladson-Billings, G. (1995). Toward a theory of culturally relevant pedagogy. *American Educational Research Journal, 32*(3), 465–492.

Newfield, J. W. (1990). Self-report. In H. J. Walberg & G. D. Haertel (Eds.), *The international encyclopedia of educational evaluation* (pp. 146–147). Oxford: Pergamon Press.

Nicholls, J. D. (1978). The development of the concept of effort and ability, perception of academic attainment, and the understanding that difficult tasks require more ability. *Child Development, 49*(3), 800–849.

Rokeach, M. (1973). *The nature of human values*. New York: The Free Press.

Ruble, D. N., & Rhales, W. S. (1981). The development of children's perceptions and attributions about their social world. In J. Harvey, W. Iches, & R. Kidd (Eds.), *New directions in attribution research* (Vol. 3, pp. 3–26). Hillsdale, NJ: Erlbaum.

Stipek, D. J. (1981). Children's perceptions of their own and their classmates' ability. *Journal of Educational Psychology, 73*(3), 404–410.

Wigfield, A. (1988). Children's attributions for success and failure: Effects of age and attentional focus. *Journal of Educational Psychology, 80*(1), 76–81.

Zimmerman, B. J., & Martinez-Pons, M. (1986). Development of a structured interview for assessing student use of self-regulated learning strategies. *American Educational Research Journal, 23*(4), 614–628.

Chapter 11

Assessing Special Needs

Major Topics

Types of Special Needs

The Assessment and Placement Process

Legal Guidelines for Identification

Developing the IEP

Assessment Methods

Standardized Instruments

Classroom Assessments

> *"This legislation covers all handicapped children without regard to where they live or which agency serves them. . . . There is no real escape for state and local agencies. The legislation seals all the cracks in services and carries out policies of zero rejection and nondiscrimination."*
>
> —Turnbull, 1986, p. 20

Prior to the 1970s, special education services were not mandated by either the states or the federal government. As a result, only about half of the children in the United States with disabilities were enrolled in school programs (Turnbull, 1986). This uneven delivery of service was one factor that precipitated federal legislation in the mid-1970s.

Another factor was the concern in the 1960s and early 1970s about the misuse of intelligence tests (Gredler, 1988). One purpose of the federal legislation was to help control the flow of misclassified children into classes for the mentally retarded (p. 58).

With the enactment of Public Law (PL) 94-142, referred to as the Education of the Handicapped Act (EHA), the federal government mandated significant requirements for the education of children with special needs. In addition to other requirements, the legislation specified the procedures to guard against inappropriate assessments and identified the components of an Individual Educational Plan (IEP) to be developed for each student. In addition, the legislation stipulated that, when possible, children with disabilities were to be educated with children who do not have disabilities (Meyen, 1996b, p. 64). That is, placement in a regular school class is preferable to placement in a special public school class and that placement is preferable to placement in any other training or program.

In 1990, PL 94-142 was amended and renamed the Individuals with Disabilities Education Act (IDEA), and updated again in 1997. This legislation redefined and clarified some terms and expanded early education services for 3- to 5-year-olds (Meyen, 1996b).

At present, most students identified as eligible for special services receive some instruction from regular class teachers and an increasing number are integrated fully into regular class settings (Meyen, 1996a, p. 16). The responsibilities of the regular classroom teacher concerning students with disabilities include (1) completing behavior rating scales and providing other information relevant to the initial evaluation of the student, (2) serving as a member of the multidisciplinary team that develops the student's individualized program (the IEP), and (3) evaluating student progress during the year on the short-term objectives in the IEP.

✦ Types of Special Needs

Special needs refers to a variety of intellectual, social, and physical characteristics that impact the child's potential for learning. At one extreme is the category referred to as gifted and talented. Other individual characteristics, however, contribute to student difficulties in learning. They range from limitations in mental functioning to physical disabilities, such as hearing impairment.

Several categories of special needs are defined by PL 94-142 (IDEA) and are earmarked for special services. Categories of particular importance for the public school system are mental retardation, learning disabilities, emotional and behavioral disorders, deafness or hearing impairment, and visual impairment. Giftedness is defined in PL 97-35 (see Table 11-1).

Mental Retardation

The dual criteria for classification as mentally retarded are (1) significantly subaverage intellectual functioning and (2) limitations in two or more areas of adaptive skill. They are self-care, home living, social skills, community use,

Table 11.1 Summary of Six Categories of Special Needs Identified in Federal Legislation

Category	Description	Characteristics
Mental Retardation[a]	Substantial limitations in functioning indicated by (1) subaverage intellectual functioning and (2) related limitations in adaptive skills, such as social skills. Ranges from mild to profound.	1. Difficulty in and maintaining attention 2. Difficulty in processing 3. Poor retention 4. Difficulty transferring skills to new formats
Learning Disabilities[b]	A disorder in one or more of the basic processes in understanding or using language that may result in problems with listening, thinking, reading, writing, spelling, or mathematical calculations. Evidenced by a severe discrepancy between achievement and intellectual ability. Excludes learning problems that primarily result from other factors.	1. Difficulty in receiving or expressing information 2. May reverse letters, words, or numbers 3. Poor attention and organizational skills
Emotional or Behavioral Disorder[a,b]	A long-standing serious condition characterized by an inability to maintain satisfactory interpersonal relationships, inappropriate behaviors or feelings under normal circumstances, a general, pervasive unhappiness or depression and physical symptoms or fears associated with personal or school problems.	1. Exhibits one of two broad sets of behaviors: (a) aggressive, acting-out behavior or (b) immature, withdrawn behavior 2. Deficient in academic skills
Hearing Impairment	A reliance on vision to understand language and the world. Hard of hearing usually allows speech understanding through hearing aids (Hunt & Marshall, 1994).	1. Lags behind peers in speech and English skills 2. Often must be taught subtle social mores and attitudes
Visual Impairment[a]	A visual handicap that even when corrected, negatively affects educational performance (Silberman, 1996).	1. Must rely on hearing and touch to experience the environment 2. Can only perceive what is reachable at arm's length 3. Difficulty in developing some concepts, such as colors
Giftedness	High-performance capability in areas such as intellectual, creative artistic, leadership, or specific academic fields; requires activities not typically provided by the school to develop capabilities (PL 97-35).	1. Early ability to manipulate symbols 2. Unusual ability to recall facts 3. Rapid acquisition of information on a range of topics (Parke, 1989) 4. Unbridled curiosity to explore new ideas

[a]The term originally used when PL 94-142 was enacted was "seriously emotionally disturbed." Currently viewed as inappropriate, the current term proposed by the National Mental Health and Special Education Coalition is "emotional or behavioral disorder" (Forness & Knitzer, 1992).

[b]Summarized from PL 94-142, *Federal Register* (1977).

self-direction, health and safety, functional academics, leisure, and work (PL 94-142 [IDEA]). These criteria are consistent with three types of intelligence identified by the American Association of Mental Retardation (AAMR). Conceptual intelligence refers to the capabilities addressed in IQ tests. Practical intelligence includes the activities required to maintain oneself independently in daily living. In contrast, social intelligence refers to the ability to understand social expectations and the behavior of others and to make appropriate decisions about one's own conduct in social situations (AAMR Ad Hoc Committee on Terminology and Classification, 1992, p. 15).

The degrees of mental retardation identified in the legislation are mild, moderate, severe, and profound. Individuals with mild mental retardation may require support services in order to graduate from high school and obtain appropriate job training, whereas moderately retarded individuals require support services and often supervision to live and work in semi-independent or independent community settings (Brown & Hoshida, 1996). Extensive educational services are required for severe or profound mental retardation.

Most individuals identified as retarded are classified as mildly retarded and typically are not diagnosed until they enter school and have difficulties with school work (Hallahan and Kauffman, 1994). Individuals with mental retardation vary in their psychological and social characteristics. Many have difficulty in attending to key information in tasks and remembering information, have delayed language development, and experience difficulties in social interactions.

Learning Disabilities

The category of learning disabilities refers to individuals with fairly normal intelligence who have severe learning problems. Federal legislation defines a specific learning disability as a disorder in one or more of the basic psychological processes involved in understanding or using language (spoken or written). Included are an imperfect ability to listen, think, speak, read, write, spell, or perform mathematical calculations (*Federal Register*, 1977). Listed in PL 94-142 (IDEA) are conditions such as dyslexia (learning disability in reading), perceptual disabilities, brain injury, and minimal brain dysfunction. Further, PL 94-142 (IDEA) specifies that the child's learning problems are not the result of (1) other disabling conditions, such as physical disabilities, emotional retardation, or emotional disturbance; or (2) environmental, cultural, or economic disadvantage. Congress did not intend that funds dispensed under PL 94-142 should be targeted to students whose learning problems derive from a disadvantaged home, poor teaching, or a lack of motivation to learn (Jacob-Timm & Hartshorne, 1994).

The basis for determining a learning disability is a severe discrepancy between the child's achievement and intellectual ability in one or more of seven areas: oral, listening, and written expression; basic reading skill; reading comprehension; and mathematical calculations or reasoning (*Federal Register*, 1977). Standardized intelligence and achievement tests as well as assessments in other areas are used for determining eligibility.

The disorders referred to as attention-deficit disorder (ADD) and attention deficit hyperactivity disorder (ADHD) are not specifically named in PL 94-142 (IDEA). However, a memorandum from the Department of Education in 1991 specified that students may be eligible for services under the learning disabilities, emotional disturbance, or other categories, (Jacob-Timm & Hartshorne, 1994).

Students identified as having learning disabilities are the largest group, over 2 million (45 percent) of those identified with handicaps to learning (U.S. Department of Education, 1991). Most of the students classified as learning disabled have difficulties in processing letters and symbols in print text. Many also are unable to produce legible handwriting and some have serious problems with mathematics.

Emotional or Behavioral Disorder

A large percentage of children have isolated instances of behavior problems, but they do not have a behavior disorder. Formerly referred to as "emotional disturbance" in the federal legislation, emotional or behavioral disorder may be characterized by any of several behaviors that occur over a long period of time to a marked degree and which affect educational performance. Included are aggressive or acting-out behaviors (e.g., disobedience, tantrums, and destructiveness of property), immature or withdrawn behavior, chronic fearfulness, and sadness or depression (Edwards & Simpson, 1996, p. 258).

Factors that determine an emotional or behavioral disorder include frequency, intensity, duration, and age-appropriateness of the behaviors (Hunt & Marshall, 1994). For example, continuous activity and exploration are typical of 2-year-olds, but not of sixth graders (McLoughlin & Lewis, 1994, p. 248). Instructional programs focus on teaching students new behaviors as well as to monitor and evaluate their behavior.

Hearing and Visual Impairments

The most pervasive effect of hearing loss is on language development (Mayer, 1996). Although individuals who are deaf or hard of hearing as a group have normal intellectual abilities, their academic achievement tends to lag 1 to 3 years behind their hearing peers (Hunt & Marshall, 1994, p. 356). The problem lies with their lack of mastery of the English language.

As indicated in Table 11-1, visual impairment refers to the condition in which the individual's educational performance is affected, even with correction.

Depending on the extent of the disability, students may require large-print materials and felt pens or materials in Braille if the student is blind. Students also may have difficulty developing some concepts, such as colors. A low incidence disability, approximately one student in a thousand is visually impaired and receives special services (Silberman, 1996, p. 353).

Giftedness

Although definitions of gifted and talented vary, children who are gifted demonstrate advanced development, such as reading at an early age, unusual ability to recall facts, rapid acquisition of information, and excelling in mathematical and verbal reasoning and learning complex concepts rapidly. Early studies implemented a score of 140+ on the Stanford-Binet Scale as the criterion for advanced development. Currently, some schools use scores of 130 to 135 to classify students as academically gifted. Some schools also use the criterion of the 95th percentile on standardized achievement tests.

Unlike other categories of special needs, federal legislation does not require educational services for gifted students. Although more than half the states stipulate special provisions for gifted and talented students, services vary from state to state. Options include enrichment, content area acceleration, "telescoping" the curriculum into a shorter time frame, and independent study.

Low Achievement (Slow Learners)

The term "slow learner" refers to the students with low I.Q. scores, although the scores are in the normal range. These students do not have specific learning disabilities that can be diagnosed by present methods. Thus, they are not eligible for special education services. However, low achievers have difficulty in following directions and completing work. Also, although many slow learners can decode words fairly well, they cannot read with enough efficiency to understand and remember the material (Brophy 1996, p. 65).

These students often are in need of a modified curriculum and individualized attention. Included are reading task directions aloud for the students and text materials with less difficult vocabulary.

Summary

The passage of PL 94-142, later renamed IDEA, mandated public educational services for students with special needs and prescribed policies for their delivery. The classroom teacher can expect to provide information during the initial evaluation of the student, serve as a member of the team that plans the student's program, and evaluate student progress during the year on the short-term objectives established for the student.

Federal legislation mandates services for several categories of special needs. Among them are emotional or mental retardation, learning disabilities, behavior disorders, and hearing and visual impairments. Mental retardation is defined as subaverage intellectual functioning and limitation in adaptive skills. In contrast, learning disabled students are achieving in school significantly below their level of intellectual functioning, and the basis for the poor achievement is typically some problem in processing capabilities. The majority of learning disabled students have difficulty with reading and others have difficulty with mathematical calculations.

Students with serious enduring behavior problems are classified as having an emotional or behavior disorder. Examples are children who are either aggressive and acting out or exhibit immature, withdrawn behavior.

Impairment in vision or hearing also impacts learning. Children who suffer hearing loss lag behind their peers in language development. However, as a group, they have normal intellectual abilities. Visually impaired children, in contrast, do not generally have delayed language development, but may have difficulty in developing some concepts, such as colors.

Although giftedness is defined in PL 97-35, the legislation does not mandate special services for these students. Gifted children exhibit advanced development, such as reading at an early age, unusual ability to recall facts, rapid acquisition of information, and excelling in verbal mathematical reasoning.

In addition to these categories, another type of academic problem in the classroom is low achievement. These students have I.Q. scores that are low, but are in the normal range. Low achievers have difficulty following directions, are usually poor readers, and have low retention.

✦ The Assessment and Placement Process

The process that is used to determine if a student is eligible for special services is governed by federal and state laws. The purpose of certifying that a student is deficient in cognitive functioning or has a disability that impedes learning is to permit the allocations of funds, resources, and personnel (McLoughlin & Lewis, 1994, p. 27). Guidelines for the assessment of the student and the development of the student's individualized program, the IEP, are major components of PL 94-142.

Legal Guidelines

When teacher efforts to remediate the difficulties of a student suspected of intellectual or learning disabilities are not successful, the student is referred to the school psychologist for assessment. Table 11-2 summarizes the requirements for the assessment that are stipulated by PL 94-142 (IDEA).

Table 11.2 Legal Guidelines for the Assessment of Students with Special Needs

Requirement	Example
Assessment should be	
1. protective of the rights of students with disabilities and their parents	School psychologist obtains written consent from the parent prior to assessment.
2. (a) technically adequate	(a) School psychologist ensures instruments are valid and reliable.
(b) administered by trained professionals	(b) School psychologist administers individual I.Q. tests; an audiologist measures hearing capabilities.
3. nondiscriminatory:	
(a) free of racial and cultural bias	A test administered to Laotian children should not include questions on U.S. colonial history.
(b) administered in the student's primary language	For a Spanish-speaking student, administer the Spanish version of the WISC intelligence test (Escala de Inteligencia Wechsler para niños—Revisada de Puerto Rico).
(c) assessment must not discriminate on the basis of the disability	A test of spelling should not require a student with impaired motor skills to write his or her answers.
4. (a) comprehensive	(a) A student referred for serious academic difficulties is evaluated with an individual I.Q. test, a standardized achievement test, a social-adjustment scale and parent and teacher interviews, and relevant processing measures.
(b) multidisciplinary	(b) The school psychologist, the regular teacher, and others contribute to the evaluation.
5. focused on student needs	The Woodcock-Johnson Psychoeducational Battery measures letter identification, oral reading, word meaning, and comprehension.

In addition to the technical adequacy of the instruments selected for the assessments, the federal legislation specifically forbids three types of discrimination. First, the instruments must be free of racial and cultural bias. Second, they must be conducted in the student's native language whenever possible. The largest number of students whose primary language is not English speak Spanish. For this group, Spanish versions of several well-known tests are available (McLoughlin & Lewis, 1994). Also important is to test deaf students who communicate using sign language in sign language.

Third, the assessment must bypass the student's disability. In assessing the intelligence of deaf students, for example, the performance scale of the Wechsler Intelligence Scale for Children–Third Edition (WISC–III) is appropriate because it does not depend on the student's verbal ability.

Finally, the assessment must be comprehensive, focused on student needs, and involve the school psychologist, the special education teacher, other specialists as needed, and the regular classroom teacher. That is, simply administering a single assessment and determining if the student's score is below a designated cut-off score does not provide sufficient information for instructional planning. Information about the extent to which the student can meet the nonacademic requirements of the classroom, that is, social adjustment skills and his or her specific academic strengths and weaknesses, is needed. As discussed in Chapter 10, the regular classroom teacher may be asked to complete a behavioral rating scale on the student. When the assessment is completed, the information is used by a multidisciplinary team to plan the student's instructional program.

Developing the IEP

The basis for the student's special education is the IEP. This document is a written commitment of the resources essential for the student's needs. A review of IEP rulings from agencies and courts by Bateman (1992) indicates that the IEP must be individualized and address all of the child's needs (not simply academic needs), and the availability of services may not be a consideration in developing the IEP. If services are not available in the district, they must be provided by another agency.

The IEP is planned by a team of individuals in a meeting for that purpose. Team membership for the first IEP meeting, specified by PL 94-142, must include the student's teacher, one or both parents (or surrogate guardian), a supervisory representative of the agency (such as the principal), and evaluation personnel (Bateman, 1992).

Table 11.3 Components of the IEP Specified in PL 94-142

Description of student's current level of performance

Annual goals

Short-term instructional objectives

Extent of participation in the regular classroom and extent of special education and related services

Duration of services (usually 1 year)

Evaluation procedures and schedules to determine, at least on an annual basis, whether the short-term objectives are being achieved

Source: Summarized from *Federal Register* (1977, August). Sec. 12a.346, Content of Individualized Education Programs. Washington, DC: U.S. Government Printing Office.

IEP components also specified in PL 94-142 (IDEA) are listed in Table 11-3. Information on the student's current performance level should address the student's unique needs that special services are to address and should be stated in concrete terms. An example is that Bobby (a third grader) reads second-grade material at the rate of 20 to 30 words per minute with five to eight errors and comprehends very little (Bateman, 1992).

The goals and objectives, based on the student's present performance levels, strengths, weaknesses, and unique learning needs, serve two purposes. They are to provide information about the appropriateness of the special services selected for the student, and to determine the student's progress (Bateman, 1992). In addition to academic areas, the goals may address social adjustment, personal responsibility, and vocational needs.

The IEP goals should not be vague or uninterpretable. For example, a statement that Alice will improve her choice of leisure time activities is inadequate. A more appropriate statement is that Alice will participate in a supervised extracurricular activity that meets regularly (Bateman, 1992).

The short-term objectives bridge the gap between the student's current performance levels and the annual goals. That is, they are teachable subcomponents of the goals and they describe specific, observable, and measurable activities (*Federal Register*, 1981). Examples are (1) construct a well-organized paragraph of six complete sentences with 0 to 2 grammatical errors and (2) read paragraphs at the third-grade level at 80 to 100 words per minute with 0 to 2 errors (Bateman, 1992, p. 36).

Bateman (1992) cautions against writing "empty" IEPs, "that rely on goals and objectives with percentages as performance levels." An example is "Sharon will have acceptable behavior 80% of the time" (p. 48). In other words, this goal allows behavior that is unacceptable 20 percent of the time. Instead of relying on percentages, Bateman (1992) suggests identifying error rates and other concrete statements of performance levels as in the examples in the prior paragraph.

When the goals and objectives are established, the team then determines (1) the types of special services the student needs and the extent to which the child will participate in the regular classroom setting, and (2) the beginning and ending dates for the services. Services typically are initiated within a few days of the IEP meeting and are projected for the remainder of the academic year.

Students with mild disabilities may be placed in the regular classroom for most of their subjects with some adjustments and also receive assistance from the special education teacher. Others may be primarily in special education classes and join their peers only for music and physical education.

Appendix C to PL 94-142 (IDEA) also states that if modifications (supplementary aids and services) to the regular education program are necessary to ensure the child's participation in the program, then they must be described in the IEP (Bateman, 1992, p. 182). Examples include special seating arrangements or the provision of assignments in writing for a hearing impaired student.

Finally, the team identifies the evaluations by which they can determine the extent to which the short-term objectives are being met. For example, the team may specify the completion of behavioral charts on the incidence of disruptive behavior in the classroom during the year, and for arithmetic, administration of a diagnostic achievement test in mathematics to be administered at the end of the school year in May. Often, the team will specify particular evaluations for each of the short-term objectives. Examples are error counts in one-paragraph essays, error rates in oral readings, and scores on teacher-made worksheets (see Table 11-4).

Summary

Certifying that a student is deficient in cognitive functioning or has a handicap that impedes learning is a decision largely governed by federal and state laws. PL 94-142 (IDEA) stipulates guidelines for the assessment of the student and the preparation of the student's IEP. First, the assessment and the planning process must be protective of the rights of students with disabilities and their parents. Second, the assessment instruments must be selected so as to be technically adequate, nondiscriminatory, comprehensive, focused on students needs, and administered by qualified personnel. Nondiscriminatory refers to freedom from racial or cultural bias, administration in the student's native language, and nonreliance on the students' disability.

Table 11.4 Partial Example of an IEP

Name: Janice Oakland Grade: 4 Date: 8/23/97

Parent/Guardian: Patrick & Mary Oakland

Phone: 869-4097

Present Level of Educational Performance: I.Q. score as measured by the WISC-III is 67.

Reading achievement is 2.1 as measured by the Woodcock-Johnson Psychoeducational Battery. Janice reads orally 2nd-grade material at a rate of 50–60 words per minute and correctly answers 30–40% of factual comprehension questions presented orally.

Mathematics achievement is 1.8 as measured by the Woodcock-Johnson Psychoeducational Battery. She can add 1-digit numbers, but lacks understanding of place value and regrouping in addition and subtraction.

Janice responds in class before thinking with telegraphic (1–2-word) responses. Her written work is impulsive with careless errors and her handwriting is barely legible.

Annual goals (partial list)

1. Janice will demonstrate 6 to 9 months' gain in reading as measured by the Woodcock-Johnson.
2. Janice will demonstrate 6 to 9 months' gain in mathematics as measured by the Woodcock-Johnson.

Short-term objectives (partial list)	Evaluation
1. Use phonics to decode unfamiliar words.	Teacher observation of oral reading
2. Answer concrete factual questions (Who? What? Where? How?) on brief stories with 0–2 errors.	Teacher observation of oral and written responses
3. By Jan. 1, read 3rd-grade material at 70 words per minute with 0–2 errors.	Informal reading inventory
4. By June 1, reading beginning 4th-grade material at 60 words per minute with 0–2 errors.	Informal reading inventory

The IEP is a detailed instructional planning document that is prepared by a multidisciplinary team. Included in the IEP are the student's current performance level, goals for the student for the year, short-term objectives, the types of services needed by the student, the amount of time to be spent in the regular classroom, the duration of services, and evaluation procedures and schedules for the short-term objectives.

Assessment Methods

Assessment serves three functions for students with special needs. They are (a) certification of eligibility for special services, (2) planning instruction, and (3) evaluating student progress.

The Role of Standardized Instruments

Intelligence and achievement tests and measures of adaptive behavior, by legal statute, play a key role in the identification of students with special needs. Student performance on an intelligence test can indicate whether the student is functioning significantly below average, a key component of determining mental retardation. Although PL 94-142 (IDEA) did not define "subaverage intellectual functioning," the American Association of Mental Retardation (AAMR) (1992) defines it as a standard score below 70 to 75 on an individually administered intelligence test (see Chapter 13 for a discussion of this score).

For other students with academic or behavioral problems, the administration of an intelligence test can rule out the possibility of mental retardation. That is, average performance on an intelligence test indicates that academic problems other than mental retardation are present.

Instead of group paper-and-pencil tests, the school psychologist selects individually administered intelligence and achievement tests. Tests that are designed to be administered to groups require reading and independent work skills. Students with academic or behavioral problems typically have difficulties in these areas.

Well-known examples of individually administered intelligence tests are the Stanford-Binet, Fourth Edition, and the Wechsler Intelligence Scale for Children, Third Edition (WISC–III). An example of an individually administered achievement test is the Woodcock Johnson-R (Woodcock & Johnson, 1989). This test addresses basic skills, different content areas, and cognitive abilities.

A well-known measure of adaptive behavior is the Vineland Adaptive Behavior Scales (Sparrow, Balla, & Cicchetti, 1984). It consists of three separate forms: two based on interviews conducted by the school psychologist and a questionnaire that is completed by the classroom teacher. The assessment yields a total score and a standard score in each of four domains: communication, daily living, socialization, and motor skills.

Depending on the student's particular problems, tests in specific areas, such as reading, mathematics, and written language, may be needed. For example, the Stanford Diagnostic Reading Test measures auditory vocabulary (the ability to recognize the meaning of words), auditory discrimination, phonetic analysis, word reading, and reading comprehension.

Classroom Assessments

The teacher faces particular responsibilities in assessing special needs students in the classroom. These responsibilities are in the areas of planning and implementing classroom tests, documenting specific classroom behaviors, and analyzing student performance in the basic skills of mathematics, writing, and reading.

Classroom tests. Two issues are important in planning and implementing tests for special needs students. First, of importance for both low achievers and students with mental, physical, or emotional disabilities is to allow sufficient time for students to complete assessment tasks and tests. The purpose of classroom tests is for the student to demonstrate his or her skills and knowledge, not to answer as many items as possible in a set time period. Sufficient time also can assist in reducing anxiety, often a problem for students with special needs.

The second issue is to plan assessments so that information on the student's knowledge and cognitive skills is not dependent on the individual's ability to produce answers on a particular type of assessment or in a particular format. On a classroom test, for example, some students may have difficulty in reading the questions or in following directions on matching items or short-answer items (Mehring, 1995, p. 14). One alternative is to prerecord the questions on a cassette so that the student can work with earphones at a listening center. Tests for students with visual perception difficulties should be administered in the resource room. In this way, students can receive assistance with matching or short-answer items (Mehring, 1995).

The types of assessments to be administered may require alternative choices. If the student has difficulty writing, for example, the teacher may use interviews of the student rather than require the student to keep a log of activities and his or her conclusions. Also, for classroom tests, students who have difficulties with written language may be tested orally (Mehring, 1995).

Documenting specific classroom behaviors. A student's IEP may identify disruptive or emotional behaviors that are to be addressed in the classroom. Two methods for documenting occurrences of discrete behaviors are event and duration recording. The focus of these recording methods is a discrete behavior, such as throwing paper wads or sleeping during class (McLoughlin & Lewis, 1994). As indicated in Figure 11-1, event recording documents the frequency of the behavior, whereas duration recording documents beginning and ending times of each incident of the behavior of interest (Alberto & Troutman, 1990). This information can be useful in determining the effectiveness of intervention strategies.

Event recording
Student: Mary S. Behavior: Throwing paper wads
Observation: Language Arts, 3/10–3/14

3/10	3/11	3/12	3/13	3/14
///	////	///	////	///

Duration recording
Student: Martin C. Behavior: Crying episodes
Observation: Math, science, and language arts classes, 11/3–11/7

11/3	11/4	11/5	11/6	11/7
8:30–8:35 1:10–1:25	9:00–9:15	—	11:04–11:18	2:06–2:10

FIGURE 11.1
Examples of event and duration recording.

Analyzing performance in basic skills. Two methods that assist the teacher in analyzing a student's basic skills are error analysis and informal reading inventories. The importance of error analysis is that it can identify areas that need attention in spelling, writing, and arithmetic computations. For example, a student's four- or five-sentence essay may be analyzed for the number of words spelled correctly, the number of misspelled words, the percentage of misspelled words, and the types of errors. Examples are phonetic spelling (kat for cat) and letter reversals (recieve instead of receive). Error analysis also is appropriate for punctuation, capitalization, and subject–verb agreement in writing.

In arithmetic computations, error analysis is applied to addition, subtraction, multiplication, and division problems completed by the student. Examples of errors include incorrect operation (adding instead of subtracting); incorrect number fact (product of 5 × 4 is 25); or incorrect algorithm (fails to carry in an addition problem) (McLoughlin & Lewis, 1994, p. 343).

Informal reading inventories. The purpose of an informal reading inventory (IRI) is to assess decoding and comprehension skills (McLoughlin & Lewis, 1994). An IRI consists of grade-referenced word lists and selections that the student reads orally. Administration of the assessment results in one of three reading levels. They are the Independent Level (student reads graded material easily with few decoding or comprehension errors); the Instructional Level (reading is more difficult for the student); and the Frustration Level (materials are too difficult for the student) (p. 299). Materials at the Instructional Level are appropriate for classroom instruction.

Summary

The three functions of assessment with students who have special needs are (1) to certify eligibility for special services, (2) to plan instruction, and (3) to evaluate student progress. Individually administered intelligence and achievement tests document the student's level of intellectual functioning and current level of academic achievement. Tests in specific areas, such as reading, mathematics, and written language, can identify specific difficulties. The Stanford Diagnostic Reading Test is an example.

In addition to assessments of intelligence and achievement, assessment of the student's adaptive behavior also is important. The purpose is to determine the student's capability to respond to the nonacademic requirements of the classroom. Other assessments also may be administered for students with particular problems, such as assessing the listening skills of visually impaired students.

Classroom assessments may be a component of the IEP and are also used during the year to determine student progress. Three issues of concern in assessing students with special needs are (1) allowing sufficient time on classroom tests, (2) choosing appropriate types of assessments in order to bypass the student's disability, and (3) choosing an appropriate format for the test. In addition to teacher-made tests, portfolio assessment, and checklists of achieved skills, teachers may use event and duration recording of behavior problems, error analysis, and informal inventories. Event and duration recordings are used for problems such as throwing paper wads and sleeping in class. Error analysis is appropriate for special skills, such as spelling and specific arithmetic computations. Informal reading levels assess the student's skills in decoding words and reading comprehension in graded reading materials.

Chapter Questions

1. McLoughlin and Lewis (1994) note that when English-language tests are administered through an interpreter to non-English-speaking students, the test norms do not apply. What are some of the reasons for this recommendation?

2. An achievement test to be administered to a deaf student includes items on rhyming words. What is the validity problem with this assessment and what legal requirement of the IEP does it violate?

3. Because the school psychologist has a crowded schedule, a member of the IEP team suggests that a paper-and-pencil intelligence test, the Otis-Lennon, be substituted for the WISC–III and that the teacher can administer it to the student during regular class time. What are the validity and legal problems with this suggestion?

4. A proposed IEP goal is that Steven will improve his study habits 75 percent of the time. What are the problems with this goal? Suggest an alternative.

5. What are some classroom behaviors that are appropriate for event recording? Duration recording?

References

AAMR Ad Hoc Committee on Terminology and Classification (1992). *Mental retardation: Definition, classification, and systems of support* (9th ed.). Washington, DC: American Association of Mental Retardation.

Alberto, P. A., & Troutman, A. C. (1990). *Applied behavior analysis for teachers* (3rd ed.). New York: Merrill/Macmillan.

Bateman, B. (1992). *Better IEPs: How to develop legally correct and educationally useful programs*. Longmont, CO: Sopris West.

Brophy, J. (1996). *Teaching problem students*. New York: Guilford Press.

Brown, F., & Hoshida, R. K. (1996). Children with mild mental retardation. In E. L. Meyen (Ed.), *Exceptional children in today's schools* (3rd ed.; pp. 433–465). Denver, CO: Love Publishing.

Edwards, L., & Simpson, J. (1996). Children with behavior disorders. In E. L. Meyen (Ed.), *Exceptional children in today's schools* (3rd ed.; pp. 251–279). Denver, CO: Love Publishing.

Federal Register (Part IV). (1977, August). Washington, DC: U.S. Government Printing Office.

Federal Register (1981, January). Washington, DC: U.S. Government Printing Office.

Forness, S. R., & Knitzer, R. J. (1992). A new proposed definition and terminology to replace "serious emotional disturbance" in Individuals with Disabilities Act. *School Psychology Review, 21*(1), 12–20.

Gredler, G. R. (1988). Assessment of learning ability: A critical appraisal. In R. M. Gupta & P. Coxhead (Eds.), *Cultural diversity and learning efficiency* (pp. 39–63). London: Macmillan.

Hallahan, D. P., & Kauffman, J. M. (1994). *Exceptional children*. Boston: Allyn & Bacon.

Hunt, N., & Marshall, K. (1994). *Exceptional children and youth*. Boston: Houghton Mifflin.

Jacob-Timm, S., & Hartshorne, T. (1994). *Ethics and law for school psychologists* (2nd ed.). Brandon, VT: Clinical Psychology Publishing.

Mayer, M. H. (1996). Children who are deaf or hard of hearing. In E. L. Meyen (Ed.), *Exceptional children in today's schools* (3rd ed.; pp. 315–350). Denver, CO: Love Publishing.

McLoughlin, J. A., & Lewis, R. B. (1994). *Assessing special students* (4th ed.). Columbus, OH: Merrill.

Mehring, T. A. (1995). Report card options for students with disabilities in general education. In T. Azwell & E. Schmar (Eds.), *Report card on report cards: Alternatives to consider*. Portsmouth, NH: Heinemann.

Meyen, E. L. (1996a). Educating exceptional children. In E. L. Meyen (Ed.), *Exceptional children in today's schools* (3rd ed.; pp. 1–50). Denver, CO: Love Publishing.

Meyen, E. L. (1996b). Foundations and status of special education. In E. L. Meyen (Ed.), *Exceptional children in today's schools* (3rd ed.; pp. 51–96). Denver, CO: Love Publishing.

Parke, B. N. (1989). *Gifted students in regular classrooms*. Boston: Allyn & Bacon.

Silberman, R. K. (1996). Children with visual impairments. In E. L. Meyen (Ed.), *Exceptional children in today's schools* (3rd ed.; pp. 351–398). Denver, CO: Love Publishing.

Sparrow, S. S., Balla, D. A., & Cicchetti, D. V. (1984). *Vineland adaptive behavior scales*. Circle Pines, MN: American Guidance Service.

Turnbull, H. R. (1986). *Free appropriate education: The law and children with disabilities* (2nd ed.). Denver, CO: Love Publishing.

U.S. Department of Education (1991). *Thirteenth annual report to Congress on the implementation of the Individuals with Disabilities Education Act*. Washington, DC: U.S. Government Printing Office.

Woodcock, R. W., & Johnson, M. B. (1989). *Woodcock-Johnson psychoeducational battery–Revised*. Chicago: Riverside.

Chapter 12

Developing a Grading System

"A B could say that you're turning in all of your homework and you're doing a good job on your quizzes, but when it comes to tests, you really can't do it. Or it could be saying that I have a lot of strengths in application and word problems, but when it comes to computation, I'm very careless. It's just a letter. It doesn't really tell you that much."

—Nicki, in Thomas & Oldfather, 1977, p. 108

Major Topics

Methods of Reporting

Purposes of Reporting Systems

Letter Grades and Pass/Fail

Checklists and Progress Ratings

Portfolios

Narrative Reports

Criteria for Reporting Systems

Planning and Implementation

Standard-Setting Frameworks

Essential Steps

The Parent–Teacher Conference

In the preceding comments, Nicki is contrasting the narrative reports used by her elementary school and the letter grades she now receives in seventh grade. Nevertheless, the meaning of a particular letter grade should be less problematic than this example. One study of 604 children in grades 1 to 6, however, indicated that even the older students did not understand the teacher's grading system (Evans & Engelberg, 1988). Similarly, 30 percent of the students in a study of four suburban high schools reported that they had received unsatisfactory marks because they had misunderstood the teacher's evaluation criteria (Natriello, 1982).

In addition to the clear communication of standards, key factors in establishing a meaningful grading system are understanding the purpose of different reporting systems and their characteristics, the criteria for establishing a fair, accurate, and consistent grading system, and the essential steps in planning and implementing a reporting system.

Methods of Reporting

Formalized evaluation and reporting systems were developed originally to sort and categorize students. Recall from Chapter 1 that the traditional view of education was that only about 5 percent of students were believed to benefit from higher education. Students who did not meet established standards of achievement were excluded from advanced schooling (Azwell, 1995).

Since those early years, both the purposes of education and reporting systems have changed. Currently, the education system is expected to teach all students who can benefit from instruction. Reporting systems also have expanded, specifically, from the use of letter grades to include checklists, progress grades, portfolios, and narratives.

Purposes of Reporting Systems

Grades and other reporting systems are formal public records developed to communicate student achievement (Hills, 1981). Although this purpose seems obvious, a later section of this chapter discusses situations and scoring practices that distort this intent.

Within the broad purpose of communicating student achievement, reporting systems, particularly grades, fulfill three major functions. They are (1) to inform parents of students' progress, (2) to serve as one source of information for educational and career planning, and (3) to provide information for administrative decisions. Among these decisions are promotion, graduation, and awarding honors.

Some educators suggest that grades also function to motivate students. However, a review of research on evaluation practices indicates that grades are motivating only for relatively high achievers (Natriello, 1987).

At present, letter grades are the predominant method of reporting student achievement. However, four other methods in use are pass/fail designations, checklists and progress ratings, portfolios, and narrative reports.

Letter Grades and Pass/Fail Designations

The majority of schools in the United States use the letter grades A, B, C, D, and F in academic subjects. Grades are useful because they serve as a summary of the student's achievement and they fulfill the requirement for record keeping. Traditional letter grading persists because (1) the system is familiar to educators, parents, and postsecondary users of student information; (2) it is administratively cost-efficient; and (3) it is beneficial for high-achieving students (Strein, 1997, p. 452).

Letter grades, however, have at least four limitations. First, they do not indicate a student's strengths and weaknesses unless supplemented by other information. This problem is reflected in the statement by Nicki at the beginning of this chapter.

Second, standards for assigning grades vary from teacher to teacher. Third, some teachers inappropriately combine achievement, effort, and other behaviors into the assignment of grades. The result, discussed in this chapter, is that the meaning of students' grades vary within the same class, the meaning of a student's grade is not clear, and the validity of the grade for reflecting achievement is lowered.

Fourth, particularly at the upper middle school and high school levels, grades may become goals in themselves. In one study of motivation, students reported diminished opportunities to improve the quality of their work because of an emphasis on grades in junior high and high school (Thomas & Oldfather, 1997). They believed that grades shifted their focus away from learning toward a concern for performance (p. 122).

An alternative to letter grades is the pass/fail designation. Although this method reduces the anxiety of grading, it provides less information than A to F grading. Pass/fail is used most often in high schools and colleges for courses a student wishes to explore outside of his or her program of study. Such courses may be particularly difficult for the student and the use of pass/fail excludes the courses from computation of the student's grade-point average.

Pass/fail or credit/no credit grading is the most common alternative recommended for students with learning disabilities. The suggestion is to grade the student on the objectives in the IEP. However, according to Strein (1997), students with learning disabilities and their parents often highly value traditional letter grades and interpret them as indicators of the child's status relative to others. Schools that use traditional letter grades for special needs students often identify them with a subscript that indicates the students are graded on a different set of standards from others.

Checklists and Progress Ratings

Some schools, particularly elementary schools, use lists of objectives or skills accompanied by some form of progress rating or grade. Objectives may include both skills in subject areas such as reading and mathematics, and social and behavior skills, such as classroom conduct and work habits. The report form for one elementary school, for example, includes items on adaptive behavior such as relationships with classmates, handling of regular classroom rules and routines, and handling work-related frustration (Darling-Hammond, Ancess, & Falk, 1995).

Progress ratings typically range from 1 to 3 to 1 to 4. One elementary school, for example, uses (1) needs a lot of help, a serious concern; (2) needs reminders, making progress; (3) handles this well; (4) this is an area of strength; and N/A—not applicable (Darling-Hammond et al., 1995, p. 230).

Sometimes the reporting format may be organized so that the teacher places a checkmark or tally in the appropriate column. Figure 12-1 illustrates an example in which each column represents a different proficiency. Although this format is easy to use, identifying progress across the four marking periods for a particular skill is somewhat difficult.

A different approach in elementary language arts is implemented in the Rochester, New York, school system. The content standards developed through the district's goals initiative consist of nine developmental stages (A to I) in reading, writing, speaking, and listening (Suponitz & Brennan, 1997). Each stage is a cluster of specific behaviors and skills that represent a particular phase in developing proficiency. For example, stage A in writing includes explains marks made on paper with crayons, markers, pencils; draws pictures and names what is drawn; combines drawing and "writing"; and shows interest in letters. Stage C includes writes in a horizontal fashion, writes legibly with spaces between words, uses invented spelling, investigates spellings of words, and writes words in a logical order to make a sentence that can be read (p. 503). At each marking period, the child receives the letter that reflects his or her present stage of development.

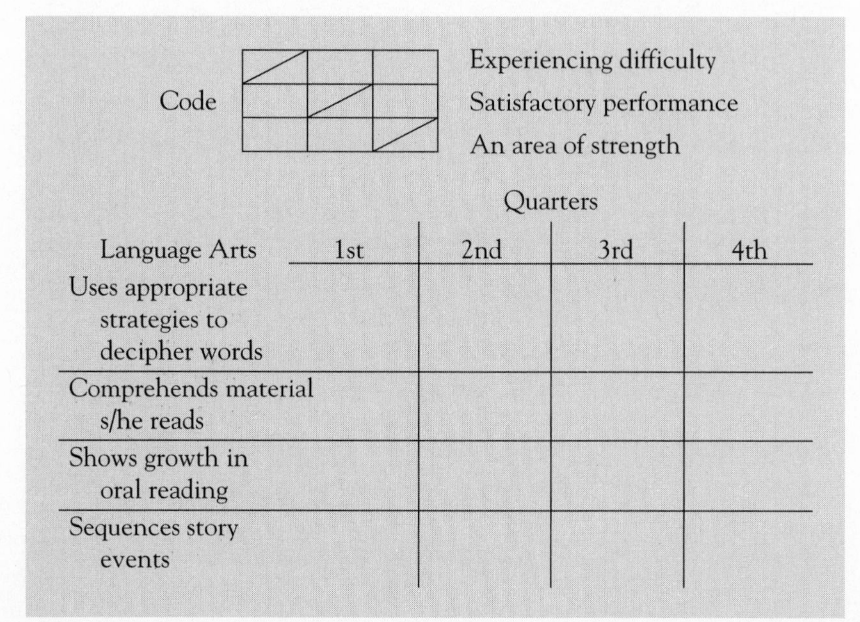

Code

Experiencing difficulty
Satisfactory performance
An area of strength

Quarters

Language Arts	1st	2nd	3rd	4th
Uses appropriate strategies to decipher words				
Comprehends material s/he reads				
Shows growth in oral reading				
Sequences story events				

FIGURE 12.1
Partial example of a progress report for the second grade.

Progress grades, in contrast, use letters. An example of a set of progress grades is E for excellent (or C for commendable), S for satisfactory, and N for needs improvement. One review indicates that 18 percent of schools use progress grades (MacIver & Epstein, 1992).

Like letter grades, progress grades and ratings may be interpreted in various ways. Of major importance is, first, to determine in advance the performances that represent satisfactory, commendable, and so on. Second, document the student's performance with concrete examples of student work and teacher observations.

Portfolios

Chapter 9 described various uses of portfolios. They are to facilitate student growth, to present student work for various purposes, to serve as a type of external assessment, and as a basis for developing reports of student achievement (the evaluation portfolio).

Two schools that use portfolios for evaluation instead of letter grading are Central Park East High School and the Bronx New School (an elementary school) in New York City (Darling-Hammond et al., 1995). These schools serve substantial numbers of low-income and minority students and students previously classified as "at risk."

The philosophy of the high school is to teach students to use their minds well. The last 2 years of work at the school are in the Senior Institute, where the student completes portfolio requirements across the 14 categories listed in the student transcript in Figure 12-2. Seven (including science and technology, mathematics, literature, and history) are presented orally before the Graduation Committee and seven are evaluated independently.

The portfolios are evaluated on quality, depth of understanding, demonstration of mastery of the particular subject area, and the use of evidence, voice, and appearance. Application of a scoring rubric of five dimensions (viewpoint, connections, evidence, voice, and conventions) results in an evaluation of distinguished (18–20), satisfactory (15–17), or minimally satisfactory (12–14). For a score of less than 12, the student must rework the portfolio.

Portfolios at the Bronx New School include writing samples that demonstrate literacy development, journals of mathematical problems, accompanied by student narratives, reading logs, reports of science experiments, drawings, and photos of other student work, such as dramatic play (Darling-Hammond et al., 1995, p. 216). Narrative reports of the student's work are sent to parents twice during the school year (January and June), followed by a parent–teacher conference. At the end of the year, the teacher selects representative samples of the student's work from the beginning, middle, and end of the year (from 12 to 20 items) to go to the next grade with the student.

Central Park East Secondary School
1573 Madison Avenue, N.Y. N.Y. 10029
Tel: (212) 860-5933
(212) 410-5216 (counselor)
Fax: (212) 876-3494
ETS Code: 332964

Coalition of Essential Schools
Community School District 4
NYC Board of Education

Last Name ____ First Name ____ Middle ____ Soc Sec # ____ OSIS # ____

Street Address ____ Borough ____ State ____ Zip Code ____

Parent/Guardian ____ Date of Birth ____ Sex ____

Previous High School (if any) ____ Date of Enrollment at CPESS ____ Expected Graduation Date ____

TRANSCRIPT OF COURSES

The following courses were taken in preparation for the Portfolio. Please refer to the Curriculum Bulletin for course descriptions and grading information. CPESS gives grades only on completion of a course of study, which requires demonstration of minimum competence. Courses are interdisciplinary and students demonstrate a variety of skills; grades therefore represent a range as follows:

Dist	=	Distinguished Work	Sat	=	Satisfactorily met requirements
MinSat	=	Minimally met requirements	Audit	=	Course not taken for evaluation
* *	=	College Course (see Curriculum Bulletin for details)			

Division II (9th) 1988/89

Course	Grade
Humanities (Lit, History, Art)	Sat+
Math	Sat+
Science	Sat+
Advisory	Dist
Community Service	Dist

Division II (10th) 1989/90

Course	Grade
Humanities (Lit, History, Art)	Dist
Math	Dist
Science	Dist
Advisory	Dist
Community Service	Dist
Spanish	Dist

Senior Inst, Fall 1990

Course	Grade
Sci Foundations, Hunter	C**
Precal & Pascal 1	Sat
Lit: Autobiography	Sat
Internship	Sat+

Senior Inst, Spring 1991

Course	Grade
Precal & Pascal 2	Sat+
Chemistry 1	Dist
Linguistics: 1000 Words	Sat+
Civil Rights History	Dist

Senior Inst, Fall 1991

Course	Grade
Chemistry 2	Dist
Mass Media	Sat+
Lit: Essay	Sat+
Science Research, Hunter	Dist

Senior Inst, Spring 1992

Course	Grade
Genetics	Dist
Rethinking Columbus	Sat
Science Research, Hunter	Dist

Standardized Tests

Regents Competency Tests

Reading	Pass
Writing	Pass
Math	Pass
Science	Pass
U.S. History	Pass
Global Studies	Pass

Languages

Spanish	Pass

CUNY Placement Tests

Reading	Pass
Writing	Pass
Math	Pass

SAT's 3/91

Test	Score
Math	600
Verbal	430

Other Tests

Test	Score
ACH ENG	520
ACH MATH	530
ACH CHEM	550

Signature, Principal ____ Date ____

SEAL MUST BE AFFIXED

FIGURE 12.2 Transcript based on student portfolios.

Narrative Reports

Some schools use narrative reports for the early years in lieu of letter grades because they describe students' strengths and weaknesses. The narrative may be based on students' portfolios or on other evaluations of student progress.

To communicate clearly to parents and other audiences, narrative reports should meet the criteria listed in Table 12-1. The report should begin with a one-sentence overview, such as "Marie has made gains in reading and mathematics this year." Specific examples of the child's accomplishments, such as "writing clearly to express her ideas" also should be included. Goals and plans for the future may include expectations that the student will begin to add details to her writing and be able to establish a beginning, middle, and an ending (Hogan, 1995). Finally, the report should be diplomatic, but accurate about any problems. For example, the report may state that Marie is enthusiastic about her work, but needs to learn to better manage her talking in class.

Summary

The broad purpose of grades and other reporting systems is to communicate student achievement. They inform parents of students' progress, assist in educational and career planning, and provide information for administrative decisions, such as promotion. Although grades are viewed by some as motivators, research indicates that they motivate only high achievers.

Letter grades, although familiar and cost-efficient, have at least four limitations. They do not indicate student strengths and weaknesses, the basis for their assignment varies from teacher to teacher, and sometimes varies with the same teacher. Fourth, they may become goals in themselves, shifting the student's focus

Table 12.1 Criteria for Narrative Reports to Parents

1. Include one paragraph on each topic, such as reading, mathematics, and social behavior.
2. Include specific examples of the child's accomplishments.
3. Describe meaningful, relevant behavior.
4. State goals and plans for the future.
5. Reflect sensitivity to the emotional impact on parents and children.
6. Present accurate information in a polished, professional manner.

Source: Summarized from Hogan (1995).

away from learning. Although pass/fail grading is an alternative, it provides less information than the range of letter grades.

Alternatives to grades include checklists and progress ratings, portfolios, and narrative reports. Some elementary schools use lists of objectives or skills in academic and adaptive behavior areas and a set of numerical ratings (e.g., 1 to 4) or progress grades.

Portfolios, when used for evaluation, may be accompanied by scoring rubrics (as described in Chapter 9) or narrative reports of student strengths and weaknesses. In addition, narrative reports may be based on portfolios or other evaluations of students. Narratives should state the student's progress, include specific examples, state plans for the future, present accurate information, and remain sensitive to the feelings of parents and children.

Criteria for Reporting Systems

Five essential criteria for reporting systems are listed in Table 12-2. They are focus and four criteria identified by Ory & Ryan (1993): fairness, accuracy, consistency, and defensibility. Several factors are involved in ensuring that each of these criteria is met, and they are discussed in the following sections.

Table 12.2 Criteria for Reporting Systems

Criterion	Definition
Focus	The system reports information about student learning.
Fairness	Each student has an equal opportunity for each grade.
Accuracy	All tests, papers, assignments, and projects are thoughtfully selected, planned, and scored according to the goals for instruction.
Consistency	All ratings, scores, and grades are determined in the same manner and according to the grading plan established at the beginning of the semester.
Defensibility	Chance or extraneous factors do not explain differences in grades or ratings, i.e., the preceding four criteria are met.

Source: Fairness, accuracy, consistency, and defensibility are summarized from Ory and Ryan (1993).

Focus

The focus of the selected reporting system should be on student learning. Two issues are important in accomplishing this goal. First, evaluation of students during the marking period must address behaviors and actions that clearly are indicators of learning. For example, communicating effectively in writing includes clearly identifying key questions and ideas in one's writing, supporting generalizations and ideas with specific, relevant, and accurate information, and using appropriate vocabulary. Inappropriate indicators of writing achievement are working quietly at one's desk and participating willingly in writing activities. Instead, they are indicators of work habits and classroom conduct. If these social behaviors are to be evaluated, they should be reported separately from achievement in academic subjects.

Second, the grading system should not be used to reward students for completion of activities. This problem is most likely to occur when letter grades are used. The most extreme examples, reported by Brookhart (1993) are those teachers whose image of grades is that of grades as currency. The emphasis is on the activities students perform, not the particular actions that indicate different levels of achievement. In other words, grades are treated as a kind of "academic token economy and function in classroom management as the reward for work done" (p. 142). Examples include turning in homework and completing a specified number of problems during seatwork.

Instead of assigning grades or points for only the completion of homework, the teacher may choose one of two options. One is to grade the homework according to criteria established that reflect learning. These criteria may address both the correctness of answers and the strategies used by students. The difficulty with this practice is that some students may have assistance at home and others may not. The other option is to treat homework as a formative exercise, for the purpose of generating feedback to students. However, some teachers state that, unless homework is graded, students will not complete the assignments. If homework is basically busy work, does not challenge student thinking, and does not contribute to essential learning in the class, students will be reluctant to undertake assignments. In other words, to be effective, homework should fulfill a specific and important role in classroom learning.

Fairness

The key to fairness is that each student has an equal opportunity for a grade (Ory & Ryan, 1993, p. 114). Included are ensuring an adequate range and variety of tasks for students to demonstrate their learning and the method used to determine student grades. The various methods that may be used are discussed in the following section.

Accuracy

Accuracy depends on (1) adequate opportunities for students to demonstrate their learning and (2) valid and reliable assessments of that learning. Essential to meeting this criterion are (1) a range and variety of tasks that reflect class objectives and (2) avoidance of the practice of assigning letter grades directly to separate assessment tasks. Letter grades represent a range of scores; for example, two student essays that both received a B may vary in quality by as much as 10 points. In other words, if a point score is assigned to all student work, the final grades of the two students may vary. Therefore, the actual rating or score should be assigned to student products instead. Then grades are determined at the end of the marking period by summing the points earned by the student on the various assessment tasks.

Also of importance is to avoid the use of nonacademic projects for extra credit to improve students' grades. An example is constructing a model of the Eiffel Tower for French class. Completion of the project does not demonstrate knowledge of the subject matter.

Consistency

Lack of consistency can occur in three ways. One is a discrepancy between task assignments and criteria set for the task (Natriello, 1982). An example is stating that the task focus is student strategies for problem solving but only the answer is scored.

Two other sources of inconsistency occur in the differential applications of achievement criteria (a) to the performance of different students and (b) across time to the work of a particular student. Inconsistent grading occurs most often when teachers assign letter grades directly to student products instead of applying scoring criteria and assigning a point score. The direct assignment of letter grades also has a high risk of being arbitrary. This places students in a bewildering position. Some who have worked very hard are likely to build up resentment about the class. Natriello (1982) found that high school students who experienced more inconsistencies in their evaluations were also more likely to become disengaged from school.

Defensibility

If the criteria of appropriate focus, fairness, accuracy, and consistency are met, then the assignment of the student's grade is defensible. That is, the reporting system evaluates students according to thoughtfully selected tasks that represent learning and achievement, students have opportunities to demonstrate their learning on a variety of tasks, and extraneous or chance factors do not account for differences in grades.

Summary

The five essential criteria for reporting systems are focus, fairness, accuracy, consistency, and defensibility. The focus should be on student learning and should not include irrelevant information. Also, grades should not be viewed as currency that is exchanged for completed work.

Fairness refers to equal opportunity for each student for a grade. Included are an adequate range and variety of tasks and the method used to determine grades (discussed in the following section).

The requirements for accuracy are (1) to provide a range and variety of assessment tasks that address the learning in the objectives and (2) to score student work reliably. Also important is to avoid the assignment of points or grades to nonacademic projects that are unrelated to student learning.

The sources of lack of consistency are (1) discrepancies between task assignments and scoring criteria and (2) discrepancies between the quality of student products and the evaluation. Inconsistent evaluation occurs most often when letter grades are assigned directly, instead of a point score. The fifth criterion for a reporting system, defensibility, is met when the other four criteria are met.

✦ Planning and Implementing a Reporting System

Developing an effective reporting system does not begin with the assignment of marks or scores. Instead, it is the final step in a process that begins with planning for instruction and assessment and includes instructional activities as well. Also important, when grading is completed, is communicating student progress to parents in the parent–teacher conference.

Standard-Setting Frameworks

Three possible frameworks for assigning grades are norm referencing, self-referencing, and criterion referencing.

Norm referencing. Often referred to as "grading on the curve," norm referencing assumes that (1) student performance in a class always spans the range from A to F and (2) specification in advance of the percentage of students that will be assigned each grade is an adequate method of representing student accomplishment. In other words, student performance is meaningful when expressed in terms of the achievement of others. An example of norm-referenced grading is deciding that the top 20 percent of the student scores earn an A, the next 30 percent receive a B, the next 30 percent receive a C, the next 15 percent receive a D, and the lowest 5 percent receive an F.

One problem with this approach to grading is that there are no rules for establishing the percentages. Although one may base the percentages on the performance of prior classes, each group of students is different. If one class, for example, consists of several high achievers, the grades of others will be lower as a result of their presence.

Another problem is that this model of assigning grades does not meet the fairness criterion. That is, the student's opportunity to earn a particular grade is determined, in large measure, by the performance of others.

Use of this method is also referred to as a competitive classroom structure, because success for one student reduces the chances for success for other students (Ames, 1984, 1992; Crooks, 1988). This structure threatens peer relationships because it leads to an "us and them" mentality (Crooks, 1988, p. 466).

Self-referencing. One approach to self-referencing is to compare a student's performance to preconceptions of his or her aptitude or ability level. One problem with this approach is that assessments of aptitude can only be made reliably in a general way. Aptitude to master specific skills or objectives cannot be predicted. In addition, the grade reflects some hypothetical goal, not the student's actual achievement. The elusive goal is to work up to one's potential. One result of implementing this model is that a student who has mastered fewer concepts and principles than a second student receives a higher grade because he or she was initially judged as less capable.

Another approach to self-referencing is to base grades on the amount of improvement. However, this method penalizes the student who has achieved reasonably well at the beginning of the marking period because the opportunity for improvement is limited. That is, a student whose assessment scores early in the marking period are in the 80 to 85 percent range has less room for improvement than the students whose scores are 70 to 75 percent of the total. Further, students soon learn the system and may perform poorly initially in order to improve their final grade.

The problem with the self-referencing approach is that it does not meet the fairness criterion. The student's opportunity to earn a particular grade is restricted by either a preconception of his or her capabilities or by initial performance in the class.

Criterion referencing. This method of assigning grades is similar to the continuum model of criterion-referenced assessment introduced in prior chapters. In the continuum model, the teacher or curriculum committee specifies the levels of mastery of complex tasks, such as writing an evaluation essay. In assigning grades, in contrast, the teacher must aggregate information about student performance from several assessments. When criterion referencing is applied to assigning grades, the teacher first specifies the mastery levels associated with each grade. Of major importance is that the teacher decide on a consistent meaning for each grade (Frisbie & Waltman, 1992). For example, an A may represent excellent or superior achievement of the concepts, principles, and capabilities expressed in the objectives for that marking period. Further, a B may reflect performance beyond the minimum, whereas a C reflects minimum competency. Finally, a D reflects a lack of learning of essential concepts, principles, and skills, and an F designates that most of the essential learnings were not achieved.

In this model, students who have achieved the designated capabilities specified at the beginning of the marking period will receive good grades, regardless of the performance of other students. Therefore, the possibility exists that all the students may receive A's and B's.

The teacher then identifies the key behaviors or tasks that are the focus of instruction, and the related assessments to be used for grading purposes. The teacher decides the pieces that will contribute to the final grade and the weight to be assigned to each piece (Frisbie & Waltman, 1992). Some student work, such as formative exercises or tests, homework, or oral responses in class typically are for the purpose of making decisions about needed instruction or special assistance. Other activities, such as unit tests, research reports, and other projects often are included in determining student grades. These assessment tasks are referred to as summative assessments.

The next decision is to weight each assessment that is to be used in grading. In general, assessments that address more objectives and/or a range of content are considered to be more important than other assessments. For example, a final examination is worth more points toward a final grade than unit tests. Also, assessments that require the integration and application of knowledge and skills are weighted more heavily than assessments that focus on recall or identification of concepts (Nitko, 1996). For example, an assessment that requires students to identify problems in a girl's diet, recommend dietary changes, and provide a rationale for the recommendations should be weighted more heavily than an assessment that requires only the recognition of dietary deficiencies.

Consider, for example, the objectives in Table 4-3. They are to describe the characteristics of goal statements, identify the errors in proposed statements of goals, and evaluate proposed goal statements in one's curriculum area for utility in planning curriculum and assessments. Describing the characteristics of goal statements may be assessed informally during class. Logical summative assessments for grading are a test that presents statements of proposed goals, for which students identify the errors. Depending on the number of statements and errors illustrated in the statements, the test may be worth 15 to 20 points. The most complex objective, evaluating proposed goal statements, may be assessed in an essay examination. Depending on the expected depth and breadth of student answers, the examination may be worth, for example from 20 to 40 points.

Of importance is that the identification of the total points an assessment is worth is not an arbitrary decision. Factors that influence the decision include the importance and complexity of the skills required by the assessment, length, and the relationship of the assessment to others in the grading process.

The points assigned to the summative assessment tasks are then summed for the marking period. Then the teacher determines the number of points for each grade. Suppose, for example, that the assessment tasks for the unit on goals and objectives are as follows:

Assessment Tasks	**Points**
Unit Tests (2)	40
Essay evaluations (2)	80
Student Plan (1)	40
Total	160

The points that may be assigned to each grade may be A—144 to 180; B—128–143; C—112–127; D—96–126; F—less than 126. The rationale for this allocation is that an A represents excellent achievement of the concepts, principles, and capabilities expressed in the objectives which means earning 90 percent or higher of the total points. A B grade, performance beyond the minimum, is reflected in 80 to 89 percent of the total points, and so on.

One potential difficulty with criterion referencing, however, is that a student may perform poorly on one of the summative assessments and yet earn a good grade. The key to avoiding this problem is to clearly communicate performance criteria to students and to provide practice and feedback during instruction.

Another potential difficulty with this method is the students whose total scores place them on the borderline between two grades. Nitko (1996) suggests collecting additional information to assist in the decision and, if still in doubt, assign the higher grade. The problem of borderline point totals, however, is most likely to occur when (1) the summative assessments address a range of content or knowledge rather than targeting particular capabilities and (2) scoring guidelines are unclear.

Criterion referencing also may be used when portfolios are evaluated for grades. For example, at Central Park High School, a portfolio that earns 18 to 20 points is graded as distinguished, whereas 15 to 17 is satisfactory. The scoring rubric for the portfolio consists of five dimensions (viewpoint, connections, evidence, voice, and conventions) that are each scored from 1 to 4 (Darling-Hammond et al., 1995).

An advantage of criterion referencing is that each student has an opportunity to earn each grade, regardless of the performance of other students. Therefore, the possibility exists that all the students may earn A's and B's. Also, because students are not competing for a limited number of good grades, there is no penalty for helping other students during instruction. Disadvantages are that to the extent that the capabilities to be learned are not well-defined or the assessment tasks are selected arbitrarily, the resulting grades will fail to meet the accuracy criterion.

Essential Steps

The essential steps in planning instruction, assessment, and grading are listed in Table 12-3. Clearly stated goals and identified objectives or key capabilities to be learned are the framework for assessment.

Step 3 is to identify achievement tasks that reflect the capabilities to be learned, both nongraded activities for feedback and graded tasks. For example, assessments may include teacher ratings of pupil skills, such as oral reading, and scores on comprehension and vocabulary tests. If the reporting system uses progress ratings or progress grades, identify the levels of performance for the identified capabilities for the key assessments. For example, what constitutes excellent, satisfactory, and needs improvement in using appropriate strategies to decipher words?

If assessments are to be equally weighted in calculating course grades, then the number of points assigned to each should be the same. If, on the other hand, a task such as evaluating goal statements is to be weighted twice as much as the other assessments, then the total possible score for the goal evaluation assessment should be twice the number of points assigned to the other assessments.

During instruction, four key practices can prevent student confusion and enhance learning. First is to clearly articulate the broad objectives to students *and* the ways they are to be met. Second, of particular importance during instruction is instructional overlap—the fit between the criterion established for learning and the instruction the student receives (Leinhardt & Bickel, 1987). This practice is a major factor in the quantity and quality of student learning (p. 195). For example, if the goal is for students to read prose with understanding, then games and drills of word components lack congruence with this goal (p. 195).

Third, provide feedback to students on nongraded situations so that they can redirect their efforts. To be effective, the feedback should be encouraging and correct student errors.

Finally, recall from Chapter 11 that low achievers and other students with processing deficits have difficulties with complex reading materials. These students often work hard and have few successes and teachers feel they must include effort in the grade. An alternative is to provide textbooks and other materials at

Table 12.3 Essential Components of an Effective Reporting System

Planning

1. Clearly state learning goals or broad objectives that focus on learning.
2. Specify (a) the objectives for the units to be taught in the upcoming marking period or (b) the key capabilities on which students are to be assessed.
3. Identify the assessments to be used for information about student learning and those to be used for grading.
4. Identify (a) the levels of performance for progress ratings or progress grades or (b) the number of points associated with each assessment for course grades.
5. For course grades, sum the points for the assignments to be graded and describe performance levels for course grades.

Instruction

6. Clearly articulate to the students the broad objectives and ways they are to be met.
7. Ensure instructional overlap between assessments and teaching (Leinhardt & Bickel, 1987).
8. Provide opportunities for students to develop skills and capabilities in nongraded situations with feedback.
9. Provide materials and texts at lower levels of reading difficulty for low achievers and others with processing difficulties (see Chapter 11).

Assessment

10. Implement specific assessments (during the marking period) congruent with items 1 through 4 and record students' performance.

Grading

11. Determine progress ratings or grades and calculate course grades at the end of the marking period in accordance with Steps 4 and 5.

lower reading levels for these students. This practice along with formative exercises reinforces student effort, lowers frustrations, and assists students in mastering key concepts and principles.

During the marking period, usually 6 or 9 weeks, implement the assessment tasks that are to be scored and record the students' earned scores. At the end of the marking period, calculate each student's grade according to the mastery levels set in Step 3.

The Parent–Teacher Conference

An important supplement to formal reports of student achievement is the parent–teacher conference. Sixty interviews of parents of early elementary school children conducted by Shepard and Bliem (1995) indicated that the parents learned most about their child's progress by talking with the teacher (p. 26). In another study involving 285 parents of fourth graders, 38 percent of the group indicated that the single most useful source of information about their child's achievement was the regularly scheduled parent–teacher conference (Waltman & Frisbie, 1994).

Prior to the conference, determine the particular goals, for example, to discuss a particular problem or to suggest home study activities. Conduct the conference in a friendly positive way, beginning with the student's strengths. Include concrete examples of the student's work, particularly when discussing the areas that need improvement. The student's standardized test scores may also be a part of the conference and guidelines for the discussion are discussed in Chapter 13.

The tone of the conference should be that of sharing information, which includes listening to parents' concerns and insights about the student. Finally, a course of action should be planned cooperatively with the parents.

Summary

Developing an effective reporting system that meets the criteria of focus, fairness, accuracy, consistency, and defensibility begins with planning instruction and assessments and includes instructional activities and assessment tasks. Clearly articulated objectives and mastery levels and identified types of assessments are essential planning steps. Communicating objectives and ways they are to be met, ensuring instructional overlap, nongraded assessments with feedback, and a variety of instructional materials are important during instruction. Implementing assessments, recording student scores, and calculating grades in accordance with the identified mastery levels concludes the process.

An important adjunct to evaluating students is the parent–teacher conference, an important information source for parents. The conference should be conducted in a positive, friendly manner, beginning with student strengths and concrete examples of their work. Listening to parents' concerns and cooperatively planning a course of action for any identified problems are also essential.

Chapter Questions

1. In developing objectives and related assessments for fourth-grade mathematics, the teacher identifies "gathering and using mathematical data" as an outcome and "presenting an oral report using data" as the expected achievement to be graded. Discuss the problems with these choices.

2. A social studies course provides only one graded assessment for the three key objectives. Which of the four criteria does this practice fail to meet? Why?

3. Aileen earned scores that total 90 out of 100 points, but earned a C in geography. What standard-setting model does this grade reflect and discuss the problems with it.

4. A task is described to students as an opportunity for creativity and exploration, but it is scored for a grade on a strict formula. Which criterion does this practice fail to meet and why?

5. Suggest some ways to develop an assessment system that will assist in preventing the problem of grades becoming goals in themselves.

References

Ames, C. (1984). Competitive, cooperative and individualistic goal structures. In R. E. Ames & C. Ames (Eds.), *Research on motivation in education: Vol. 1. Student motivation* (pp. 177–207). New York: Academic Press.

Ames, C. (1992). Classrooms: Goals, structures, and student motivation. *Journal of Educational Psychology, 84*(3), 261–271.

Azwell, T. (1995). Messages about learning. In T. Azwell & E. Schmar (Eds.), *Report card on report cards* (pp. 3–10). Portsmouth, NH: Heinemann.

Brookhart, S. M. (1993). Teachers' grading practices: Meaning and values. *Journal of Educational Measurement, 30*(3), 123–142.

Crooks, T. J. (1988). The impact of classroom evaluation practices on students. *Review of Educational Research, 58*(4), 438–481.

Darling-Hammond, L., Ancess, J., & Falk, B. (1995). *Authentic assessment in action: Studies of schools and students at work*. New York: Teachers College Press.

Evans, E. D., & Engelberg, R. A. (1988). Student perceptions of school grading. *Journal of Research and Development in Education, 21*(2), 45–54.

Frisbie, D. A., & Waltman, K. K. (1992). Developing a personal grading plan. *Educational Measurement: Issues and Practice, II*(3), 35–42.

Hills, J. R. (1981). *Measurement and evaluation in the classroom*. Columbus, OH: Merrill.

Hogan, E. (1995). Communicating in a culturally diverse community. In T. Azwell & E. Schmar (Eds.), *Report card on report cards* (pp. 22–34). Portsmouth, NH: Heinemann.

Leinhardt, G., & Bickel, W. (1987). Instruction's the thing wherein to catch the mind that falls behind. *Educational Psychologist, 22*(2), 177–207.

MacIver, D. J., & Epstein, J. (1992). Middle grades education. In M. C. Alkin (Ed.), *Encyclopedia of educational research* (6th ed.; pp. 834–844). New York: Macmillan.

Natriello, G. (1982). *Organizational evaluation systems and student disengagement in secondary schools*. (Final report to the National Institute of Education.) St. Louis, MO: Washington University.

Natriello, G. (1987). The impact of evaluation processes on students. *Educational Psychologist, 22*(2), 155–175.

Nitko, A. (1996). *Classroom assessment of students*. Columbus, OH: Merrill.

Ory, J. C., & Ryan, K. E. (1993). *Tips for improving testing and grading*. Newbury Park, CA: Sage.

Shepard, L. A., & Bliem, C. L. (1995). Parents' thinking about standardized tests and performance assessments. *Educational Researcher, 24*(8), 25–32.

Strein, W. (1997). Grades and grading practices. In G. B. Bear, K. M. Minke, & A. Thomas (Eds.), *Children's Needs II: Development, problems, and alternatives* (pp. 467–475). Bethesda, MD: National Association of School Psychologists.

Suponitz, J. A., & Brennan, R. T. (1997). Mirror, mirror on the wall, which is the fairest test of all? An examination of the equitability of portfolio assessment relative to standardized tests. *Harvard Educational Review, 67*(3), 472–506.

Thomas, S., & Oldfather, P. (1997). Intrinsic motivation, literacy, and assessment practices: "That's my grade. That's me." *Educational Psychologist, 32*(2), 107–123.

Waltman, K. K., & Frisbie, D. A. (1994). Parents' understanding of their children's report card grades. *Applied Measurement in Education, 7*(3), 241–251.

Chapter 13

Interpreting Norm-Referenced Tests

Many of the misuses [of tests] stem from a desire for shortcuts, quick answers, and simple routine solutions for real-life problems. All too often, the decision-making responsibility is shifted to the test; the test user loses sight of the fact that tests are tools, serving as valuable aids to the skilled practitioner, but useless or misleading when improperly used.

—Anastasi, 1985, p. xxiii

Major Topics

<u>Methods of Scoring</u>

- Raw Scores
- Grade-Equivalent Scores
- Percentile Ranks
- Standard Scores
- Role of the Normal Distribution
- Comparison of Scoring Methods

<u>Interpreting Student Performance</u>

- Standard Error
- Confidence Bands
- Using Test Results
- Composition of the Reference Group

Chapter 2 briefly introduced the use of norm-referenced achievement tests as a means to obtain estimates of a student's performance compared to that of a large number of his or her peers. Chapter 11 discussed the role of individually administered intelligence and achievement tests to determine if a student's intellectual functioning is significantly subaverage (one aspect of the legal definition of mental retardation) or to establish a baseline of achievement potential in the identification of learning disabilities.

Important in interpreting the information from norm-referenced tests used for these purposes is understanding the types of scores that are typically reported, their limitations, and their meanings.

Methods of Scoring

Ways of scoring norm-referenced tests include raw scores and different types of comparison or derived scores. Included are grade equivalents, percentile ranks, and standard scores.

Raw Scores and Derived Scores

A raw score is the number of points earned by an examinee on a test, whether teacher-made or commercially published. Within the classroom, raw scores on teacher-made tests are useful in determining the mastery of particular skills and computing grades. Further, one way to obtain a general estimate of a student's relative performance is to compare the individual's score with other scores in the class. For example, if the student's score of 65 points is the second highest on the test, the performance is very good. In contrast, if 65 is fourth from the lowest score, with 20 scores above it, the performance is very poor.

However, raw scores on teacher tests are not dependable indices of performance across classrooms because the types and content of classroom tests vary. Therefore, raw scores on teacher tests cannot be used for between-class comparisons.

To obtain an estimate of student performance beyond the classroom, schools administer norm-referenced instruments developed for state or national use. As mentioned in Chapter 2, norm-referenced tests assess a broad domain of knowledge and are designed to identify fine differences in examinee performance. In addition, development of these tests includes administration of the particular instrument to a representative sample of the population for whom the test is intended. The scores of subsequent examinees are compared to the performance of this representative sample, referred to as a norming or reference group.

The student's raw score on the standardized test is converted to some type of derived score that indicates the student's standing on the test relative to the reference group. Suppose, for example, that the test developers intend to use the derived scores referred to as percentile ranks. The midpoint or the fiftieth percentile is assigned to average performance in the reference group. That is, if average performance on the test is a raw score of 60, the midpoint of the percentile ranks, the fiftieth percentile, is assigned to that score. Subsequent test takers who earn a score of 60 are reported, in terms of the reference group, as scoring at the 50th percentile.

In addition to percentile ranks, other types of derived scores are grade-equivalents and standard scores. They are referred to as derived scores because they are conversions from the students' raw scores.

Grade-Equivalent Scores

Reported primarily at the elementary school level, a grade-equivalent score has two components. The first indicates the grade and the second is the month of the school year, which range from 0 to 9. A fourth-grade student's raw score of 74 in reading comprehension, for example, may correspond to the performance typical of a student in the fifth grade, second month. The grade-equivalent score, therefore, is 5.2. In other words, the score indicates that this student is a year advanced in reading.

Although apparently simple to understand, grade-equivalent scores are easily misinterpreted. Table 13-1 illustrates their limitations. One is that they are easily viewed as standards to be achieved. However, if some second-grade children earn a grade-equivalent score of 3.0 in language arts, other second graders should not be expected to reach that level. Children, particularly in the elementary grades, progress at different rates.

Table 13.1 Limitations of Grade-Equivalent Scores

Limitations	Example
1. The score is not a standard that all should achieve.	1. Some of the fourth-grade pupils scored 5.1 on a norm-referenced reading test. Expecting other pupils who scored from 3.1 to 3.8 to attain this score by May is unrealistic.
2. The score does not indicate the appropriate grade placement for the student.	2. A score of 4.8 for a third-grade student does not mean that he or she mastered fourth-grade science.
3. Score units are not equal at different grade levels.	3. The gain in reading from grade 1.0 to 1.5 is much greater than the gain from grade 8.0 to 8.5 (McLoughlin & Lewis, 1994, p. 59).
4. All students will not gain 1.0 grade equivalent per year.	4. A student who is a very slow reader is not likely to increase his or her score 1.0 in a year.

Similarly, grade-equivalent scores are not indicators of appropriate grade placement. A grade-equivalent score of 3.1 in reading for a second-grade child does not mean that the child should be promoted to third grade. It simply means that the child is advanced in reading comprehension and, very likely, vocabulary, in comparison to the average second grader.

A third problem is that, because the scores are delineated by months, they are often assumed to be equal units. However, for example, the gain in reading from grade 1.0 to grade 1.5 is much greater than the gain from grade 8.0 to 8.5 (McLoughlin & Lewis, 1994). Finally, grade-level scores tend to give the impression that all students' scores should increase 1.0 in a year's time. Above-average students tend to gain more than 1.0 in a year and poor students typically gain less than 1.0.

The problems with grade-equivalent scores have led to calls to discontinue their use. McLoughlin and Lewis (1994) suggest that professionals should select tests that provide other types of derived scores in addition to or instead of grade-equivalent scores.

Percentile Ranks

One of the most widely reported derived scores is the percentile rank or score. Briefly, a percentile rank for a particular raw score indicates the percentage of individuals in the reference group who scored lower than that particular raw score. For example, if a raw score of 38 equals a percentile rank of 46, then 46 percent of the reference group earned raw scores lower than 38. That is, the student's raw score is higher than approximately 46 percent of the reference group.

Although percentile ranks are easy to interpret, they also have disadvantages. Table 13-2 lists the limitations. One is that they should not be mistaken for percentage of items answered correctly. For example, answering 62 percent of the items on a test correctly may be one of the best performances on the test. Thus, the student's corresponding percentile rank is 96 because he or she outperformed 96 percent of the reference group.

Another disadvantage of percentile ranks is that they are not equal units of measure. Because most scores on a norm-referenced test cluster near the midpoint or center of the set of scores, the percentile ranks around the midpoint are closer together than the percentiles at the upper and lower extremes of the raw scores. In other words, the difference between the percentile ranks of 45 and 55 (the middle) represents a much smaller difference in actual test performance than the difference between the percentile ranks of 85 and 95 (or between 5 and 15). (These particular inequalities are illustrated graphically in the discussion of the normal curve in this chapter.)

Table 13.2 Limitations of Percentile Ranks

1. The score may be misinterpreted as percentage of items answered correctly.	1. Answering 62% of the test items correctly does not mean a percentile score of 62.
2. Scores are not equal units.	2. The difference in raw scores between the 45th and 55th percentiles is less than the difference between the 85th and 95th percentiles (or between the 5th and 15th).
3. Scores only have meaning in terms of a particular reference group.	3. A student's percentile score is 83 compared to all high school seniors in the state, but 35 compared to seniors in private preparatory schools.

A third disadvantage is that percentile scores only have meaning in terms of a particular reference group. Therefore, simply to report that a student may have a percentile score of 83 is not informative. Instead, as indicated in Table 13-2, he or she may earn a percentile score of 83 compared to a representative sample of all high school seniors. However, compared to seniors in private preparatory schools, the student's percentile rank may be 35. In other words, a student's relative standing varies, depending on the knowledge and abilities of the particular reference group.

Standard Scores

One group of derived scores, referred to as standard scores, overcomes the unequal unit problem of percentile ranks. Standard scores are determined by taking into consideration two characteristics of a set of scores, the mean and the standard deviation. The mean is the arithmetic average of the scores and the standard deviation is a measure of the spread of the scores. Specifically, it is the average amount that scores differ from the mean of the group on the particular test. A small standard deviation indicates that the scores cluster around the mean. In contrast, large values of the standard deviation indicate that scores are spread out away from the mean. For example, two classes on a course achievement test may have the same mean. However, the class with the standard deviation of 6.3 is more heterogeneous with regard to the test than the class with a standard deviation of 3.8.

Standard scores express student performance in terms of (1) the distance of the score from the mean of the group and (2) the standard deviation of the set of scores. Three well-known types of standard scores are z-scores, T-scores, and stanines.

z-scores. The z-score is referred to as the basic standard score, because it is the building block for all standard scores (Hopkins, Stanley, & Hopkins, 1990). A student's z-score is calculated by (1) subtracting the mean of the set of scores from the student's score and (2) dividing by the standard deviation. For example, suppose a student's score on an end-of-course examination is 50. If the class mean is 40 and the standard deviation is 5, the student's standard score on the test is 50−40 divided by 5 or 2.0. That is, the student's score is two standard deviations above the mean. In other words, z-scores are raw scores expressed as standard deviation units from the mean.

The z-score is particularly useful in comparing a student's performance in two different subject areas. Suppose a student earns a 67 in English and a 59 in mathematics. If the mean and standard deviation on the English test are 70 and 3, then the z-score on that test is −1.0. The English score is one standard deviation below the mean. For mathematics, however, with a mean of 35 and a standard deviation of 8, the student's z-score is 3.0 or three standard deviations above the mean. The z-scores for the tests in these two subject areas indicate a substantial difference in performance.

T-scores. A disadvantage of z-scores, as indicated by the prior example, is that scores below the mean are expressed as negative scores. The T-scale avoids this problem by using a mean of 50 and a standard deviation of 10. To convert a z-score to this scale, simply multiply it by 10 and add the result to the mean of 50. The z-scores of 3.0 and −1.0 in the prior example become T-scores of 80 and 40. As in the z-score form, 80 is three standard deviations above and 40 is one standard deviation below the mean.

Stanines. The standard scores referred to as stanines range from 1 (low) to 9 (high). The name, a combination of "standard" and "nines," reflects that the scores represent nine partitions of the total set of scores earned by the reference group. Unlike percentile scores and other standard scores, each stanine represents a bandwidth of raw scores. For example, stanine 5 is at the center of the distribution and reflects the percentile ranks from 40 to 59. Thus, stanine 5 reflects average performance. On an achievement test, stanine 4 reflects performance somewhat below average and stanines 2 and 3 indicate serious academic deficits.

One advantage of stanines is that they are easily understood. Also, because each stanine represents a band of scores, another advantage is that they prevent the assignment of undue precision to a single score. That is, a score on an assessment is not error-free; a band of scores that includes the student's score is a more accurate estimate of the student's skills and capabilities.

Role of the Normal Distribution

Standard scores on norm-referenced tests and the use of standard deviation units are best illustrated in relation to the ways that large sets of scores are distributed among the test takers. For the purpose of comparing small and large sets of scores, Figure 13-1 illustrates the distribution in graph form of 28 test scores on a classroom test.

As indicated, the range of frequencies (from 1 to 28) is shown on the vertical axis and the possible scores on the test (1 to 20) are on the horizontal axis. Each point on the line indicates the frequency of a particular score and the line joining the points indicates the shape of the particular distribution. In this example, the shape is irregular or asymmetrical, in part because the test is short (20 items) and the sample is small (28 subjects).

In contrast, the shape of the distribution of a large sample of test scores on a broad-range achievement or an intelligence test approximates a particular type of symmetrical distribution referred to as a normal distribution or normal curve. Figure 13-2 is an example of a normal curve. The frequencies, if included, would be labeled on the vertical axis and the scores would be indicated on the horizontal axis.

As indicated in Figure 13-2, a normal curve is symmetrical; that is, each half is a mirror image of the other. A normal curve also differs from other distributions

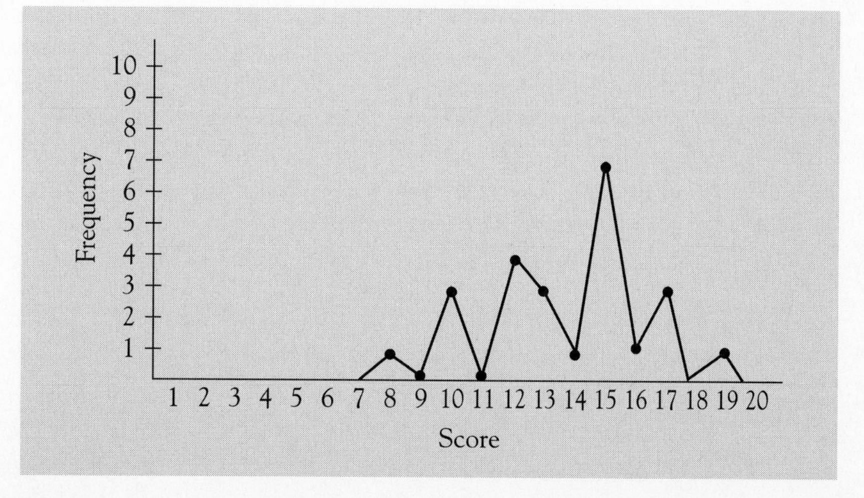

FIGURE 13.1 Distribution of scores on a classroom test (N = 28).

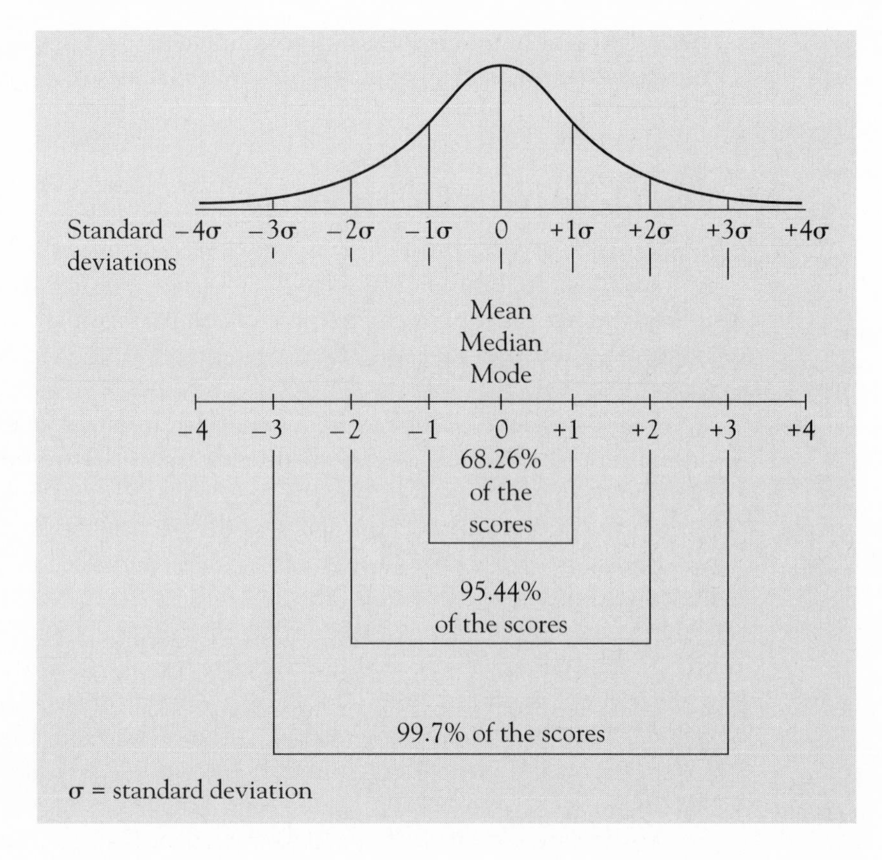

FIGURE 13.2 Normal distribution. Properties of the normal curve: (1) The distribution is symmetrical. (2) The arithmetic average (mean), the midpoint of the set of scores (median or 50th percentile), and the most frequently occurring score (mode) are the same score and occur precisely at the center of the distribution. (3) The percentage of cases in each standard deviation is known.

of data in other ways. For example, researchers and others often describe the center of a distribution by using either the arithmetic average of the set of scores (the mean), the midpoint of the scores (the median or 50th percentile), or the most frequently earned score (the mode). For the data from the classroom test (Figure 13-1), the mean is 14.2, the 50th percentile is 15, and the mode is 15. In contrast, for a normal distribution, the mean, median, and mode are exactly the same score and they occur precisely in the center of the distribution.

In a normal distribution, 99.97 percent of the scores are encompassed by three standard deviations above the mean and three standard deviations below the mean. In addition, a fixed percentage of cases occurs in each standard deviation. Specifically, 68 percent of the students' scores occur between −1 and +1 standard deviations. As indicated in Figure 13-2, the greatest concentration of cases occurs in this portion of the distribution. Further, 95.44 percent of the cases are between −2 and +2 standard deviations with 99.7 percent between −3 and +3 standard deviations.

These relationships are useful in the interpretation of standard scores from norm-referenced tests. Consider the interpretation of performance on the Wechsler Intelligence Scale for Children–III (WISC–III). The mean for the WISC-III is 100 and the standard deviation for the test is 15. Recall from Chapter 11 that one criterion for classification as mentally retarded is a standard score below 70 to 75 on an intelligence test. The score of 70 is two standard deviations below the mean of 100. This performance level is below that of 97+ percent of the reference group.

Comparison of Scoring Methods

Percentile ranks and the different types of standard scores are different methods for apportioning the scores represented by the normal curve. Figure 13-3 illustrates these methods and the relationships among them. Stanine 5, for example, includes the raw scores that are within 1/4 of a standard deviation above and below the mean. With the exception of stanines 1 and 9, which are the "tails" of the normal curve, each stanine includes the raw scores in one-half of a standard deviation.

Figure 13-3 also illustrates the unequal nature of percentile ranks. The percentile scores at the center of the distribution are smaller, in terms of the raw scores that are represented, than the percentile ranks from 80 to 90 (and those from 10 to 20). Stated another way, a change of a few points of a raw score near the center of the distribution is more likely to result in a change in the student's percentile ranks than a change of a few raw score points at other points on the

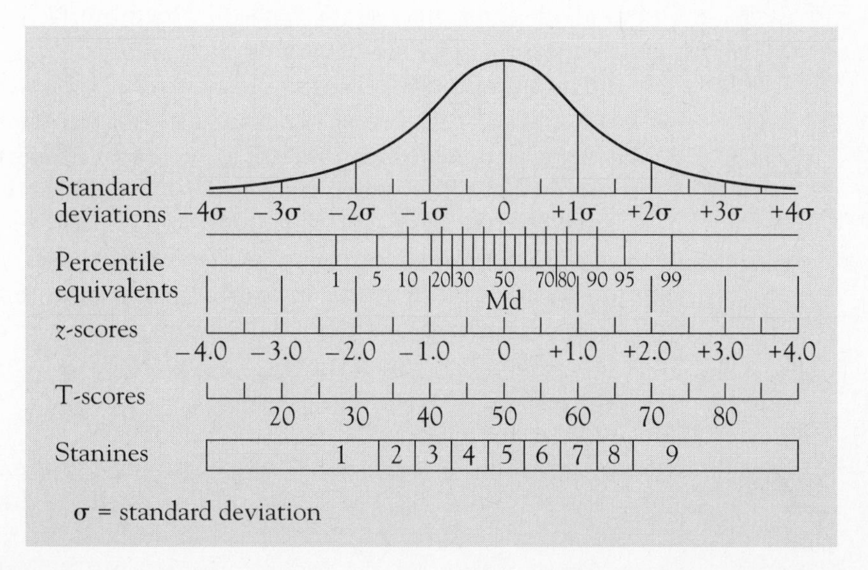

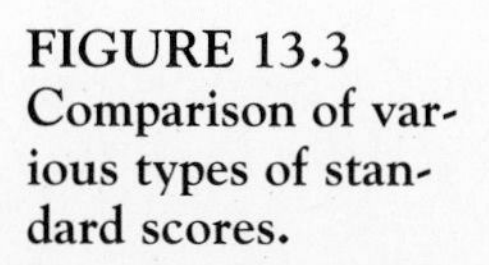
FIGURE 13.3 Comparison of various types of standard scores.

score range. This characteristic is illustrated in the relationship between stanines and percentile ranks. Stanine 5, for example, represents percentile scores from 40 to 59, whereas stanine 2 reflects the range from the 4th to the 10th percentile.

Summary

Raw scores and derived scores are two general methods of scoring student performance on ability and achievement tests. The raw score is the number of points earned by an examinee. Derived scores are obtained by comparing a student's raw score to the performance of students in a representative reference group. A derived score that indicates the examinee's standing relative to the reference group is assigned to the student's raw score.

The major types of derived scores are grade-equivalent scores, percentile ranks, and standard scores. Grade-equivalent scores, reported in grade levels and months, have several limitations. They are the tendency to view the scores as (1) standards for all students, (2) indicators of appropriate grade placement, (3) indicators of equal units of growth, and (4) expectations of an increase of 1.0 per year for all students.

Percentile ranks indicate the percentage of students in the reference group that scored lower than the examinee. Although easy to interpret, they have three limitations. Specifically, percentile scores may be misinterpreted as percentage of items answered correctly, they only have meaning in terms of a particular reference group, and they are not equal units. That is, the percentile ranks between 45 and 55 represent a smaller difference in raw scores than the percentile ranks between 85 and 95 (or between 5 and 15).

Standard scores, in contrast, indicate the distance of the student's raw score from the mean in standard deviation units. A score of 85 on the WISC–III, for example, is one standard deviation (15 points) below the mean of 100. Stanines, one type of standard score, range from 1 to 9, with stanine 5 as the average. Unlike percentiles and other standard scores, each stanine represents a bandwidth of raw scores. Thus, they prevent overinterpretation of student performance.

Of importance in interpreting scores on norm-referenced tests is that the scores of the reference group approximate a normal curve. That is, the score distribution is symmetrical, the mean, median, and mode are the same score, and the percentage of cases in each standard deviation are known. Specifically, 68 percent of the cases occur between +1 and −1 standard deviations and 95 percent occur between +2 and −2 standard deviations.

The interrelationships between the various types of derived scores are easily seen on a diagram of the normal curve. Stanine 5, for example, represents percentile scores from 40 to 59, whereas stanine 2 reflects the range from the 4th to the 10th percentile.

Interpreting Student Performance

Important issues in interpreting norm-referenced scores are the interpretation of error in the scores and the use of confidence bands, interpreting student portfolios, and the composition of the reference group.

Standard Error and Confidence Bands

Any test score is only an estimate of the examinee's true knowledge, skills, or capabilities. Factors such as the individual's mental and physical state, the physical surroundings, the sentence structure and language of the test, and other factors influence the individual's performance. In other words, if the test were administered several times (which is not practical), the scores earned by the examinees would vary somewhat from one administration to another. The test, in other words, is an imperfect measure of the individual's capabilities.

In other words, the student's true score, the score that reflects the student's actual ability, is not known. This problem would not be a major issue if one is only considering one student's performance on only one test. However, on occasion, the teacher may be interested in comparing a student's performance with that of others in the class. Also of major importance is that teachers and parents are interested in comparing a student's performance in different subject areas or in different skills areas related to learning. For example, in diagnosing a child's problems with reading, one question is if the student's skills differ in auditory discrimination, phonetic analysis, word reading, and reading comprehension. That is, which observed differences in the child's scores are the result of chance factors and which reflect differences in actual ability?

The key to answering this question is the extent of measurement error associated with a particular test. Referred to as the standard error of measurement, this information is usually included in the manual for a standardized test and it can be calculated for other tests.

The standard error is used to set limits around the student's obtained score. The purpose is to establish a band of scores that we are reasonably confident includes the student's true ability or achievement score. This band of scores, referred to as a confidence band, is determined by adding and subtracting the estimate of the standard error to the student's obtained score. For example, if the standard error for a test is 4.1, the confidence band for a score of 63 on that test is 58.9 to 67.1. If it were possible to test the student repeatedly under ideal conditions, 68 percent of the student's scores would fall within this band. For this reason, it is sometimes referred to as the 68 percent confidence band. That is, we are reasonably confident that the student's true ability score is between 58.9 and 67.1.

Figure 13-4 illustrates the use of confidence bands on an achievement test taken by Ernest, David, and Bob. The students' scores are, respectively, 73, 77,

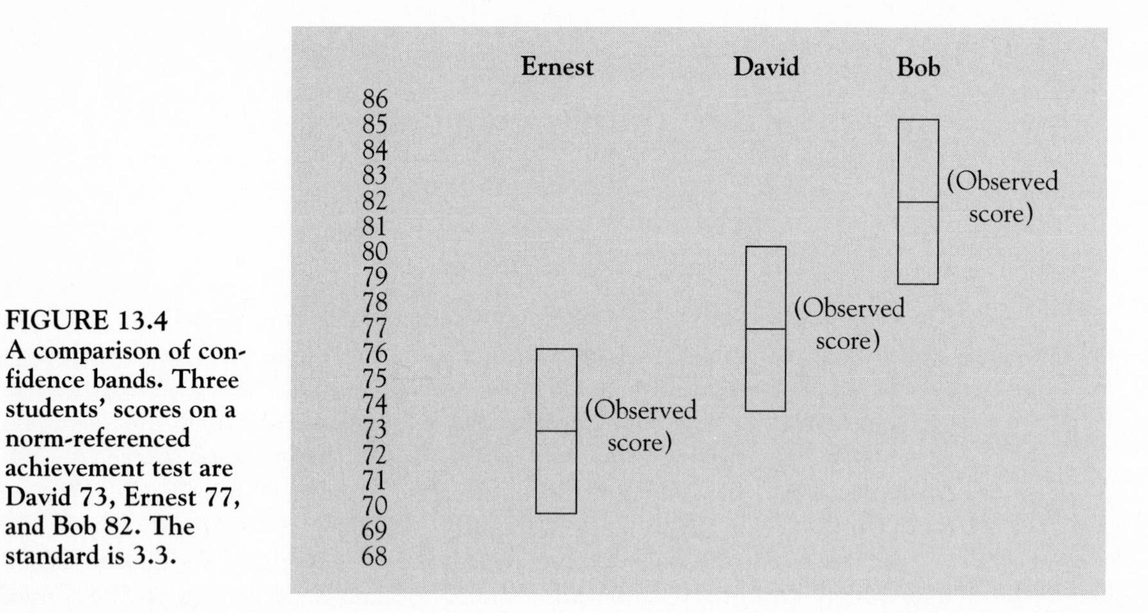

FIGURE 13.4
A comparison of confidence bands. Three students' scores on a norm-referenced achievement test are David 73, Ernest 77, and Bob 82. The standard is 3.3.

and 82, and the standard error is 3.3. As illustrated, the confidence bands for the scores earned by David and Ernest overlap as well as the confidence bands for David and Bob. When the confidence bands overlap, there is no real difference between the true achievement levels of the students. Therefore, there is no real difference between the achievement of David and Ernest and between David and Bob. However, the confidence bands indicate that there is very likely a difference in achievement on this test between Ernest and Bob because the confidence bands do not overlap. The importance of confidence bands is that they can prevent overinterpretation of student scores, that is, assuming that real differences exist when the observed differences are attributable to chance factors.

Suppose, however, that the standard error on the test is 5.1 (instead of 3.3). Would the interpretation differ? The answer is yes, because the confidence bands of all three students would then overlap. They are, respectively, 67.9 to 78.1, 66.9 to 87.1, and 71.9 to 82.1. This example illustrates the importance of adequate reliability for the scores on a test because a component of the formula for the standard error is the reliability estimate for the test. The lower the reliability, the higher the measurement error of the test. In other words, high reliability contributes to low measurement error and increased precision in estimating students' true ability levels.

On occasion, greater precision than a 68 percent confidence level may be desirable. Adding and subtracting two standard errors from the observed scores results in a 95 percent confidence band. That is, 95 percent of the obtained scores, on repeated testing under ideal conditions, would fall within the confidence band. For the students in Figure 13-4, the 95 percent confidence bands for a standard error of 3.3 are 66.4 to 79.6, 70.4 to 83.6, and 75.4 to 88.6.

Using Test Results

Two issues of importance in using tests results are analyzing student performance and communicating test results to parents.

Analyzing student performance. The use of derived scores and confidence bands makes possible the comparison of a student's performance on different tests. Figure 13-5 presents a hypothetical profile for a student on the Metropolitan Achievement Test, Seventh Edition (MAT 7). On this profile, the student's raw scores are converted to percentiles, stanines, and grade equivalents, and 68 percent confidence bands are reported for the percentile ranks. As indicated by the

METROPOLITAN ACHIEVEMENT TESTS
SEVENTH EDITION WITH OTIS-LENNON SCHOOL ABILITY TEST, SIXTH EDITION

			1992	MAT7	OLSAT	**INDIVIDUAL REPORT FOR**
TEACHER:	SMITH		NORMS:			**Brian Elliott**
SCHOOL:	LAKESIDE ELEMENTARY	GRADE: 04	SPRING	NATIONAL	NATIONAL	AGE 09 YRS 10 MOS
		TEST DATE:	LEVEL:	ELEM 2	E	
DISTRICT:	NEWTOWN	05/93	FORM:	S	2	

TESTS	NO. OF ITEMS	RAW SCORE	SCALED SCORE	NATL PR-S	NATL NCE	GRADE EQUIV	AAC RANGE	NATIONAL GRADE PERCENTILE BANDS (1 10 30 50 70 90 99)
Total Reading	85	66	632	68-6	59.9	5.9	MIDDLE	
Vocabulary	30	27	667	90-8	77.0	8.4	HIGH	
Reading Comp.	55	39	618	53-5	51.6	5.0	MIDDLE	
Total Mathematics	64	43	602	52-5	52.6	5.1	MIDDLE	
Concepts & Problem Solving	40	29	617	68-6	59.9	6.0	MIDDLE	
Procedures	24	14	579	37-4	43.0	4.3	LOW	
Language	54	33	609	51-5	50.5	4.8	MIDDLE	
Prewriting	15	10	606	47-5	48.4	4.7	MIDDLE	
Composing	15	8	602	43-5	46.3	4.5	LOW	
Editing	24	15	614	56-5	53.2	5.3	LOW	
Science	35	25	628	65-6	58.1	5.9	MIDDLE	
Social Studies	35	25	630	69-6	60.4	6.0	MIDDLE	
Research Skills	36	29	635	73-6	62.9	6.5	MIDDLE	
Thinking Skills	83	56	615	61-6	55.9	5.7	LOW	
Basic Battery	203	142	617	60-6	55.3	5.4	MIDDLE	
Complete Battery	273	192	619	62-6	56.4	5.5	MIDDLE	

FIGURE 13.5 Score profile on the MAT 7 for a hypothetical student.

stanine scores and the percentile bands, Brian's vocabulary knowledge differs significantly from his reading comprehension (the percentile bands do not overlap). Also, Brian's performance on mathematical procedures is significantly below his performance on mathematics concepts and problem solving, reading, science, and social studies. On the MAT 7, mathematical procedures assess students' ability to apply arithmetic procedures to solve addition, subtraction, multiplication, and division problems involving whole numbers, decimals, and fractions.

In this profile, the column labeled "AAC Range" reports an achievement/ability comparison. This range is reported when the MAT 7 is administered in conjunction with a group ability test, the Otis-Lennon. The AAC describes the student's performance in relation to other students with the same measured ability. Brian's achievement on math procedures and thinking skills is low compared to other students at his ability level (as measured by the Otis-Lennon).

In addition to norm-referenced scores and confidence bands, some test publishers also report criterion-referenced interpretations for subtests or particular skill areas of the norm-referenced tests. Such scores should be interpreted with caution because the items on the test represent a range of difficulty. That is, in the construction of a norm-referenced test, most of the items that all students answer correctly are discarded. Thus, scores obtained on a subset of items do not necessarily represent mastery of a particular skill.

Communicating test results to parents. As described in Chapter 12, the teacher should be prepared for the conference with the parent, communicate findings clearly and simply, and respond to questions or parent comments in a nondefensive manner.

Specific guidelines for communicating the results of norm-referenced tests are listed in Table 13-3. Begin with describing the purpose and/or focus of the test without using jargon. For example, use the phrase "sounding out words" instead of "phonetic analysis." Also, the term "ability test" instead of "intelligence test" is preferable, because the term "intelligence" sometimes evokes emotional reactions.

Then explain the type of score reported on the test. If more than one test has been administered by the school, reporting the findings with the same type of score is less confusing (McLoughlin & Lewis, 1994). Also, grade-equivalent scores are often misunderstood and standard scores may be too technical. However, percentile ranks are more easily understood than the other types of scores.

The student's performance should be reported in terms of confidence bands. Similarities and differences should be explained in terms of overlap or nonoverlap of the score bands. If test results are reported in stanines, a difference of two stanines typically indicates a significant difference in performance. A stanine of

Table 13.3 Guidelines for communicating test results

Guideline	Example
1. First, describe the focus of the test.	The skills involved in reading comprehension; this test measures sounding out words, identifying letter sounds, etc.
2. Explain briefly the type of scores used.	Standard scores may be too technical; percentiles are more easily understood (McLoughlin & Lewis, 1994).
3. Report the student's score as a confidence band and describe the meaning generally.	Mary scored between the 40th and 47th percentile; her performance is average compared to a national sample.
4. Clarify similarities and differences in confidence bands.	Mary's performance on word attack skills is higher than her vocabulary skills (if the bands do not overlap).
5. Relate the test information to planned use of findings.	I'll be working with Mary on her vocabulary skills and sending home some worksheets with her. I hope you will be able to help her with them.

7 in word attack skills, for example, is significantly different from a stanine of 5 in reading comprehension.

Finally, plans for using this information in instruction should be discussed briefly. As indicated in Table 13-3, these plans may include both classroom and home activities. For the profile of Brian Elliott, for example, the teacher would discuss plans to address his deficits in mathematical procedures.

In summary, the purpose of these guidelines is to communicate clearly with parents and to avoid misconstruing the results.

Composition of the Reference Group

An important factor in the interpretation of a student's performance on a test is the characteristics of the reference group. Essential characteristics are (1) all significant subgroups of the population should be represented adequately if the group is to be a national sample, (2) the performance of the group should be recent, and (3) the sample size should be adequate. One of the problems with the Gesell Readiness Test (discussed in Chapter 3) is that the reference group consisted of a small sample of upper-middle-class white children in New Haven, Connecticut. The sample size was inadequate, the sample was not representative of the students in the nation, and the performance scores are over 40 years old.

Published tests sometimes include comparison scores for different reference groups. For example, the MAT 7 reports scores on the mathematical concepts and problem-solving subtest for grades 4 to 8 both with and without calculators.

Of importance in the selection of a norm-referenced instrument is that the test manual should provide detailed information about the reference group for the test. For example, the manual for the Woodcock-Johnson Psychoeducational Battery–Revised indicates that the reference group consisted of 6,359 subjects from more than 100 communities. Included were 705 preschool children, 3,245 students in kindergarten through twelfth grade, 916 college students, and 1,493 adults who were not enrolled in secondary or postsecondary schools (McLoughlin & Lewis, 1994). In addition, the elementary and secondary school students were randomly selected from the grade lists of regular classes, excluding students with less than 1 year in an English-speaking classroom (p. 164).

Summary

Because tests are not perfect assessments of student abilities and skills, a test score is only an estimate of the student's true capabilities. For this reason, the standard error of measurement of the particular test is used to create a confidence band around the student's observed score. The 68 percent confidence band, calculated by adding and subtracting one standard error to each score, represents the range that would include 68 percent of the obtained scores on repeated testing. If the confidence bands for two scores overlap, there is no real difference between the true achievement or ability levels represented by the observed scores. In other words, observed differences are the result of chance factors. Confidence bands are frequently used to compare student performance on subject-area subtests of comprehensive achievement batteries. Nonoverlapping score bands or differences of two stanines indicate real differences in achievement.

In communicating test results to parents, the teacher should briefly present an overview of the test, avoid jargon, and briefly discuss plans for any identified deficits.

Also of importance in the selection of norm-referenced tests and in the interpretation of scores is the reference group used for generating the comparison scores. Essential characteristics of that group are adequate numbers, representativeness of the target population, and recency.

Chapter Questions

1. The federal legislation referred to as Title I allocated federal funds for the development of innovative instructional programs for low-achieving, low socioeconomic students. One suggested method for establishing program effectiveness was to compare the students' scores on standardized tests with the expected growth of students at their grade level. Discuss the problems with this suggestion.

2. The mean of a set of scores is 45 and the standard deviation is 4. What are the z-scores for the raw scores 62 and 21?

3. The profile for Brian Elliott (Figure 13-5) indicates his achievement in mathematical procedures is low compared to students at the same ability level. Why would Brian not be identified as learning disabled?

References

Anastasi, A. (1985). Mental measurement: Some emerging trends. In J. V. Mitchell (Ed.), *Ninth mental measurements yearbook: Volume I* (pp. xxiii–xxix). Lincoln, NE: The University of Nebraska, The Buros Institute of Mental Measurements.

Hopkins, K. D., Stanley, J. C., & Hopkins, B. R. (1990). *Educational and psychological measurement and evaluation* (7th ed.). Englewood Cliffs, NJ: Prentice Hall.

McLoughlin, J. A., & Lewis, R. B. (1994). *Assessing special students* (4th ed.). Columbus, OH: Merrill.

Chapter 14

Ethical and Legal Issues in Assessment

Parents in one community file a legal challenge to a reading passage on a statewide test on the basis that it promoted smoking. The passage described a grandfather smoking a pipe on the front porch.

—National Council on Measurement in Education, 1994.

The preceding situation reflects one of the legal issues currently associated with high-stakes testing—that of parental rights to review and challenge test items that they believe contradict their basic beliefs. Discussed in this chapter are parental rights and other legal issues associated with high-stakes testing and the teacher's ethical responsibilities in testing.

Ethical Responsibilities in the Classroom

Students have the right to be tested in fair and equitable ways and to expect that the results will be interpreted appropriately. The preparation of students for taking a test, test administration, and

Major Topics

Clasroom Responsibilities

Preparation of Students

Test Administration

Interpretation of Test Results

Legal Issues Related to High-Stakes Assessments

Notice and Adverse Impact

Instructional Validity

Opportunity for Success

Parental Rights

Accommodations for Disabled Students

Definitions of Disability

Alternatives to Accommodation

Guidelines for School Districts

making appropriate inferences from test scores are important teacher responsibilities related to this right.

Preparation of Students

One major classroom expectation related to tests is that students will be motivated to do their best. Table 14-1 lists several guidelines for teachers to enhance motivation. Of major importance is that students perceive the test as fair. That is, the test is not designed to trick them, but is a mechanism for them to demonstrate their learning. Adequate time to prepare for a test also is important, therefore, adequate notice and a review prior to the test should be provided. Finally, encouraging physical well-being for a standardized test is also appropriate.

A second expectation for students is that they will not become discouraged during the test. Therefore, teachers should familiarize students with test formats that differ from their classroom experience (such as selected-response, matching, and multiple-choice items). The purpose is to prevent a factor extraneous to student performance, for example, an unfamiliar format, from confusing students.

Standardized tests present some different challenges from those of classroom tests. Among them are special answer sheets and time limits. Appropriate preparation activities that include teaching young pupils (1) to transfer their responses to answer sheets or to bubble in their answers and (2) to finish within time limits (Smith, 1991). These preparation activities can contribute to lowering student anxiety at the time of the test.

In addition, a norm-referenced test will include some difficult items that many of the students cannot answer. The teacher should explain that the tests are intended for use in many different classrooms and that students are not expected

Table 14.1 Guidelines for Motivating Students to Take Tests

1. The teacher should view his or her tests as a mechanism for students to demonstrate their knowledge and skills.
2. Announce a test in advance and inform students of the general type and content and approximate length.
3. Do not administer a test on the same day that a unit is completed.
4. Provide a review of the main ideas and skills taught in the unit.
5. For standardized tests, encourage students to get a good night's sleep and eat breakfast before the test (Haladyna, Nolan, & Haas, 1991; Smith, 1991).
6. For standardized tests, send a note to parents about the importance of the child's physical well-being for the test (Haladyna et al., 1991; Smith, 1991).

to be able to answer all the items. The teacher also should instruct his or her students to spend little time on items for which they cannot determine the answer. Instead, they should go on to subsequent items on the test.

These activities are intended to ensure that students can demonstrate their best performance. However, other test preparation activities inflate student scores without raising the achievement level of students. These score-inflating practices are unethical. Included are developing a curriculum based on test content, developing objectives based on test items and teaching them, and presenting items to students that are similar to those on the test (Haladyna et al., 1991; Mehrens & Kaminski, 1989; Smith, 1991). Each of these activities can increase test performance without any change in the construct represented by the test. For example, developing objectives to teach students a particular type of word problem on a mathematics test does not address students' reasoning and problem-solving skills (the construct to be measured by the task). The result, in other words, is misleading test scores.

Another unethical preparation practice described by researchers (Haladyna et al., 1991; Mehrens & Kaminski, 1989; Smith, 1991) is the use of commercial test preparation materials. Such materials specifically review the skills to be tested, using formats that appear on the test itself. Mehrens and Kaminiski (1989) conducted a content analysis of one set of commercial materials for a widely used standardized test of basic skills. They concluded that use of the materials was equivalent to administering a parallel form of the test itself and explaining all the answer choices to the students (p. 30).

Test Administration

Teachers and administrators are responsible for selecting and/or developing assessment methods that are appropriate for instructional decisions and to ensure fairness in the testing conditions. For example, as indicated in Chapter 2, a broad-range achievement test would not be selected if the purpose is to assess student capabilities in organizing and researching information for a complex problem and developing a solution. Similarly, a standardized test that emphasizes phonics is inappropriate for assessing the achievement of pupils in a whole-language curriculum. In other words, a test that emphasizes ideas, concepts, and skills that are not a focus of the school curriculum should not be administered.

Particularly important in administration is that the teacher should provide a positive environment for the test (see Table 14-2). As stated in Chapter 2, tests should not be used as tools for classroom management or to punish students. Also, in reference to the test, the teacher should not make comments such as "If you don't work fast, you won't finish" or "This is a difficult test, so pay attention."

Table 14.2 Guidelines for Test Administration

1. For classroom tests, provide clear and easily understood directions.
2. Do not schedule a test on the day of the "big game" or some other major school event.
3. Provide a positive physical and psychological environment.
4. Implement procedures to discourage cheating.
5. Do not provide cues or hints to individual students.
6. Remain in the classroom during the test.
7. For standardized tests, read the directions exactly as written; do not paraphrase or amplify.
8. For standardized tests, strictly observe the stated time limits.

Equally important is that, with the exception of students with debilitating conditions, students should take the test under the same conditions. Therefore, directions should be clear and cues and hints should not be provided to individual students. If an item on a teacher-constructed test is vague or confusing, it should be clarified for the entire class.

To discourage cheating, the teacher should require that books and other unneeded materials be removed from students' desks. Also, the teacher should quietly observe the class during the test. For a major test, such as a final examination, the pages may be assembled in different sequences. Finally, for a standardized test, the requirements stated in the manual should be followed explicitly.

Interpretation of Test Results

Much of the misuse of tests stems from making inferences from the scores that go beyond the information they provide. For example, a test score is not a measure of the "whole person." That is, a low score does not indicate that a student is an unworthy person. Similarly, a high score does not indicate intellectual superiority. Yet, often so much importance is attached to test scores that testing generates anxiety and self-doubts. Further, low performance has been cited as a contributor to low self-esteem and a lack of self-efficacy (Bandura, 1986; Weiner, 1980).

Table 14-3 presents four important guidelines for using test scores appropriately. The first two address the error that is associated with any test score. As stated in Chapter 13, use only score bands as indicators of student performance. Second, verify the student's score through other types of evidence, such as homework, class performance, and scores from other tests.

Table 14.3 Guidelines for Interpreting Test Scores

1. Do not attribute an unwarranted precision to the test score. Student performance should be considered only in terms of score bands.
2. Do not use the test score as the only item of evidence. Instead, verify the score through the use of other types of information.
3. Do not overgeneralize the student's performance. Interpret the test score only in terms of the specific test.
4. Do not evaluate a student's score in isolation. Instead, the student's educational background, language proficiency, aptitude, and other factors should be used in interpreting student performance.

Guidelines 3 and 4 address the tendency to overinterpret a test score. Because even standardized tests that are similarly labeled do not measure a construct exactly the same way, performance should be reported in terms of the particular test that was administered. In addition, the student's educational background, language proficiency, and other relevant factors should be used in interpreting student performance.

One particular problem associated with norm-referenced standardized tests is the interpretation of test norms. Unfortunately, the public often views test norms as standards to be met. Instead, as discussed in Chapter 2, the norms are simply the derived scores of a sample of typical students on the test. Further, the tests are designed so that 50 percent of the examinees are above the midpoint of the scores and 50 percent are below. In addition, given the range of difficulty of the items on the test and the likelihood that some information on the test is not in the curriculum, student performance should not be viewed as an indicator of the effectiveness of the curriculum.

Summary

Several practices should be observed to ensure that scores on a test reflect the students' best performance. Motivating students through advance notice of the test, providing a review, and treating tests as integral to learning are important prior to test administration. Also important is introducing students to unfamiliar formats or response sheets and to expect difficult items on a standardized norm-referenced test.

However, practices that inflate student scores without influencing actual achievement are unethical. Included are redesigning the curriculum based on test content, developing objectives based on test content, and using commercial test preparation materials.

During test administration, the teacher should provide a positive and fair environment for the test takers. Tests should not be used as punishment, directions should be clear, hints should not be provided to students, and practices should be observed to discourage cheating. The requirements for standardized tests (e.g., observing time limits and reading directions precisely) should be strictly observed.

Finally, test scores should not be overinterpreted. They should not be overgeneralized beyond the limits of the particular test and they should be interpreted in light of both the student's background and other evidence about student performance.

✦ Legal Issues Related to the Nature and Use of High-Stakes Assessments

The term high-stakes assessment refers to tests or other performance samples that are used for key academic decisions about students or teachers. Grade promotion, graduation from high school, and teacher certification are critical decisions in which assessment often is a requirement. Five legal issues related to the nature and implementation of assessments for critical decisions may be identified. They are notice, adverse impact, instructional validity, opportunity for success, and parental rights (Phillips, 1996a). These issues also may provide insights into potential problems with assessments of content and performance standards associated with Goals 2000 (p. 5).

Notice and Adverse Impact

Notice and adverse impact are two related yet separate legal issues. Notice refers to adequate advance notification of the standards and requirements for key academic decisions, such as the awarding of a high school diploma. Adequate notification became an issue in the *Debra P. v. Turlington* case (1979–1984) in the state of Florida. The plaintiffs challenged the fairness of requiring black students who had attended segregated schools at some time during their education to pass a functional literacy test for graduation.

The court ruled that a high school diploma is a property right. That is, a diploma conveys certain benefits, such as employability, on students. Further, the Fourteenth Amendment provides that individuals cannot be deprived of a property or liberty interest by a government entity unless the basis for the denial is fundamentally fair (Phillips, 1994a, p. 108). That is, procedural due process must be observed. Therefore, the court ruled that students who might be deprived of the property rights associated with a diploma must receive adequate prior notice of any required assessment (Phillips, 1994a, p. 51). In the *Debra P.* case, the court postponed the use of the test in Florida for 4 years until all black students had attended only integrated schools (Fischer & Sorenson, 1991).

The procedural due process decision of this case, in other words, is that advance notice of a testing requirement for a diploma must allow for sufficient preparation of students. That is, students must be given adequate opportunity to learn. In two subsequent cases in Georgia and New York, the courts ruled that less than 2 years is inadequate notice (Phillips, 1996a).

Adverse impact refers to the potentially negative effects of new or revised standards on historically disadvantaged groups (Phillips, 1996a, p. 6). For example, many performance assessments are open-ended tasks that require analysis, interpretation, and writing. As indicated in Chapter 8, some data from NAEP assessment indicate that students differ by ethnicity in their rates of attempting open-ended items (Baker, O'Neill, & Linn, 1993). Therefore, if such tasks are to be part of grade promotion or graduation requirements, they must be addressed by both regular classroom instruction and remediation efforts.

Of importance is that differential performance alone is not sufficient to claim adverse impact and therefore invalidate a graduation standard. In Illinois, several disabled students successfully completed their IEPS, but failed the graduation test. They were, therefore, denied high school diplomas and they challenged the testing requirement for the diploma in *Brookhart v. Illinois State Board of Education* (1983). The court ruled that disabled students could be required to pass a test prior to receiving a high school diploma. However, the court also ruled that less than 1½ years was insufficient notice for disabled students (Phillips, 1994a).

Instructional Validity

Chapter 3 described content validity as the adequacy with which the items or tasks on an achievement test sample the particular subject area. The *Debra P.* case raised the issue of both the content and instructional validity of the functional literacy test in Florida. Specifically, a federal appeals court in 1981 noted that the state should administer an examination on the material that was taught in the same way that a teacher administers a final examination of the material he or she has taught in a particular class. This requirement, according to the court, constitutes instructional validity (Fischer & Sorenson, 1991, p. 100).

The case was sent back from the appeals court to the lower court to decide the issue of instructional validity. Of course, proving that each student has been taught tested skills is impossible. Thus, the court had to determine whether the preponderance of the evidence supported a finding of instructional validity (Fischer & Sorenson, 1991, p. 101). The evidence included expert testimony based on an extensive survey of reports from school districts, teachers, and students. The data indicated that (1) the skills were included in local curricula, (2) the majority of teachers confirmed that the skills were taught, (3) 99 percent of the students surveyed statewide indicated they had been taught the skills, and (4) the state also had implemented broad and effective remediation efforts (Fischer & Sorensen, 1991). The district court ruled in 1983 that the test was instructionally valid and this ruling was upheld on appeal.

The instructional validity issue for high-stakes assessments has two current implications for districts and states. First, the adoption of new graduation standards implies revisions in the curriculum (Phillips, 1996a). Second, ample time must be allowed so that teaching practice can change to incorporate the new skills and context. For example, complex performance assessments often introduce skills and capabilities that are not traditionally a part of the subject area. As illustrated in Chapter 8, performance assessments in mathematics and science may require writing. However, writing is a relatively new assessment component in these subjects. Also, such a skill cannot be taught in a short time period (Phillips, 1996a, p. 6). Therefore, if such performance assessments become a part of graduation standards, ample time must be provided for writing to become an integral component of mathematics and science courses.

Opportunity for Success

The guarantee of fundamental fairness of assessments for graduation for all students is derived from the due process clause of the Fourteenth Amendment (Phillips, 1994b). Opportunity to learn, demonstrated by the *Debra P.* case, is one aspect of fundamental fairness. Another aspect, referred to as opportunity for success by Phillips (1994b), refers to protection from assessment procedures that are invalid, arbitrary, capricious, unfair, or that foster unequal chances for success. Of importance is that opportunity for success does not guarantee equal outcomes; it only ensures standardized conditions of administration (Phillips, 1996a, p. 7).

The use of performance assessments in high-stakes testing introduces new concerns in the opportunity-for-success issue. Two concerns include the use of different equipment by different students and the training that students receive on equipment (Phillips, 1994b, p. 2). Suppose, for example, that students are to determine the amount of wall-to-wall carpeting needed for their classroom and that one class must use rulers because yardsticks are not available. The use of rulers, however, adds to the difficulty of the task and also increases the likelihood of error. Students who fail that task, when it is the basis for a high-stakes decision, could claim unfair treatment because their task was more difficult (Phillips, 1994b, 1996a).

Similarly, any equipment that requires training that is used for an assessment may negatively impact student performance if the training was lacking (Phillips, 1994b). An example is a set of mathematical tasks that are to be completed using a calculator when students have not had prior access to calculators (Linn, Baker, & Dunbar, 1991). As indicated in Chapter 8, such a situation is not a problem on an assessment such as NAEP when the purpose is to obtain data about the general performance level of students in the United States. However, it can be a problem for high-stakes decisions about individual students.

In addition to tasks that use equipment, some performance assessments include group activities, outside assignments, and pretask activities. All of these features can jeopardize fairness. The problem with a cooperative group assessment is that students may not contribute equally to the outcome. Suppose that one academically strong student dominates a group science experiment and one weak student contributes very little. The question of fairness involves whether the weak student should receive credit for accomplishing the task (Phillips, 1996a, p. 8).

The use of outside assignments, such as writing an essay, in high-stakes performance assessments raises the question of unequal resources. Some students' products, for example, may be influenced by parents, siblings, or tutors (Phillips, 1994b, p. 2). Also, some may have access to computer software and laser printers that can enhance the appearance of the finished product. Other students risk being penalized as a result of these and other different opportunities.

Finally, some assessments may include discussions of relevant reading material or other pretask activities. Discussions in different classrooms may highlight different information or lead to different clues about the subsequent assessment (Phillips, 1994b).

Parental Rights

As indicated at the beginning of this chapter, statewide assessment programs and performance assessments in large school districts have recently experienced legal challenges related to the content of test items. In one case, parents objected to a social studies item that required interpretation of a graph that displayed percentages by religious affiliations. The plaintiffs maintained that estimates required value judgments or activities that violate the students' religious beliefs.

The legal challenge to the tests was based on the premise that they violate First Amendment guarantees of free speech and religion. The contention is that the tests ask personal questions and require students to address questions that are counter to their religious beliefs (Phillips, 1996a). In a recent Texas case, *Maxwell v. Pasadena I.S.D.* (1994), the court found no violation of First Amendment rights to the free exercise of religion. However, the court did rule that the parents' fundamental right to direct their children's education had been violated. Therefore, the court ruled that the state cannot administer tests to Texas students unless the parents are provided an opportunity to review the tests 30 days after the administration.

The decision in this case is currently under appeal (Phillips, 1996b, p. 2). However, in the interim, the Texas legislature enacted a law that requires the annual release of all items to students. Two effects of this action are (1) an increase in budget expenditures ($6 million) for maintenance of the technical quality of the instruments and (2) an increase in the material available for inappropriate teaching of specific test content (Phillips, 1996a, p. 10).

These challenges to tests reflect a perception of "hidden agendas" in statewide testing (National Council on Measurement in Education, 1994). That is, the court challenges appear to arise from a distrust of secure tests and the litigation is an effort to bring about disclosure of test questions. Nevertheless, districts and states should conduct a sensitivity review of all objectives and assessment items prior to use and replace potentially controversial items with others (National Council on Measurement in Education, 1994). Important screening areas are personal values, religious content, and controversial topics (p. 2). A graph that displays percentages of religious preferences should be replaced with a graph that illustrates the types of automobiles owned by a random sample of Americans (Phillips, 1996a, p. 10).

In addition, districts and states that plan to permit the review of secure assessment materials geared to mandated standards should establish specific procedures for reviews. Among them are (1) the signing of a nondisclosure agreement by any person who is allowed to review the materials, including staff who supervise the reviews; and (2) supervision of each review by two staff members (Phillips, 1996a).

Content Disclosure

The prior section described the Texas legislation that requires the annual release of all standardized test items to students and two major effects. One is the required budget increase to maintain instrument quality and the other is an increase in available material for directly teaching test content.

In 1996, New York State enacted legislation on content disclosure of tests used for postsecondary and professional school admissions. The intent is to provide a copy of the test form and a scoring key for particular administrations to students who request it. The legislation applies to computerized test administrations as well as paper-and-pencil tests (Lissitz, 1997, p. 2). Among the tests that are affected are the Scholastic Aptitude Test, the Graduate Record Examination Advanced Tests, and the Test of English as a Foreign Language. Among the unanswered questions are (1) are some types of items more resistant to disclosure and reuse effects, and (2) is there a time frame after which an item can be reused?

Summary

The increasing use of assessments for high-stakes decisions has led to various legal challenges related to this purpose. To date, the five legal issues that have been identified are notice, adverse impact, instructional validity, opportunity for success, and parental rights.

Notice refers to adequate advance notification about the standards for major academic decisions, such as awarding a high school diploma. If passing a particular test is to be part of the standards, students must be notified sufficiently in advance so that they have ample opportunity to learn the required knowledge and skills on the test (referred to as the opportunity-to-learn requirement). Courts in two separate states have ruled that less than 2 years is not adequate notification.

Adverse impact refers to the potentially negative effects of new or revised standards on groups that have been historically disadvantaged. In such situations, the new standards must be addressed by both regular classroom instruction and remedial efforts. However, poor performance alone is insufficient to claim adverse impact and thereby set aside the standard.

Instructional validity, as defined by the legal system, asks if students have been taught the skills tested on examinations required for a high school diploma. Evidence accepted by the courts includes expert testimony on curriculum content and confirmation by students and teachers that the skills have been taught. If performance assessments become requirements for grade promotion or a high school diploma, then essential skills that are new requirements must become an integral component of instruction.

The requirement to provide adequate notification of new standards in high stakes decisions addresses the opportunity-to-learn aspect of fairness in assessment. The other aspect of fairness, that is, opportunity for success, protects students from assessment procedures that are invalid, arbitrary, capricious, unfair, and that set up unequal chances for success. Potential problems associated with the use of performance assessments for high stakes decisions include (1) the unavailability of needed equipment for some students, (2) lack of training on essential equipment, (3) unequal contributions by participants in a group activity, (4) unequal access to other resources for outside assignments, and (5) differences across classrooms in the instructional quality of pretask activities.

The most recent challenge to statewide tests is that of the nature of item content. A Texas court ruled that particular items that appeared to violate students' religious beliefs did not violate First Amendment guarantees of free speech and religion. However, the court stated that the state of Texas cannot administer tests to students unless the parents have an opportunity to view the tests 30 days after the administration. Although the decision is currently under appeal, states and districts may wish to review items and replace those that may be potentially controversial.

Accommodations for Students with Disabilities

Chapter 11 discussed the special needs of students in classroom testing. This section discusses the issues involved in accommodations for students with disabilities in district and statewide testing. In past years, many states excluded disabled students from assessments that were used as indicators of the attainment of state standards. However, part of the mandate in Goals 2000 is the development of high-level standards for all students (Phillips, 1996a, p. 11).

As described in Chapter 11, legislation in the 1970s and an Office of Civil Rights ruling stipulated that (1) any handicapped individual who is otherwise qualified must be included in programs or activities that receive federal assistance and (2) programs must make reasonable accommodations for their physical or mental limitations. Because public schools receive federal assistance in some form, these provisions apply to tests for graduation and others administered by public institutions, such as the Scholastic Aptitude Test and the Graduate Record Examination.

Definitions of Disability

The disabilities mentioned in Section 504 of the Rehabilitation Act include both physical and mental abilities. Early requests for testing accommodations typically were made on the basis of blindness, wheelchair confinement, or temporary incapacities, such as a broken arm (Phillips, 1994a, p. 94). Accommodation for these problems requires the removal of physical barriers that prevent examinees from entering the test site or from demonstrating their learning.

Beginning in the 1980s, the major focus of requests for accommodations has shifted to mental disabilities. Recent requests are for disabilities such as attention-deficit disorder, dysgraphia, dyscalculia, dyslexia, and processing deficits. This shift has led to problems in the interpretation of the phrase "otherwise qualified." That is, a physical disability, such as blindness, is clearly extraneous to the testing of an intellectual skill, such as comprehension of text. The student simply demonstrates the capability using Braille materials. In contrast, mental disabilities may not be extraneous to the testing of an intellectual skill and are not likely to be independent of the skills that are being tested.

Court cases in recent years illustrate this issue. In one federal case, a medical school student had requested an oral examination in biochemistry instead of the required multiple-choice examination. In another federal case, the plaintiff, a law student with orthopedic and neurologic difficulties, had requested a part-time schedule and at-home testing. The courts viewed granting these requests as preferential treatment rather than the elimination of disadvantageous conditions (Phillips, 1993a, p. 21). Therefore, the schools were not required to modify the examinations.

Two other federal cases have challenged the test itself for mentally disabled students. In *Brookhart v. Illinois Board of Education* (1983) several disabled students failed the test required for a diploma. They filed a lawsuit challenging the testing requirement. Among the findings of the court was that school administrators are required to provide disabled students with accommodations such as Braille or wheelchair access (Phillips, 1994a, p. 110). However, the court also ruled that administrators were not required to change test content. Such a change results in substantial modification of the test and does not constitute reasonable accommodation.

Another aspect of the testing issue surfaced in *Anderson v. Banks* (1981). In this lawsuit, counsel for the mentally retarded students contended that the students had not been taught the skills that were tested in the examination for graduation. The court ruled that the students' disability was not extraneous to the skills being tested; therefore, the students were not otherwise qualified. That is, these students were unable to benefit from general education and were prevented from learning the required skills because of their disability (Phillips, 1994a). In other words, the courts have upheld the right of states and school districts to apply the same competency standards to nondisabled and disabled students.

Alternatives to Accommodation

Administrators, on occasion, may experience strong pressure to grant accommodations that significantly alter the interpretation of the standard (Phillips, 1996a, p. 12). In such situations, granting the accommodation may result in testing a different skill than the test is intended to measure (Phillips, 1994a). For example, allowing a reader on a test of reading comprehension changes the test to one of listening comprehension. The policy dilemma, therefore, becomes a question of whether to permit the disabled student to substitute a different skill than that measured by the test (Phillips, 1993a, p. 2).

Alternatives to the dilemma involve changing the assessment for all students (Phillips, 1996a, p. 12). For example, a reading comprehension standard might be restated as text understanding. This change allows students to (1) read the material and answer written questions or (2) have the material and the questions read to them. Other possible accommodations for all students are more generous time limits and the use of equipment, such as calculators for math tests.

Phillips (1996a) notes that allowing all students access to useful accommodations is also fair to low-achieving students. They are not entitled by law to supportive accommodations, but often do not have the opportunity to demonstrate their capabilities (p. 12).

Guidelines for School Districts

As the classifications of mental disabilities increase, requests for accommodations also are likely to increase. Therefore, development of a detailed policy and written procedures for the review of requests is essential (Phillips, 1993b, 1994a).

First, the district should develop written instructions for accommodations requests and the availability of these instructions should be communicated clearly in brochures and other materials (Phillips, 1993b, p. 2). Second, all requests should be made on a standardized form provided by the district that is supplemented by supporting materials. Directions for completing the form should include the deadline for submission and the testing office to which the form is to be submitted (Phillips, 1993b).

Third, the supporting materials should include three types of information. They are (1) the documentation of the disability by a licensed professional who is experienced in the diagnosis and treatment of the particular disability, (2) documentation of the individual's credentials (vita that includes education, experience, and professional credentials), and (3) a description of any accommodations that the applicant received in his or her schooling.

The nature of the disability and the need for the requested accommodation should be explained in a letter signed by the licensed professional. In addition, the letter should state that this description is based on an actual evaluation of the applicant in person by the licensed professional (Phillips, 1993b, 1994b).

Fourth, all requests should be reviewed on a case-by-case basis and decisions made on the basis of already developed written criteria. To ensure consistency, one designated individual in the testing agency should review and make a decision on all requests. A qualified consultant may provide assistance in borderline cases (Phillips, 1993b, p. 2). Finally, the district should provide an expedited review process for denied requests and a formal appeals procedure for appeals that were upheld in the expedited review (Phillips, 1993b, 1994a). The appeal should be available following a written request and should include an administrative hearing.

Summary

Legislation in the 1970s established the basis for reasonable accommodations for physical or mental limitations of individuals in testing who are otherwise qualified. In recent years, requests for accommodations of mental disabilities have increased. Federal courts, however, have ruled that schools are not required to change test content or to substantially modify a test when the modification results in preferential treatment. Courts have also upheld the rights of states to apply the same competency standard to both nondisabled and disabled students. Alternatives to the dilemma of granting an accommodation that substantially changes the test involve changing the nature of the assessment for all students.

Given the increase in requests for accommodations, school districts should develop written policies and procedures for the review of requests. Important features to include are written instructions for applicants, standardized request forms, documentation of the disability by an experienced licensed professional (and documentation of his or her credentials), need for the accommodation, and a description of any accommodations received in school. Review of requests should be made using written criteria on a case-by-case basis. Procedures for expedited review of denied requests and subsequent appeals also should be provided.

Chapter Questions

1. A school district is planning to include a performance assessment that addresses students' skills in organizing, summarizing, and communication data as a part of the test for a high school diploma. Discuss the preparation that the district must undertake to address key legal requirements prior to implementation of this assessment.

2. Discuss the similarities and differences between opportunity to learn and opportunity for success as interpreted by the courts.

3. A teacher maintains that he clarifies items on his tests that are vague and he feels he should do the same for items on standardized tests that students find confusing. What is the problem with this proposed practice?

4. What are the implications of the legal decision that a high school diploma is a property right?

5. The performance assignment identified in question 1 will be designed to be completed using word processing computer software and a spreadsheet program. If you were a parent asking to legally challenge this assessment, what might be the basis for your challenge and why?

References

Anderson v. Banks, 520 F. Supp. 472 (S.D. Ga. 1981).

Baker, E., O'Neill, H., & Linn, R. (1993). Policy and validity prospects for performance-based assessment. *American Psychologist*, *48*(12), 1210–1218.

Bandura, A. (1986). *Social foundations of thought and action*. Englewood Cliffs, NJ: Prentice Hall.

Brookhart v. Illinois State Board of Education, 697 F. 2d 179 (7th Cir. 1983).

Debra P. v. Turlington, 474 F. Supp. 244 (M.D. Fla. 1979), *aff'd in part, rev'd in part*, 644 F.2d 397 (5th Cir. 1981); *on remand*, 564 F. Supp. 177 (M.D. Fla. 1983), *aff'd*, 730 F2d 1405 (11th cir. 1984).

Fischer, L., & Sorensen, G. (1991). *School law for counselors, psychologists, and social workers* (2nd ed.). New York: Longman.

Haladyna, T. M., Nolan, S. B., & Haas, N. S. (1991). Raising standardized achievement test scores and the origins of test score pollution. *Educational Researcher, 20*(5), 2–7.

Linn, R., Baker, E., & Dunbar, S. (1991). Complex performance-based assessment: Expectations and validation criteria. *Educational Researcher, 20*(5), 15–21.

Lissitz, R. W. (1997). The New York standardized testing legislation. *National Council on Measurement in Education Quarterly Newsletter*, *5*(1), 2.

Maxwell v. Pasadena I.S.D. No. 92017184, 295th District Court of Harris County, TX, Dec. 29, 1994.

Mehrens, W. A., & Kaminski, J. (1989). Methods for improving standardized test scores: Fruitful, fruitless, or fraudulent? *Educational Measurement: Issues and Practice*, *8*, 14–22.

National Council on Measurement in Education (1994). Content challenges to assessment programs. *National Council on Measurement in Education Quarterly Newsletter*, *2*(3), 2.

Phillips, S. E. (1993a). Update on testing accommodations I. *National Council on Measurement in Education Quarterly Newsletter*, *2*(1), 2–3, 6.

Phillips, S. E. (1993b). Update on testing accommodations II. *National Council on Measurement in Education Quarterly Newsletter*, *2*(2), 2–3.

Phillips, S. E. (1994a). High-stakes testing accommodations: Validity versus disabled rights. *Applied Measurement in Education*, *7*(2), 93–120.

Phillips, S. E. (1994b). Opportunity for success. *National Council on Measurement in Education Quarterly Newsletter*, *3*(1), 2.

Phillips, S. E. (1996a). Legal defensibility of standards: Issues and policy perspectives. *Educational Measurement: Issues and Practice*, *15*(2), 5–13, 19.

Phillips, S. E. (1996b). Parental rights to view statewide assessments. *National Council on Measurement in Education Quarterly Newsletter*, *3*(4), 2.

Smith, M. L. (1991). Meanings of test preparation. *American Educational Research Journal*, *28*(3), 521–542.

Weiner, B. (1980). *Human motivation*. New York: Holt, Rinehart, & Winston.

Appendix
Descriptive Statistics

The purpose of descriptive statistics is to provide summary information about a set of scores. The three types of descriptive statistics discussed in the following pages are (1) measures of central tendency, (2) measures of variability, and (3) calculation of a Pearson product-moment correlation coefficient for two sets of test scores.

Measures of Central Tendency

A measure of central tendency is an average or typical score in a set of scores. The measures of central tendency are the mean or arithmetic average of all the scores, the median or midpoint of the scores, and the mode, the most frequently occurring score.

The Mean

The mean, symbolized by $\overline{X}$, is calculated by summing a set of scores and dividing the sum by the number of scores.

The formula for the computation is

$$\overline{X}=\frac{\Sigma X}{N}$$

where Σ is the sum of, X is any score, and N is the number of scores. In Table A-1, the mean for the 28 test scores is 14.214.

The Median

The median is the point in a set of scores that divides the scores into two equal halves. That is, the median is the midpoint of a set of scores. To identify the midpoint, (1) arrange the scores in order from highest to lowest and (2) count up or down to the midpoint. When the number of scores in the set is odd, the median is the middle score. When the number of scores is even the median is halfway between the two middlemost scores. In Table A-1, the number of scores is even, and the two middlemost scores are 15. Therefore, the median is 15.

The Mode

The mode is the most frequently occurring score in the data set. In Table A-1, the mode is 15. Sometimes, a set of scores may have two modes; for example, if six people each earned scores of 17 and 13. In such cases, the data set is described as bimodal.

✦ Measures of Variability

Measures of central tendency provide information about typical scores in a data set. Also important is information about the spread of scores. For example, the means of two classes on an arithmetic test may each be 78, but the score spread of class A is from 45 to 90 and the spread of class B is from 56 to 116. Thus, the pattern of performance in the two classes differs.

Three often-used measures of variability are the range, the quartile deviation, and the standard deviation.

The Range

The most easily calculated measure of variability is the range; simply subtract the lowest score from the highest. For the data in Table A-1, the range is 12 (20 − 8). For class A and class B in the preceding paragraph, the ranges are 45 and 60.

A disadvantage of the range is that it is unreliable because it is based on only two extreme scores. For example, suppose that, with the exception of one high score (98), all the scores in a class lie between 60 and 84. However, because only the highest and lowest scores determine the range, the calculation for this class is a range of 38 points (instead of 24 points).

The Quartile Deviation

Instead of calculating the range of the total set of scores, the quartile deviation is based on the range of the middle 50 percent of the scores. Referred to as the interquartile range, the middle 50 percent of the scores consists of the scores from

Table A.1 Measure of Central Tendency for a Set of Test Scores (N = 28)

Annotation (left)	Score	Annotation (right)
	8	
	10	
	10	
	10	
	12	
	12	
	12	50% of scores
	12	
	13	
	13	
	13	
	14	
	15	
	15	
	15	Median = 15 (halfway between the two middlemost scores)
Mode = 15 (most frequent score)	15	
	15	
	15	
	15	
	15	
	15	50% of scores
	16	
	17	
	17	
	18	
	18	
	18	
	20	

$\Sigma X = 398$

$N = 28$

$$\overline{X} = \frac{\Sigma X}{N} = \frac{398}{28} = 14.214$$

the 25th to the 75th percentile. The quartile deviation is half of this range of scores. It indicates the distance above and below the median, which includes approximately the middle 50 percent of the scores.

To calculate the quartile deviation, (1) determine the 25th and 75th percentiles, referred to as Q_1 and Q_3, and (2) divide by 2. For the data in Table A-1, $Q_1 = 12$ and $Q_3 = 15.5$ (the 75th percentile is halfway between score 15 and score 16). The calculation is as follows:

$$Q = \frac{Q_3 - Q_1}{2} = \frac{15.5 - 12}{2} = \frac{3.5}{2} = 1.75$$

The Standard Deviation

The most used measure of variability is the standard deviation. Briefly, it is an average of the extent of deviation of a set of scores from the mean. Calculating the standard deviation by hand is a laborious process, therefore, a calculator is needed. In addition, some calculators are programmed to calculate descriptive statistics, including the standard deviation. This section illustrates the steps that are involved, using the data in Table A-1.

The information required to calculate the standard deviation is (1) the squares of all the scores; (2) the sum of all the scores, which is the squared; and (3) the number of scores.

The formula for the standard deviation is

$$\text{S.D} = \sqrt{\frac{\Sigma X^2 - \frac{(\Sigma X)(\Sigma X)}{N}}{N - 1}}$$

The steps are as follows:

1. Sum the scores (ΣX): $\Sigma X = 398$
2. Square the sum $(\Sigma X)(\Sigma X)$: $(\Sigma X)(\Sigma X) = (398)^2 = 158{,}404$
3. Square each individual score (X^2): See Table A-2.
4. Calculate the sum of the squared scores (ΣX^2): $\Sigma X^2 = 5{,}874$.
5. Place this information in the formula and complete the calculations.

Table A.2 Squared Individual Scores for Data in Table A-1 (N = 28)

8	64
10	100
10	100
10	100
12	144
12	144
12	144
12	144
13	169
13	169
13	169
14	196
15	225
15	225
15	225
15	225
15	225
15	225
15	225
15	225
15	225
16	256
17	289
17	289
18	324
18	324
20	400
$\Sigma X = 398$	$\Sigma X^2 = 5,874$

$$S.D = \sqrt{\frac{\Sigma X^2 - \frac{(\Sigma X)(\Sigma X)}{N}}{N-1}}$$

$$= \sqrt{\frac{5874 - \frac{(398)(398)}{28}}{28-1}}$$

$$= \sqrt{\frac{5874 - \frac{158{,}404}{28}}{27}}$$

$$= \sqrt{\frac{5874 - 5657.286}{27}}$$

$$= \sqrt{\frac{216.714}{27}}$$

$$= \sqrt{8.0264} = 2.833$$

✦ Pearson Product-Moment Correlation

Essential data for calculating a Pearson product-moment correlation on two sets of test scores are the square of each score on test one (X^2), the square of each score on test two (Y^2), the sum of the X^2 and Y^2 columns, the cross product of each score (XY) (each X multiplied by the corresponding Y score), and the sum of the XY column (see Table A-3). This procedure is used in calculating split-half, parallel forms, and test-retest reliability.

$$r = \frac{\Sigma XY - \frac{(\Sigma X)(\Sigma Y)}{N}}{\sqrt{\Sigma X^2 - \frac{(\Sigma X)^2}{N}}\sqrt{\Sigma Y^2 - \frac{(\Sigma Y)^2}{N}}}$$

$$= \frac{42{,}958 - \frac{(631)(670)}{10}}{\sqrt{40{,}549 - \frac{(631)^2}{10}}\sqrt{45{,}786 - \frac{(670)^2}{10}}}$$

$$= \frac{42{,}958 - \frac{422{,}770}{10}}{\sqrt{40{,}549 - \frac{398{,}161}{10}}\sqrt{45{,}786 - \frac{448{,}900}{10}}}$$

Table A.3 Data for Calculating a Pearson Product-Moment Correlation for Two Sets of Test Scores

	Test 1		Test 2		
	X	X^2	Y	Y^2	XY
Alice	74	5,476	79	6,241	5,846
Bob	58	3,364	51	2,601	2,958
Carl	61	3,721	63	3,969	3,843
Darla	73	5,329	76	5,776	5,548
Ellen	64	4,096	69	4,761	4,416
Fran	67	4,489	72	5,184	4,824
George	43	1,849	49	2,401	2,107
Harry	59	3,481	70	4,900	4,130
Iris	62	3,844	73	5,329	4,526
Jack	70	4,900	68	4,624	4,760
Σ	631	40,549	670	45,786	42,958

$$= \frac{42{,}958 - 42{,}277}{\sqrt{40{,}549 - 39{,}816.1}\,\sqrt{45{,}786 - 44{,}890}}$$

$$= \frac{681}{\sqrt{732.9}\ \sqrt{896}}$$

$$= \frac{681}{(27.072)\ (29.933)}$$

$$= \frac{681}{8.10346}$$

$$= 0.8404 \text{ or } .84$$

a strong relationship between these two sets of scores.

Glossary

adverse impact: a legal issue in high-stakes assessment that refers to the potentially negative effects of new or revised standards on historically disadvantaged groups.

affective characteristics: hypothesized unobservable characteristics that involve beliefs, feelings, and perceptions.

alternate-response item: item that provides only two answer choices.

alternative or authentic assessments: assessments that are related to real-world tasks.

anecdotal records: a factual description of actions and events noted by an observer, typically, the classroom teacher. Consists of brief, concrete notations that focus on one student at a time.

assessment: all the systematic methods and procedures that are used to obtain information about behaviors.

qualitative: verbal descriptions of behaviors.

quantitative: yield numerical estimates of behaviors (also referred to as measurements).

behavior rating scale: an affective primary trait scale that typically addresses social adjustment behaviors.

bias errors: typically used in reference to rating scales; includes rating tendencies that result from particular attitudes or beliefs of raters.

central tendency error: the tendency to rate all individuals near the center of a rating scale.

checklist: a set of specific behaviors that reflects a competency or activity of interest that is checked as present or absent by the observer.

confidence band: a score range that we are reasonably confident includes the student's true ability level.

constructed-response question: a test question that requires the student to develop an answer instead of choosing an answer from available options.

continuum scale: see rating scale

criterion-referenced measurement: a method of yielding test scores that is designed to assess particular skills and capabilities. Student performance is reported as skills mastery either as pass/no pass or a level of performance on a skills continuum. A student score depends on a preestablished standard (not the performance of others).

derived score: any of several score types that are conversions from a student's raw score and that indicate the examinee's standing relative to a reference group.

duration recording: a method of documenting the beginning and ending times of each incident of a particular behavior, such as crying episodes.

essay question: a test question that poses a problem that requires the student (1) to identify relevant information essential to addressing the problem and (2) to select, organize, and integrate the information in a composed response of one to several paragraphs.

event recording: a method of documenting the frequency of a discrete behavior, such as throwing paper wads.

formative assessment: assessment implemented for the sole purpose of providing feedback to teachers and students about errors and misunderstandings; assessment is not included in the student's course grade.

generosity error: the tendency to rate all individuals at the high end of a rating scale.

goals: statements of the idealized outcomes; they are ultimate outcomes that specify neither the time nor the criteria for achievement.

grade-equivalent score: a score that indicates the performance level of a student on a norm-referenced test in terms of grade level and month; not recommended for use because of frequent misinterpretations.

halo effect: the influence of the rater's general impression of an individual on the rating of particular skills or behaviors.

high-stakes assessment: tests or other performance samples used to make major academic decisions about individuals, such as grade promotion, the awarding of a high school diploma, or teacher certification.

informal observations: spontaneous, unstructured information about student behavior that typically is not verbalized in oral or written form; typically used by teachers to make on-the-spot decisions during instruction.

instructional objectives: statements that (1) clarify, in specific terms, the intent of curriculum goals and (2) serve as guidelines for instruction.

logical error: a type of personal bias on rating scales that involves the inappropriate association of two characteristics as similar and rating them in the same way.

mastery test: see criterion-referenced measurement.

matching item: test item that presents several problems accompanied by a single list of possible answers.

measurement: (1) the process by which a score or rating is determined; (2) a structured situation that includes samples of particular characteristics or behaviors and that yields a numerical score or rating.

minimum competency testing: the use of standardized criterion-referenced tests to assess the mastery of basic skills.

multiple-choice item: a test item that consists of a stem (either a question or incomplete statement) and four to five response choices.

norm-referenced measurement: a method of yielding test scores that is based on assessment of a broad domain, uses items on a range of difficulty, and compares examinee performance on the test to the average performance of students in an identified reference group. The student's score may be reported in the form of a grade-equivalent, percentile, stanine, or other type of standard score.

opportunity to learn: a legal requirement of high-stakes assessment that mandates both instruction in the assessed capabilities and sufficient time for students to develop them.

opportunity for success: protection in high-stakes assessment from procedures that are invalid, arbitrary, capricious, unfair, or that foster unequal chances for success.

parental rights: (1) the legal guarantee established in federal legislation that ensures parental input in the assessment and instructional planning for children who qualify for special services, and (2) court decisions that ensure parental review of test items used in assessments for high-stakes decisions about students.

percentile score: the percentage of individuals in the reference group that scored lower than a given raw score on a norm-referenced test.

performance assessments: assessments that require the demonstration of understanding and skill in applied, procedural, or open-ended settings.

portfolio assessment: a collection of student work over time that reflects growth, breadth in the subject area, and, when used in the classroom, includes student reflections.

primary trait scale: see rating scale

rating scale: an instrument for documenting the degree to which particular characteristics or behaviors are present.

continuum scale: instrument consists of one set of scale points, each of which reflects a level of proficiency of a complex skill.

primary trait (dimensions-of-performance scale): instrument lists characteristics or dimensions of performance that are each accompanied by a scale (such as 1 to 7) with verbal anchors for scale points.

raw score: the number of points earned by a student on a test, whether teacher-made or commercially published.

reliability: the consistency of student scores (1) on different tasks or items on the same topics or skills or (2) assigned by different raters or observers.

response set: the tendency to rate all dimensions or characteristics on a scale in the same manner as the first few items.

severity error: the tendency to rate all individuals at the low end of a rating scale.

short-answer question: a test question that requires a word, phrase, or, at most, a few sentences as an answer.

special needs students: students for whom any of a variety of intellectual, social, and physical characteristics impact their potential for learning.

standard deviation: a measure of the spread of a set of test scores.

standard error of measurement: the estimate of measurement error associated with a particular test.

standard score: the distance, in standard deviation units, of the student's score from the arithmetic average (mean) of the scores of the reference group.

stanine: a type of standard score that ranges from 1 to 9.

structured-response item: test item for which the student must choose an answer from the options provided.

summative assessment: a cumulative assessment administered for the purpose of grading student achievement in a course.

table of specifications: a test blueprint that lists key concepts or topics across the top and levels of skills in the far left column. Test items are written for designated cells in the table (the intersections of topics and skills).

test: a set of tasks or questions that often is administered to a group of students in a specific time period. Tasks or questions typically address the cognitive capabilities learned in a particular course, subject area, or discipline.

test score pollution: a change (usually an increase) in test scores that is related to school or classroom practices and that has no connection to the concepts or capabilities represented by the test.

triangulation: the process of obtaining evidence from multiple data sources and multiple methods in order to check one's inferences about observations.

validity: the appropriateness, meaningfulness, and utility of the particular inferences that are made from test scores. Methods for establishing validity begin during test development with the conceptual framework and continue through use of the assessment.

Photo Credits

1 Elizabeth Crews/Stock Boston
2 James Shaffer
3 Paul J. Sutton/Duomo Photography
4 James Shaffer
5 James Shaffer
6 Elizabeth Crews/Stock Boston
7 Elizabeth Crews/Stock Boston
8 Bob Daemmrich/Stock Boston
9 Kathy McLaughlin/The Image Works
10 James Shaffer
11 Grant LeDuc/Stock Boston
12 James Shaffer
13 Arthur Grace/Stock Boston
14 Glen Korengold/Stock Boston

Author Index

Subject Index